ETHNICITY

AND

HEALTH

* * * * *

VOLUME VII

ETHNICITY AND PUBLIC POLICY
SERIES

iii

iv

ETHNICITY

AND

HEALTH

WINSTON A. VAN HORNE
EDITOR

THOMAS V. TONNESEN
MANAGING EDITOR

THE UNIVERSITY OF WISCONSIN SYSTEM
INSTITUTE ON RACE AND ETHNICITY

The University of Wisconsin System
Institute on Race and Ethnicity
P. O. Box 413, Milwaukee, WI 53201

International Standard Book Number ISBN 0-942672-12-7 (cloth)
International Standard Book Number ISBN 0-942672-13-5 (paper)
Library of Congress Catalog Card Number: 88-51124

"Health is wealth."
A proverb

". . . the tongue of the wise *is* health."
Proverbs, 12:18

FOREWORD

We all have had the experience of some event(s) or occurrence(s) from our distant past flashing back repeatedly into our consciousness for no apparent rhyme or reason. While pondering my thoughts for this foreword, one of these from my life came to mind, although at least here the connection can be understood.

As a lowly freshman in college, too many years ago to admit, our Spanish professor asked the members of her class to write down what was the one thing each of us most desired in life. How this was relevant to our learning Spanish, I still do not know, and I do not even remember the specific answers which we read aloud, although they rather predictably focused on material things. What I do recall most vividly, though, is the answer which our professor gave, for none of the students chose it. Her answer — "good health." When I first heard her selection, I smugly said to myself, "No wonder, look at how old she is." But as I listened to her explain her reasons, pointing out that little in life could be enjoyed, especially material possessions, in the absence of good health, it began to make eminent sense to me. It made such an impression that now, whenever this tiny snippet from my life comes to the forefront of my mind, I am almost embarrassed that I failed to think of writing "good health" back then, although I suppose one should not be ashamed of feeling invulnerable as most eighteen-year-olds do.

And when was the last time this brief snapshot of an occurrence redeveloped in my brain? It was when my colleague, Winston Van Horne, first showed me one of the phrases which now appears two pages preceding this foreword — "Health is wealth." As we all know, this is an old proverb, and it is one that I had heard before, but this was the first time upon hearing it that the episode with my former Spanish professor came to mind. As I read it — "Health is wealth" — I could almost see and hear this nun tactfully admonish us for our collective shortsightedness. "Remember," she said, "all the money in the world cannot buy health." Ah, the wisdom of it all.

Yet it was not very long after reading my colleague's choice of proverbs, and simultaneously recalling the "good health" incident from my

ix

freshman days, that a lesson which is evident in the chapters of this book began to surface. Granted, it is a fact that health is wealth, something that is, and justifiably so, valued. But is it also a fact that money cannot buy health, as my Spanish professor stated so matter-of-factly? As I asked myself this last question in light of the contents of this volume, I realized that the obverse of the proverb can also hold true — "Wealth is health."

On first impression the title of this book, "Ethnicity and Health," may lead someone to believe that its chapters will discuss such genetic proclivities as sickle-cell anemia among blacks or, historically, tuberculosis among American Indians. But this, of course, is not what the book does at all. Central to the book's theme is not that various racial and ethnic groups have different health needs and outcomes because of biological factors, but rather that these differences are heightened and often exacerbated because of cultural ones. This is not at all meant to diminish the role that biology and genetics play in matters of health, but instead to say that culture and diversity for too long have not been given their due when questions of health and, most importantly, health care are discussed. Perhaps above all else, the authors of the chapters which follow call out collectively for the recognition of cultural diversity and orientations in the delivery of health care.

But what about my phrase "Wealth is health?" In what way does it illuminate the contents of this book? One need not engage in deep thought to realize that wealth, especially in a society such as the United States which has a predominantly private health care system, acts as a determinant of health, both preventively and curatively. Who could argue that wealth or, more specifically, its absence — poverty — is not a factor in stress and mental health in the black community, the subject of Lawrence Gary's chapter; infant mortality among American Indians, the subject of Joyce Kramer's chapter; teenage pregnancy, the focus of Maria Luisa Urdaneta's and Tom Thompson's piece; the health care needs of the minority elderly, the theme of Toni Tripp-Reimer's and Bernard Sorofman's essay; and homicide in black communities, the concern of Julius Debro's contribution? Wealth/poverty is a contributory element in all of these health issues, and it hovers over Victor Rodwin's discussion of equity in private versus public health care systems, as well as may be a factor in some American Indians retaining traditional health practices, the subject of Laura Adams' and Merritt Knox's chapter. The point here is that although there is no one-to-one correspondence between wealth and health, the former can surely, if used wisely, aid those who possess it to better avoid the absence of health and/or ameliorate an unhealthy state. To this extent one's socioeconomic status, something which cannot easily be divorced from culture, has a direct bearing on one's health, and thus points to a more equitable distribution of economic resources as an important way to achieve better health for all. It is this underlying theme that I find flowing through the chapters of this volume, and it will cause me to think a bit differently the next time my brain decides on its own to resuscitate the anecdotal experience with my former professor.

This volume, although the seventh in our *Ethnicity and Public Policy* series, is only the second produced under the banner of the University of Wisconsin System Institute on Race and Ethnicity. We have been more than pleased with the evolution of the Institute in the past year, and we trust our readers will feel likewise about this volume.

The more one is involved in book publishing, the more he/she realizes the vital contributions of those "behind the scenes" in bringing a work to fruition. In many ways the authors or editors whose names appear on the title page are only the proverbial tip of the iceberg. For this book, the many hours that Claire Parker has toiled cannot go unmentioned. Editors' written comments may seem perfectly clear at the time they are made, yet they can take on the appearance of hieroglyphics when viewed in their totality a few days later. Nevertheless, Ms. Parker has magically transformed these scribblings into coherent copy every time, and this truly is an art.

Two individuals who have been with us since nearly day one of the series, Joanne Brown and Linda Jallings, have most likely again had their patience tried, and we are grateful that they once more agreed to take the test and provide us with their considerable copy editing and production skills respectively. Thelma Conway has assumed responsibility for the marketing and sales of books in the series without skipping a beat, and this too is an important piece of the puzzle.

It nearly goes without saying that the Institute and the *Ethnicity and Public Policy* series could not proceed without the continued support of the University of Wisconsin System administration. One of the individuals who has been most instrumental in this regard, Vernon

Lattin, will soon be taking leave of the Badger State for the Grand Canyon State, and we wish here to express our gratitude and bid him a fond farewell. John Schroeder and George Keulks have afforded like assistance at the institutional level, and Ron Hedlund and Bill Murin have been key in aiding the Institute through its work in its first full year. Despite the recent efforts of these individuals, though, we must call upon them immediately to summon their talents and energies for the next volume in our series, *Black America: 20th Century Assessment — 21st Century Prognosis*. There is no rest, even for those who are not wicked.

Thomas V. Tonnesen

University of Wisconsin-Milwaukee

CONTENTS

PREFACE

Eugene S. Farley, Jr.

University of Wisconsin-Madison

The fun of writing a preface is the considerable freedom one has in deciding how to structure one's observations. Since a specific aspect of the book's central theme of ethnicity and health is covered in each of its individual chapters, I have decided to deal with broader, more philosophical aspects of diversity and ethnicity. I want to suggest a different conceptual framework within which to consider ethnic diversity and human experience. I should like to show that:

- Diversity and ethnicity are basic to our species. Many of us want to be different in belief, looks and actions from others; that is, unique.

- Conversely, conformity, resistance to diversity and a demand to be "like me" are also ingrained in our species.

- How we accept and respond to diversity determines much of how we function as a species and as societies.

- To survive as a species, we need to understand and accept diversity and recognize it as a strength. To do this we must change the paradigm which seemingly dictates much of human social dialogue and interaction.

- A new paradigm, emphasizing sustainability of the environment and survival of our species, is needed.

- Health care providers are in a position to help develop this new paradigm and frame the social dialogue accordingly.

The study of ethnicity and public policy will help humanity gain a needed understanding of its own diversity.

The United States population derives from the many ethnic groups which make up our species. All of us living in this country, except the American Indians, came here because we either wanted to leave or were forced to leave the places of our origin. We were a mixed group. We came seeking our own religious freedom (although with differing degrees of tolerance for others); we came to find wealth and adventure; we came in chains guaranteed to keep us slaves, and as bonded servants with future freedom presumably assured; we came for solitude, for peace, for brotherly love, for starting new ways of living and new societies; we came to find space and land, to live and to grow; we came as people willing to kill for a "just" cause, and as people refusing to kill ever; we came from all lands, from all races, religions and beliefs; we came and made a country; we were heroic, noble, honorable and pure; we were corrupt, selfish, destructive and cruel; we were diverse, we represented the world; we were different; we were "ethnic."

As we try to understand ethnicity, we must look at ourselves. Each of us is part of an ethnic group of one kind or another. Each is affected by the history, belief system and mores of that group. Diversity in America, as in this world, is our reality. It is a basic fact of all human existence. It is our strength. Diversity allows us to develop perspective and insight. It enhances creativity, provides new ways of seeing ourselves and the world, and helps us adapt to the varying conditions of existence.

How we perceive and cope with diversity determines how it influences our lives. As inhabitants of this earth, our role is as a participating spectator of life. As members of society and its institutions, we have the ability either to work together, accepting our differences, or to diffuse our energies and destroy our strength by demanding conformity. Individuals and societies blessed with diversity can make it a threatening problem if they demand conformity.

Those who want to eliminate our diversity often disparage or give a negative meaning to our differences. Many of us act as though the difference between groups is the problem of the other group—not ours. We view ourselves as the norm, and the others as deviant. Groups that come from different historical, cultural, religious and/or racial backgrounds or traditions than the observer are identified as "ethnic groups." In reality we are all ethnics; we represent some grouping of people who are or have been separate or different from other groupings of people. Though the majority of any population often fails to recognize itself as an ethnic group in this sense, it too is one. In a situation where individuals from the majority group are isolated from another, the latter become a "minority" and may be perceived as culturally or ethnically distinct themselves.

Man's seemingly inherent drive to emphasize differences, using them to elevate one group and to degrade another, and man's tendency to destroy himself and his environment, raise the question: Is mankind fatally flawed? Some interpret this as a religious question, relevant to the religious concept of original sin. Others interpret it as a biological question, with an evolutionary answer coded in our genes. Still others interpret it as a philosophical question, with the answer hidden in our environment. Unfortunately, recognition of the question does not unite mankind. The context in which the question is interpreted determines how one attempts to answer it, and over time the various attempts to answer the question have affected the development of cultures, ethnic groups and religions, and unquestionably led to killing and wars.

As one looks at ethnic diversity and mankind's response to it, one may also ask the question: Is man's brain adaptive or maladaptive? Does it favor species survival or extinction? Man's brain has the "brilliance" to create the ultimate weapon that can destroy all life on earth. Can it also help man develop the social conscience or wisdom which will prevent the use of this weapon to destroy all in the name of saving life? (To paraphrase from the Vietnam War era: "We had to destroy the village in order to save it.") Or is mankind's brain so flawed that it can never develop the prerequisites needed for survival in the face of such a weapon?

The answers history gives us are not reassuring. Mankind's history of recurrent destruction, although combined with a history of great building and growth, has prevented or delayed the ability of its members to work together fully toward uninterrupted progress. Yet growth and development are necessary if we are to insure the survival of our species within the limits of the bountiful, but finite, resources of this planet and, possibly in the future, other planets.

If we are to assure the long-term existence of our species, we as members of mankind must use our individual and collective brains to work within the constraints of the resources and environment of this planet. We have the potential to create, develop and survive. Will we use this potential or will we, with increasing rapidity, pollute and destroy the environment so it can no longer support us?

If we as a species are to improve our chances for survival, we need to learn to communicate in ways which improve our understanding of cultural and ethnic diversity and the wonder of our existence. This communication must occur in ways which reduce the chances for destructive individual and societal behavior. How can our species do this? Sadly, through all of recorded history much of human dialogue has revolved around good vs. evil, the haves vs. the have nots, the rich vs. the poor, God vs. the devil, freedom vs. control, black vs. white, Jews vs. Gentiles, Muslims vs. Christians, Muslims vs. Hindus, ad infinitum! This list has been expanded to now include communism vs. capitalism, East vs. West and North vs. South.

If diversity is our strength, why have so many people, groups and institutions viewed it as a problem over the millennia? In its history mankind has shown a great willingness, almost a need, to develop reasons to differentiate people in a way which allows one group to control, dominate or destroy another. Human beings have the remarkable ability to identify or create differences and to use those differences as an excuse to fight among themselves.

Conflict seems to be the driving force behind much of human activity. Power and authority are often obtained and maintained by capitalizing on the differences of others. In Nazi Germany, fear of communists and Jews was encouraged and exploited by Hitler and formed much of the basis for his rise to power. In the pre-civil rights American South, and lingering thereafter, political power was built on the fostering of racial fears and hatreds, thus depriving many citizens of their constitutionally guaranteed rights and freedoms.

A classic example of the above is America's phobia regarding communism and its "principal" agent, the Soviet Union. Since the second decade of the twentieth century, almost all successful presidential candidates have had to loudly proclaim their anticommunism. This fear has altered and shaped the course of our history, and been the basis for a large increase in the power of the federal government—especially the executive branch. It has led us to accept abuses of the Constitution and usurpation of legitimate government authority by "shadow governments" in the name of "national security and freedom." Fear of communism and the Soviet Union has been so ingrained in the broader society that the form and substance of our political dialogue, as well as the structure of our economy, have been constrained unduly by it. This has resulted in the growth and power of a "military-industrial complex" which rivals or surpasses that of Hitler's Germany or the present-day Soviet Union. All this shows that mobilizing support by creating a common enemy based on ethnic differences, and using diversity as a stimulus for hatred and armed conflict, are natural outgrowths of mankind's current course of political and social evolution.

Here, then, is an intriguing question: What would happen if the Soviet Union were to change, and we found that our fears were exaggerated or no longer warranted? Would we recognize and respond to such change? What would happen to power in the United States if suddenly the Soviet Union were not the enemy, or to power in the Soviet Union if the United States were no longer perceived this way? The power structure in both countries has become dependent on an exaggerated fear of the other country's differences. Marked reduction of this fear would require major changes in governmental and political actions, or the identification of new enemies. Power based on the existence of "enemies" requires "enemies" to be there. The absence of enemies would require real changes to take place within each country, both in their thinking and actual foreign policy actions. Such changes are hard to initiate and slow to evolve, but are possible.

Social Change

Conflict between two or more forces is the current paradigm for the development of human civilization. This paradigm is limited and does not fit observed needs; it therefore prevents clear communication on issues that are basic to our future—survivability of the species and the sustainability of life on this earth. A new paradigm must be developed to direct political and social dialogue, and to improve the ability of our diverse species to communicate:

> The paradigm governing scientific belief about the solar system was based on the "fact" that the sun revolved around the earth. Yet over time it became increasingly difficult or impossible to fit all the observed pieces of astronomical information into the paradigm to make a rational, coherent whole. New observations required new interpretations of facts. New interpretations required a paradigm shift based on observed data that showed that the earth revolves around the sun. Unfortunately, then as now, regardless of the evidence, groups with vested interests in the old paradigm resisted its demise. A dominant group opposing change was Orthodox Christianity, which to protect its authority, demanded the acceptance as "fact" that the sun revolves around the earth. The Church's resistance successfully delayed the development in Europe of knowledge already possessed by much of Eastern, African and middle American civilizations. However, once the scientific paradigm of the solar system did shift to include the fact that the earth revolves around the sun, observations could be understood and explained in a coherent manner and knowledge could advance.

> When observations and reality can no longer be explained by the dominant paradigm or theory, the paradigm must shift. The shift usually spurs great advances in knowledge. As facts increasingly fail to fit their accepted theory or paradigm, people who resist change make greater efforts to force or change facts to fit the old paradigm, or insist upon an orthodoxy that denies the facts. In time, observations which show the limits of the existing paradigm become so overwhelming that it changes. With the paradigm shift, new insights and knowledge are developed which lead to real progress. Eventually, the "new" paradigm may be required to change in the face of still newer facts. Yet, some will continue to deny the validity of the new paradigm in spite of observed

facts, and will adhere to a dogma or ideology which for many becomes like a religion.*

Rational dialogue on issues of basic importance to society is inhibited by the fact that the present paradigm of world development falls within the context of conflict: one ethnic group against another or one belief system against another. Given this fact, we must work to shift this paradigm to one which better fits the basic realities confronting mankind, realities which we, as a species, must resolve if we are to continue to exist. The new paradigm must state that consistent, worldwide cooperative enterprises and development can proceed only within the context of a sustainable global environment. This paradigm must recognize that the interrelationship of all life on earth is the basis for the long-term viability of human life. It must respond to society's potential for development, while also maintaining the resources, environment and ecological balance on earth.

The study of ethnicity can help develop the public dialogue essential to changing the current, flawed paradigm. Dialogue is necessary if the body politic is to understand the validity of the new paradigm. As the new paradigm is more clearly defined and understood, communication on specific issues will become more coherent and rational. This occurrence will help solve many of the conflicts and problems unresolved in the context of the present paradigm.

The new paradigm will provide a different focus on the issues of "how to get the most for oneself?," "how to maintain one's standard of living?," "how to prevent the spread of communism?," "how to increase productivity and consumption?," "how to deal with East-West, communist-capitalist or non-democracy-democracy conflicts?," and "how to keep our country powerful?" It should help us rethink these questions in light of our mutual need to ensure the life of all of earth's creatures.

What will be the source of this new, revolutionary paradigm? It will come from the observations, understandings and teachings of many individuals and groups. It will derive from the essence of most great religious, philosophical and political thought (when dogma, mythology, superstition, prejudice and unthinking response are removed from them). It will also arise from the basic tenets of democracy, responsible free enterprise, philosophical communism, socialism and pragmatic realism which recognize that there are practical limits to what can be

---

* My own quotation, excerpted from an unpublished position paper on paradigm change written in December 1987 for the Madison (Wis.) Institute. It is derived largely from Thomas Kuhn, *The Structure of Scientific Revolutions*, 2nd ed. (Chicago: The University of Chicago Press, 1970).

done to our environment without destroying it. It will recognize that man has the potential to work, develop and survive in peace and diversity within the limits of this planet. It will help people see all of mankind as an incredible resource. In the context of such developments, we will be better able to explore and, possibly in time, inhabit other planets and solar systems. Real national and international greatness can only come when all diverse groups begin to listen to, learn from and share with one another.

Ethnic Diversity and Health Care

The chapters in this book reveal the relationships between economic status, ethnicity, race, health and health care. They point out some of the major gaps in the present health care system, particularly in relation to the care of minorities and the poor. Taken as a whole, the chapters give evidence that:

1. Health care makes a difference. Where health care is available in an organized, regular manner, health statistics improve. Where such health care is not available because of financial or any other reasons, health statistics worsen.

2. Poverty frequently is associated with less health care, particularly preventive, and worse health outcomes. It often leads to less good health (mental and/or physical), and less good health can reinforce poverty.

3. The United States has the most costly health care system in the world, but this has not assured its population the best health care outcomes or statistics. Although the United States is the highest total spender on health care among Western and other industrialized nations, it is the lowest public spender: It is the most private system. The United States is the only industrially advanced country without some form of compulsory and universal entitlement to health insurance, leading to roughly 15 percent of the population being uninsured for health care services.

4. Culturally determined concepts of health and illness are important determinants of health and disease. Belief systems regarding health and illness are important in how health care providers offer their services and in how these services are received, i.e., ethnicity as well as socioeconomic status affect health and health care.

5. To be effective, health care providers must have some understanding of the belief system of their patients regarding health, illness and healing.

6. The United States must accept responsibility for the fact that it, along with South Africa, has greater disparity in its health care system and more people with limited access to health care than any other advanced nation. In this respect, we must recognize that many of our health outcome statistics are poorer than nations with far less wealth and resources. To overcome this, a system which assures regular access for all to good health care, including prevention, should be developed.

7. The experience of administering health care services to those from diverse cultural and socioeconomic groups informs one that individuals who possess an understanding of their own cultural traditions have a sense of self-worth and self-confidence which transcends culture and economics. Often these individuals share more in common with similar people from other cultures and economic groups than with people of their own background who lack this sense of understanding. They may have similar health statistics, also. Those who are "successful" in their own culture often have much in common with those who are "successful" in another.

The chapters of this volume impress one with the fact that the privatized American health care system has not yet mobilized itself to assure that each citizen has ready access to needed health care services, especially preventive. Achievement of such should assure improved health statistics for the entire population.

As a family physician and teacher of future family physicians, it is impossible to read the pages that follow without wanting to change our health care system—change it so that it responds more readily to present unmet needs and produces better health outcomes for the entire citizenry. These changes must include:

1. More rational organization of the health care system to assure:

   • access for all, unrelated to employment or ability to pay;

   • more availability;

   • more community-oriented primary care.

2. Better preparation of the provider by the medical education system to assure more appropriately trained physicians to provide:

   • preventive services;

- early detection of problems;
- appropriate and early intervention;
- culturally sensitive, person-oriented care;
- family-oriented care.

3. Greater sensitivity of the government to the unmet needs of the citizens, and a willingness to facilitate the development of health care systems, both public and private, which assure all individuals access to good medical care.

One goal of health care providers is to help individuals feel better physically and psychologically, hence they should strive to help patients develop their self-esteem. This requires them to know their patients and to be aware of, and responsive to, cultural and ethnic variations. Health care providers should be agents for social change; they are exposed to the problems and should be seeking solutions to how to provide services accessible to all. The inability of American society to deal adequately with the health problems of its diverse ethnic groups may be based on its failure to, as of yet, accept and understand what America or being American implies, as distinct from what specific ethnic or cultural group one is from.

Over the millennia, our species seems to have lacked the ability to develop the collective wisdom needed to take advantage of the opportunities available to us. Now we must change our self-destructive behavior, belief system and paradigm, which limit our ability to interpret and understand our problems.

Mankind has the intelligence, the resources and the technology to work together to respond to human need and diversity. The United States has the resources, the sociopolitical formations, and the religious, philosophical, as well as ethical traditions which should allow it to resolve many of the socioeconomic and ethnic injustices and disparities that now obtain. With these attributes well-grounded in the society, we should be capable of bringing about the paradigmatic change necessary to protect our diversity and, concomitantly, improve our health.

BIBLIOGRAPHY

The following books are referred to because they depict various aspects of problems mankind faces in dealing with its many prejudices mentioned earlier. They show some of the extremes to which "respectable" people, individually and collectively, will go to build or maintain a power base, or defend their prejudices, whether racial, cultural or political.

Fugard, Athol. *Master Harold and The Boys*. New York: Alfred A. Knopf, 1982, distributed by Random House.

In this play, Fugard presents compellingly the terrible effects of apartheid on personal thought, expression and behavior. It is a story of behavior that was a commonplace in our society prior to the passage of the Civil Rights Act of 1964 and the Voting Rights Act of 1965. It shows the emotional strains of prejudice and how this affects all people, even "nice" ones. The cost to the individual and society of personal prejudice is high. Add to this the cost of governmentally legislated and mandated discrimination, and the basis for violent revolution obtains.

Lifton, Robert J. *The Nazis Doctors: A Medical Killing and the Psychology of Genocide*. New York: Basic Books Inc., 1986.

This volume is based on interviews the author conducted with German physicians who actively participated in human experimentation in the Nazi concentration camps. He describes how some of these doctors were able to twist their thinking to believe their behavior was consistent with the highest standards of medical ethics and the Hippocratic Oath. Many literally believed they were "saving the race." It is an excellent account of the total ability of "respected" professionals, who are supposedly intelligent, educated individuals, to commit and justify all kinds of horrors in the name of scientific advancement, rather than the true reasons of blind hatred and prejudice.

Lukas, J. Anthony. *Common Ground: A Turbulent Decade in the Lives of Three American Families*. New York: Alfred A. Knopf, 1985, distributed by Random House.

Through interviews with families representing various ethnic groups and "sides" involved in the court-ordered integration of Boston's public schools, the author has been able to humanize the parties and show where they had common interests. It is an excellent documentation of the thinking and action of ordinary citizens who perceive themselves merely to be struggling for the well-being of themselves and their children. In presenting several viewpoints of the same problem, he shows the destructiveness of prejudice and how it prevents individuals and groups from acting in concert for the common good.

Shirer, William L. *20th Century Journey: A Memoir of a Life and the Times*. Vol. 1: *The Start: 1904-1930*. New York: Simon and Schuster, 1976, and Shirer, William L. *20th Century Journey: A Memoir of a Life and the Times*. Vol. 2: *The Nightmare Years: 1930-1940*. Boston: Little, Brown and Co., 1984.

In these two books, Shirer, a well-known journalist and correspondent, discusses developments in the United States early in this century, as well as events in Europe where he served as a correspondent before and during the rise of Adolph Hitler. He provides an excellent historical overview of issues important to Hitler's rise to power. He gives a graphic view of how virulent anticommunists built upon anti-Semitism and people's fear of communism to destroy democratic movements and gain massive support for totalitarian government. These books give historic testimony to the fact that mankind can be swayed into irrational, destructive behavior, justified by prejudice, fear, hate and ignorance.

Tuchman, Barbara W. *A Distant Mirror—The Calamitous 14th Century.* 1st trade ed., New York: Alfred A. Knopf, 1978.

An excellent, sweeping overview of events of the fourteenth century, which has many dramatic comparisons with the present century. It provides a perspective in time which allows one to see the massive irrationality and destructive nature of human behavior then and now.

Tuchman, Barbara W. *The Guns of August.* New York: The Macmillan Co., Inc., 1962.

This book illustrates the irrationality that led to World War I. It shows how insignificant differences between peoples and nations were magnified in order to mobilize the populace to fight.

Zinsser, Hans. *Rats, Lice and History.* The Atlantic Monthly Press Books. Boston: Little, Brown and Co., 1935, 3rd ed., 1963.

This work deals with the history of typhus epidemics and their effect on history. It clearly depicts how mankind, through wars and mass destruction, created the ideal conditions for the spread of the disease agents and the disease itself. Even though mankind did not know the causes of the diseases and epidemics, it did associate them with the disruption and destruction of war. In spite of this, mankind failed to alter its behavior and continued to fight, plunder and kill during the peak of the worst epidemics. As a result, disease, as much as might and intellect, often determined the outcome of battle.

INEQUALITIES IN PRIVATE AND PUBLIC HEALTH SYSTEMS: THE UNITED STATES, FRANCE, CANADA AND GREAT BRITAIN*

Victor G. Rodwin

New York University

Introduction

Over fifteen years ago, in a comparative study of the United States, Sweden and England, Odin Anderson characterized the quest for greater equity in health as an "endless search for the dream."[1] The validity of this statement depends not only upon empirical evidence, but also upon one's concept of equity. It will be argued here that it is possible to attain what may be called a "weak concept" of equity. The search for what may be termed a "stronger concept" of equity, however, so far has proved elusive—at least in the United States, France, Canada and Great Britain.

Inequalities in health—both in relation to outcomes (health status) and to the availability and use of medical care—have been studied quite thoroughly.[2] There is extensive work on alternative concepts of equity,[3] and there is a large number of empirical studies which document inequalities in health status and measure access to medical care in relation to various concepts of equity.[4] One gap in this literature, however, is the absence of a standard of comparison by which to assess the extent of health inequalities in the United States.

This chapter will attempt to assess the extent of health care inequalities in the United States as compared to the situation in other, more "public" health care systems. It is not possible to make systematic comparisons because each country relies on different categories in defining such concepts as socioeconomic status and health status. Never-

*The author wishes to express gratitude to Howard Berliner, John Forester, Marc Rodwin and Tom Tonnesen for their comments on an earlier draft of this chapter.

theless, since the comparative approach is not well developed, it is possible to make a modest contribution in this direction.[5]

The initial presumption was that problems of inequality are more severe in the relatively private, market-based health care system of the United States than in the more publicly controlled systems with a national health service, such as in Great Britain, or with national health insurance, such as in Canada and France. This turns out to be true when grounded in the weak concept of equity. However, regarding a stronger concept of equity, the evidence suggests that inequalities are pervasive in all of these systems.

On the Concept of Equity in Health Care

Enough able minds have addressed the concept of equity in health care so as to make all but the most ignorant or courageous analysts hesitate to take on the subject anew.[6] For purposes of this discussion, it is sufficient to begin with three well-known distinctions: first, between equity and equality; second, between equity in levels of health or health care and equity in financing; and third, between the weak and the stronger concepts of equity— both of which will be relied upon to interpret the empirical evidence presented subsequently.

Equality means "the same" in the sense that George Orwell played with the concept in *Animal Farm*.[7] Many would probably support the ideal of promoting measures to make health status equal among all. For example, there should be no strong objections to making life expectancy between the sexes, or even between social classes, equal. Few, however, would expect such efforts to succeed given the differences among groups and individuals in their genetic makeup, income and educational levels. No one, not even the most fanciful utopian, would presume that the use of health care services should be equal among individuals. People who are sick should receive more medical care services than those who are well. How much more they should receive is not merely a technical issue. To the extent that this question raises issues of social justice, it becomes an issue of equity.

The second distinction, between equity in levels of health or health care and equity in financing, involves the interrelationships between costs and benefits. Attitudes and perspectives, of patients, providers and/or taxpayers, often vary. From the point of view of financing, it is crucial to distinguish the distribution of costs between those who actually receive services and the larger set of all who pay for them.[8] But this discussion is concerned only with equity in achieving levels of health and in receiving health care services.

A weak concept of equity in health care would suggest that everyone is entitled to, and actually receives upon request, a basic minimum of health care services. Norman Daniels associates this concept with the presuppositions about equity which underlie Alain Enthoven's Consumer Choice Health Plan for national health insurance in the United States.[9] Such a notion also resembles the view advocated by the President's Commission for the Study of Ethical Problems in Medicine, which concluded that equitable access "requires that all citizens be able to secure an adequate level of care without excessive burdens."[10]

A stronger concept of equity presupposes far more ambitious aims. For example, in the best of all possible worlds, one might wish that despite severe inequalities in income and wealth, an ideal health care system would somehow provide sufficient remedial effects so as to make death (mortality) and disease (morbidity) independent of an individual's socioeconomic status. Likewise, one might want the use of services by consumers and the diagnostic procedures and therapeutic treatment provided by health care professionals (and even the *manner* in which these are provided) to be related only to the patient's medical condition, not to his or her ability to pay. Such a concept of equity assumes an equitable distribution of health care services— "one in which illness is the major determinant of the allocation of resources."[11]

Both the weak and the stronger concept of equity in health care can be applied to outcomes (health status) as well as to inputs (use of health care resources). The weak concept of equity justifies a range of inequalities based on differences in income and preference. The stronger definition, however, suggests that *with respect to health status*, equally situated individuals should be treated equally (horizontal equity) and unequally situated individuals should be treated unequally (vertical equity). Also, the stronger equity concept suggests that there should be equal access to health care services, i.e., that the ways in which patients differ in their geographic residence or socioeconomic status should not lead to systematic differences in their use of services or treatment.

Both concepts of equity mirror a set of values; both will be used as criteria by which to evaluate the health care systems in the United States, France, Canada and Great Britain. After distinguishing between public and private health care systems and classifying health systems along a public/private continuum, the nature of health inequalities in these systems from the perspective of the weak and the stronger concepts of equity will be assessed.

Public Versus Private Health Systems

Health care systems vary in the public/private mix of their financing and organization.[12] The United States, for example, is known to differ from Canada and Western Europe because it is at the private end of the public/private spectrum.[13] In comparison to France, Canada and Great Britain, the United States is the highest health care spender (public and private combined), but it has the lowest share of public expenditures on health as a percentage of its gross domestic product (GDP). (See Table 1.) As to sources of financing, the United States health system relies the most on direct consumer payments and private health insurance, and the least on public insurance and government revenues. The United States has the most "private" system in still another respect, for it spends the smallest share of health expenditures in government-administered institutions.

At the opposite extreme, Great Britain is the lowest health care spender (public and private combined), yet it retains a relatively high share of public expenditures on health care as a percentage of GDP. Great Britain also has the smallest role for direct consumer payments and, in spite of recent growth, a very small private health insurance industry.[14] Direct government financing plays the largest role. In terms of organizational structure, Great Britain is the most "public" system: It is, after all, a national health service (NHS).

France and Canada represent two models of national health insurance (NHI). Both fall midway between the extremes of the United States and Great Britain. Canadian NHI is financed largely by government revenues, and health services are provided, for the most part, in private, fee-for-service practices and private, not-for-profit hospitals. French NHI, by contrast, is financed largely by social security payroll taxes, and health services are provided in private, fee-for-service practices and in a mix of public and private, for-profit hospitals, which is dominated largely by the public ones. In contrast to France, Canada and Great Britain, the United States is the only industrially advanced nation that lacks a system of compulsory and universal entitlement to health insurance. As a consequence, roughly 15 percent of the population is uninsured for health care services.[15]

France established a system of NHI covering all industrial workers in 1928. In a spirit of solidarity, the system was extended to all salaried workers following World War II, followed by agricultural workers in 1961 and the self-employed in 1975. By 1978, virtually all of the population was covered under a compulsory universal NHI scheme.[16] Benefits include the services of general practitioners and specialists in office-

TABLE 1

THE PUBLIC/PRIVATE MIX IN HEALTH CARE FINANCING AND ORGANIZATION

	Expenditures as Percent of GDP		Health Expenditures by Source of Funding (Percent)				Percent of Total Expenditures Spent in Government-Administered Institutions
	Total Expenditures on Health	Public Expenditures on Health	Direct Payments by Consumers	Private Insurance	Insurance	Government/ Social Security	
	(A)	(B)	(C)	(D)	(E)	(F)	(G)
United States	10.6	4.5	27.1	25.0	11.0	31.0	19.0
France	9.3	6.6	19.6	3.0	69.0	7.0	37.2
Canada	8.2	6.1	19.5	2.0	9.0	66.0	20.7
Great Britain	5.9	5.2	5.8	1.0	5.0	87.0	73.3

Sources: The data in columns (A) and (B) are for 1982, from Organization for Economic Cooperation and Development, *Measuring Health Care* (Paris: OECD, 1985). Data in columns (C) through (G) are for 1975, from Robert J. Maxwell, *Health and Wealth: An International Study of Health Care Spending* (Lexington, MA: Lexington Books, 1981). The magnitudes have not changed significantly since then.

based practices as well as in hospitals, laboratory tests and diagnostic procedures, prescription drugs, dental services, coverage for work accidents, sick days, and maternity leave and care. Beneficiaries are reimbursed substantially, but not in full. Although there are no deductibles, patients must contribute a small copayment for each day spent in a hospital and a coinsurance payment allowable for outpatient services—roughly 20 percent of the negotiated fee. Approximately one-fourth of French physicians have opted to engage in "extra-billing," which drives up the level of coinsurance beyond 20 percent.

Canada passed federal legislation which encouraged its provincial governments to adopt hospital insurance in 1957 and insurance for medical care (outside the hospital) in 1966. By 1970, all Canadian provinces had established a system of health insurance which provided universal coverage for Canadian residents and a comprehensive benefit package comparable to that provided in France, with the exception of prescription drugs.[17] In France, coverage for drugs is far broader than Canada, but Canadian NHI provides first-dollar coverage: there are neither deductibles nor out-of-pocket copayments for patients. What is more, in contrast to France, extra-billing is more restricted and patients are not required to advance payment for ambulatory care and then wait for reimbursement. Providers are reimbursed directly by the provincially-controlled health insurance funds.

The British NHS was enacted in 1946 and established in 1948. The 1944 white paper preceding its enactment proclaimed that "everybody in the country should have an equal opportunity to benefit from medical and allied services."[18] Thus, the NHS entitles all British subjects and legal residents to receive "needed" medical care free of charge at the point of consumption. The health system is organized as a tripartite structure. Hospital care is provided within districts which receive budgets from regional health authorities. General practitioner services, as well as dental and ophthalmic services, are organized by family practitioner committees who contract with these professionals to take responsibility for providing services to a designated population. Finally, public health services and certain categories of home care and social services are provided by local authorities. The system is almost entirely financed through general revenue taxation, and the physicians and hospitals must meet the demand for health care services within clearly defined budgetary constraints.

The Weak Equity Criterion

According to this criterion, all citizens should be able to secure a basic minimum of health care services or, to reiterate the expression used by

the President's Commission, an "adequate level of care without excessive burdens."[19] The United States is the only country in this comparison that fails to pass this test.

In France, Canada and Great Britain, the entire population is entitled to use medical care services. There is no category equivalent to the
American term "uninsured." There are occasionally coinsurance requirements in France and occasional copayments in Great Britain,
such as for drugs. Occasionally there are problems in obtaining access
to more specialized services in France, Canada and Great Britain, but
such problems are systematic only in the latter where rationing of certain specialized services such as kidney dialysis is standard practice.[20]
Furthermore, there are never any financial barriers to receiving primary care services (on both an outpatient and an inpatient basis) in
the three countries, and one would be hard pressed to find examples of
hospitals "dumping" patients to other facilities on financial grounds.[21]

Of course, it is difficult to define what constitutes an "adequate level
of care." Given some definitions, it is entirely possible—even probable—that France, Canada and Great Britain do not provide adequate
levels of care to certain segments of their populations. But only the
United States has a health care system in which a significant portion of
the population is uninsured and, because of this status, contains systematic differences in patterns of medical care use. What is more, only
the United States has experienced a recent trend where the percentage
of the uninsured has been rising, and the gap in patterns of medical care
use between the insured and the uninsured has been widening.

These characteristics disclose the existence of a two-tiered health
care system in which the adequacy of the care provided for the bottom
tier appears to be eroding. The argument that the United States fails to
meet the weak equity criterion rests on the proposition that the uninsured, a lower tier in the American health system, receive less than an
adequate level of care. A less than adequate level of health care in this
context is a relative judgment: first, in relation to the level of care received by those in the higher tier; and second, to the level of care received by the lower tier over time. On both grounds, recent studies in
the United States suggest that the uninsured are receiving less than an
adequate level of health care services.

In a comparison of health services received by the uninsured with
those received by the publicly insured (under Medicaid), Robert Blendon and his colleagues have shown that the level of care is significantly
different. [22] Their survey data (collected before Arizona became the
only state with no Medicaid program) indicated that low-income people received substantially less medical care from physicians if they re-
sided in Arizona or in other states with only limited Medicaid pro-

grams. In Arizona, poor children saw physicians 40 percent less frequently, and poor rural residents saw physicians 22 percent less frequently than poor residents of states with Medicaid programs. Moreover, the proportion of poor Arizona residents who were refused care for financial reasons was almost double that in states with Medicaid programs.

These findings are consistent with an earlier study which analyzed data from the 1977 National Medical Care Expenditure Survey. In this study, Karen Davis and Diane Rowland demonstrated that lack of health insurance matters: Financial access to ambulatory care, in comparison to physical and racial barriers, was the most important factor affecting use. They showed first, that the insured received 54 percent more ambulatory care (visits to clinics, doctors' offices or hospital outpatient departments) than the uninsured; second, that adjusting for health status, the insured in poor health saw a physician 70 percent more often than the uninsured in poor health; and third, that the same differentials applied to hospital care—the insured received 90 percent more hospital care than the uninsured.[23] This last point reinforces similar findings by Gail Wilensky and Marc Berk.[24]

A recent study by Kenneth Thorpe and Charles Brecher indicates that the uninsured poor in cities with public hospitals receive significantly more hospital care than the uninsured poor in cities without such facilities.[25] This conclusion could be used to argue that public hospitals, and perhaps other health care facilities as well, may serve to attenuate the disparities in access to medical care. However, it does not deny the findings by Blendon and his colleagues, nor those by Davis and Rowland, that public facilities and programs for the poor do not eliminate the systematic differences in the use of medical care by the insured and uninsured.

When one compares the care received by the uninsured over time, the evidence appears to support the argument that the uninsured are receiving less than an adequate level of care. Such a conclusion is all the more significant when one considers that between 1975 and 1983, following changes in Medicaid eligibility requirements, the proportion of Americans under the poverty level who were insured by Medicaid fell from 63 to 46 percent, and the number of Americans with no insurance increased by more than 20 percent.[26]

In the most recent report on the access of Americans to health care, Harold Freeman and his coauthors compare the results of their surveys between 1982 and 1986. They note that the gap between the uninsured and the insured in average number of physician visits increased from 19 to 27 percent during this period. While the gap in receipt of hospital care narrowed, there is still a 19 percent difference in admission rates between the uninsured and the insured. Although between 1982 and 1986 the overall use of medical care (physicians and hospitals) by Americans declined, these surveys indicate that low-income individuals and minorities in poorer health were affected disproportionately.

To underscore the above, physician visits for low-income individuals in poorer health declined by 8 percent, while visits for the nonpoor of similar health status increased by 42 percent. Also, the average number of physician visits for low-income adults under age sixty-five declined by 30 percent, but there was no such change for the nonpoor. Minorities experienced similar relative declines. In 1982 the gap between physician visits by blacks and whites in fair and poor health was 12 percent, with whites having a higher number of visits. In 1986, probably as a result of cutbacks in Medicaid expenditures and eligibility criteria, this gap increased to 33 percent.

Freeman, et al. also note that 13 percent of the uninsured claimed they did not receive medical care for economic reasons. The equivalent percentage for the entire population was six, and for low-income individuals, blacks and Hispanics respectively, 9 percent, 9 percent and 7 percent. Finally, the 1986 survey uncovers significant "underuse" of medical care. For example, of the total population surveyed, 41 percent who had serious symptoms did not contact a physician. The equivalent figure for the uninsured was 67 percent.[27] (See Table 2.)

What must be emphasized about the uninsured is who they are. Predominantly, they are poor. Thirty-two percent of the poor compared to 10 percent of the nonpoor have no public or private coverage.[28] The percentage of whites with private insurance was eighty compared to fifty-seven for blacks. This is not surprising since private insurance is, for the most part, provided by employers, and the unemployment rate is significantly higher among blacks. Disproportionately more blacks (20 percent) than whites (12 percent) had neither public nor private health insurance.

Although, as will be pointed out, there has been great improvement in the United States in reducing the disparities in use of medical care by socioeconomic status, the evidence presented above suggests that serious gaps remain. Moreover, the uninsured have systematically different patterns of health care use in comparison to the insured. Assuming the insured receive an adequate level of care, the contrast suggests that the uninsured most likely receive *less* than an adequate level. Even if the level of care received in 1982 were defined as adequate,

TABLE 2

INDICATORS OF POTENTIAL UNDERUSE OF MEDICAL CARE,
1986

Problem	Percent of Population Groups with Problem				
	Total U.S.	Low Income	Black	Hispanic	Uninsured
Individuals with chronic illness without physician visit in a year	17	18	25	22	20
Among individuals with one or more physician visits in a year, those with serious symptoms who did not see or contact a physician	41	42	39	53	67
Pregnant women without prenatal care during first trimester	15	30	17	27	20
Individuals with hypertension without blood pressure check in a year	20	15	30	30	22
Individuals with no dentist visit in a year	38	57	50	47	--

Source: Adapted from Howard E. Freeman, Robert J. Blendon, Linda H.
Aiken, Seymour Sudman, Connie Mullinix and Christopher R. Corey,
"Americans Report on Their Access to Health Care," *Health Affairs* 6:
1 (Spring 1987): 6-18.

the data from surveys taken since then which have been summarized
here suggest that what the uninsured are receiving today is less than
adequate.

The Stronger Equity Criterion

According to the stronger equity criterion, an equitable health care
system should achieve sufficient remedial effects such that health outcomes, as well as patterns of medical care use, would be independent of
an individual's socioeconomic standing. By this criterion, neither the
United States, France, Canada nor Great Britain comes close to

achieving equity. Let us review the evidence, first concerning health
outcomes, and next in relation to the use of medical care.

Inequalities in Health Outcomes

Whether health outcomes are measured in terms of mortality, morbidity or health status, and whether socioeconomic status is measured by
income, occupation or level of education, much the same picture
emerges in all of these countries: Those at the bottom are worst off.
They have the highest rates of death, disease and functional disability.
Consider, for example, infant mortality rates.

In the United States, there is no routine data collection procedure
linking infant mortality to the income of the infant's parents. Several
studies, however, provide strong indications. For the period 1964 to
1966, Philip Hauser and Evelyn Kitagawa showed that infant mortality rates were highly correlated to family income.[29] Another study,
comparing poverty and nonpoverty areas of nineteen large American
cities from 1969 to 1971, suggests that infant mortality rates were 50
percent higher in the poverty areas.[30] Often, since there are no data by
socioeconomic status and since it is well known that poverty rates
among blacks are higher than among whites, race is used as a proxy for
income. When this occurs, the differentials appear even more pronounced. Between 1950 and 1980, the ratio of infant mortality rates of
blacks to whites increased from 1.6:1 to 1.9:1. [31]

In France, demographers have a long tradition of documenting disparities in infant mortality rates among occupational groups. Although the disparities have narrowed—at least during the period between 1950 and 1970—the mortality rate of infants whose fathers are
manual workers is still more than twice that of infants whose fathers
are professionals or upper-level managers. [32] Moreover, the ratio of the
mortality rate of infants whose mothers are Algerian to that of infants
whose mothers are French was 1.7:1 during the period from 1966 to
1970, a decrease of only .2 compared to the period 1956 to 1960.[33] This
disparity is not limited just to Algerians and to infant mortality. The
immigrant or nonimmigrant status of the mother also is highly correlated with premature births and perinatal mortality.[34]

Canada, as in the United States, has no routine data collection on
infant mortality rates by income or occupational group. Once again,
though, a number of studies provide reasonably strong indications. For
example, in Toronto, Ursula Anderson found that the lower-income
population had infant mortality rates two-and-one-half times higher
than the higher-income population.[35] In Montreal, there are no studies

of infant mortality by socioeconomic group, but Russell Wilkins showed that the average life expectancy was significantly lower in poorer neighborhoods than in wealthier ones.[36] For the entire province of Quebec, it seems clear that infant mortality rates are related to the income as well as to the ethnic origin of the parents. For example, Nouveau Quebec, one of the poorest regions in the province and one which is populated largely by Inuits (Eskimos), has infant mortality rates that exceed the average for the province by a factor of three.[37]

In Great Britain, data on infant mortality by social class have been collected since the beginning of this century. As in France, the disparities in infant mortality rates by social class have narrowed considerably.[38] Nevertheless, from 1970 to 1972 the infant mortality rate of those in the lowest class was over twice that of those in the highest class.[39] Moreover, from 1930 to 1972 the overall percentage decrease in neonatal mortality rates was higher for the two highest classes than for the two lower ones.[40]

Such patterns of differential health outcomes by socioeconomic status can be shown for a variety of indicators such as standardized mortality rates, age-specific mortality rates and life expectancy. What is more, there is a range of health status indicators which are also highly correlated socioeconomically. For example, measures of various activity limitations such as "restricted activity days" or "bed disability days" indicate that the poor tend to suffer disproportionately—at least in the United States, Canada and Great Britain where such data, based on surveys, are readily available.[41]

Inequalities in the Use of Medical Care

As in the case of health outcomes, whether the use of medical care is measured by physician visits, hospital admissions or length of stay, and no matter how socioeconomic status is measured, there are common patterns of inequality in the United States, France, Canada and Great Britain. The use of physician services is an example.

Following the establishment of Medicare and Medicaid in the United States, NHI in France and Canada and the NHS in Britain, there was evidence of redistribution of ambulatory care services. Those in the lower-income brackets increased significantly their use of physician services; those in the upper-income brackets slightly decreased theirs.[42] In interpreting these changes, however, given that the poor tend to be sicker than upper-income groups, it is crucial to adjust the data on physician visits for differential health status.[43] In all four countries, although the poor tend to visit physicians more frequently than those with more income, once these adjustments are made, there is still evidence of significant inequalities.

In the United States, based on the 1969 Health Interview Survey, Karen Davis adjusted data on physician visits for differences in need and found that all persons with family incomes under $5,000 made 3.7 annual adjusted visits to physicians, while those with family incomes over $15,000 made 5.2.[44] In a later study based on the 1976 to 1978 Health Interview Survey, Joel Kleinman, Marsha Gold and Diane Makuc adjusted data on physician visits for differences in health status and found similar inequalities. Depending on the measure used to assess health status, they found that the poor have between 7 percent and 44 percent fewer physician visits than those with income above twice the poverty level. Moreover, they found that the poor are far more likely to use hospital clinics and less likely to use private physicians' offices.[45]

In France, similar findings based on survey data reveal the extent of inequalities under NHI. Although there are no data available on physician visits by socioeconomic status that are adjusted for levels of health status, Georges Rösch and his colleagues used an indicator of morbidity to so adjust data from a survey of medical care consumption patterns in the Paris region.[46] They found that, holding morbidity constant, upper-level managers had a consumption index equal to over twice that of manual workers. Subsequent studies have not updated this work, but the 1970 and 1980 French national surveys of medical care use reveal strikingly different patterns by socioeconomic standing.

For example, both in 1970 and in 1980, manual workers made significantly more visits to general practitioners than upper-level managers. Conversely, upper-level managers made far more visits than manual workers to specialists, radiologists, dentists and physical therapists.[47] Such differentials in patterns of medical care use are also found between ethnic groups in France, even for such basic services as prenatal care. Only 9 percent of French women do not complete their required four prenatal visits, but this figure reaches 20 percent for all immigrant women and 25 percent for all North African women living in France.[48]

In Canada, also, there are indications that NHI does not meet the stronger equity criterion regarding the use of physician services. In a study of the universal and comprehensive medical insurance plan in the province of Saskatchewan, Robin Badgely and others concluded that although use of medical services by all groups had increased, there was little change in the relationships between one's socioeconomic position and the use of medical services.[49] Subsequently, for the period 1963 to 1968, Beck found considerable inequalities in access to physicians' services by income class, particularly for specialist services, complete ex-

aminations and laboratory testing.[50] Although the disparities were reduced over the time of the study, they were not removed.

In a study of the use of physician services in the metropolitan area of
Montreal, Philip Enterline and his colleagues noted the change from a
positive correlation of use with socioeconomic status a year before
Medicare, to a negative correlation a year after its introduction.[51] Similarly, in a national study of medical and hospital use, Statistics Canada noted that lower-income people had a higher incidence of medical
care use than those in higher-income groups.[52] Neither of these studies,
however, adjusted for health status between these groups.

The one Canadian study that has made the adjustment for health
status provides mixed results.[53] For those patients who had reported
being sick in the past four weeks, a higher percentage of patients in the
low economic class reported seeing a doctor than in the high economic
class. Conversely, for those patients who reported not being sick in the
past four weeks, a higher percentage of patients in the high economic
class reported seeing a doctor than in the low economic class. Moreover, a significantly higher proportion of patients in the high economic
class (85 percent) reported seeing their doctor in a private office than
those in the low economic class (60 percent). Nearly all those who did
not see their doctor in a private office went to hospital clinics or emergency rooms.[54]

In Great Britain, as in the United States, France and Canada, data
from the General Household Survey, reported in *The Black Report*,
generally confirm that use of general practitioner services is higher for
groups with a lower socioeconomic status than for those with a higher
one. [55] After adjusting these data for differential health status, though,
with the exception of one important study by Elizabeth Collins and
Rudolf Klein, most of the evidence suggests that the higher classes
make more use of general practitioner services than the lower classes.[56]
But even this evidence probably underestimates the disparities because, as Richard Titmuss argued, the well-to-do know how to make
better use of the system.[57] They know how to get through the "gate-
keeper" to confer with hospital-based consultants, i.e., specialists.

In addition to knowing how to use the system, *The Black Report*
emphasizes that the higher socioeconomic groups make more use of
preventive and health promotion services.[58] For example, Ann Cartwright notes that there are clear class gradients in the proportion of
mothers receiving prenatal care.[59] Similar gradients apply for the provision of dental services.[60] *The Black Report* also notes that hospital
outpatient departments and emergency departments are used more by
the working class than by the middle class. Furthermore, the lower so-

cioeconomic groups receive less consulting time than do the upper ones.[61]

Such patterns of differential socioeconomic use of physician services can also be shown for hospital admission rates and lengths of stay. As a general rule, the poor tend to have higher admission rates and lengths of stay—not only in the United States but in France, Canada and Britain, as well.[62] This relatively high use of hospital services no doubt reflects the poorer heath status of lower-income groups and their different patterns of using ambulatory care services.

Methodological Problems in Comparing Inequalities

In applying the stronger equity criterion to the evaluation of health care systems, it is tempting to draw conclusions about the extent of health inequalities in the United States as compared to France, Canada and Great Britain. Such a cross-national approach would attempt to compare the extent of inequalities across each system at approximately one point in time. An alternative, longitudinal approach would compare rates of change within each system toward or away from equality. Both approaches, along with the methodological problems they engender, are called out in Table 3 pertaining to infant mortality, and in Table 4 with respect to physician visits.

The problem in working with data derived from national surveys is the risk related to sampling errors and the validity of the instrument itself. The problem in relying on local studies, on the other hand, is whether any valid inferences can be drawn for the whole country. The more overwhelming problem, however, in assessing the extent of health inequalities across countries is the unavailability of comparable data. Each country and each study has its own way of measuring socioeconomic status, and since studies of health inequalities are not done with great frequency, it is difficult to find comparable studies that focus on the same point in time.

The problem of comparing different measures of socioeconomic status is particularly vexing. It is difficult enough to develop measures which reflect levels of income, wealth, occupational status, education and a host of other factors. What makes cross-national comparisons so problematic is that each country has either developed or explicitly not

TABLE 3

DISPARITIES IN INFANT MORTALITY BY SOCIAL CLASS AND ETHNICITY

(Rates for lowest class compared to rates for highest class)

| | Social Class or Proxy Thereof | | | | | | | |
	Lowest	Highest	1950	1964	1970	1974-78	1980	1983
USA	Income Below $3,000	Income Above $10,000		1.61 (32.1:19.9)				
	Black	White	1.64 (43.9:26.8)	1.84 (42.0:22.8)	1.83 (32.6:17.8)	1.80 (26.2:14.2)	1.94 (19.6:10.1)	1.97 (19.2:9.7)
France[a]	Manual Laborers	Professionals/Executives	2.76 (61.7:22.3)	2.46 (36.2:14.7)	2.49 (30.4:12.2)			
Quebec[b]	Inuits (Eskimos)	French				3.80 (39.5:10.2)		
Britain[c]	Class IV & V	Class I & II	1.74 (33.5:19.2)	1.64 (20.8:12.7)	1.63 (17.8:10.9)			

Sources: U.S. data: Income data are from the United States Public Health Service, National Center for Health Statistics, Series 22, No. 14, cited by Evelyn Kitagawa and Philip Hauser, *Differential Mortality in the United States: A Study in Socioeconomic Epidemiology* (Cambridge, MA: Harvard University Press, 1973). Data by race are also from NCHS; see U.S. Department of Health and Human Services, Public Health Service, National Center for Health Statistics, *Health: United States 1985* (Washington, D.C.: U.S. Government Printing Office, Pub. No. (PHS) 85-1232, 1985), p. 54.
French data: Marcel Corzé, "Mortalité infantile des générations 1950-1951 et 1955 à 1960, suivant le milieu social et la résidence," *Études et Documents Démographiques*," No. 9 (Paris: INSEE, 1965); Solange Hémery and Marie-Claude Gérard, "Mortalité infantile en France selon le milieu social," in International Union for the Scientific Study of Population, *Proceedings: International Population Conference 1973* (Liege: IUSSP, 1973), Vol. 3, pp. 171-184; and adapted from Ministre de la Santé, *Propositions pour une Politique de Prevention: Rapport au Ministre de la Santé* (Paris: Les Presses du Palais-Royal, 1982), p. 33.
Quebec data: Robert Pampalon, *Géographie de la Santé au Quebec* (Quebec: Government of Quebec, Ministry of Health and Social Services, 1985, pp. 369 and 391.
British data: J. A. Heady and M. A. Heasman, *Social and Biological Factors in Infant Mortality*, Studies on Medical and Population Subjects No. 19 (London: HMSO, 1966), cited in Sir Douglas Black, et al., and Peter Townsend and Nick Davidson, eds., *Inequalities in Health: The Black Report* (New York: Penguin, 1982), Table 3.9.

[a] The data listed under 1964 are for the period 1961-1965; those listed under 1970 are for the period 1966-1970.

[b] These infant mortality rates are for two regions in Quebec, Nouveau Quebec and Canton de l'Est. Ninety-six percent of the population in Nouveau Quebec are Inuits; 85 percent of the population in Canton de l'Est is French. The poverty index, calculated by Robert Pampalon, is 2.25883 for Nouveau Quebec (the poorest region in the province) and 0.61456 for Canton de l'Est.

[c] Data are for England and Wales.

TABLE 4

ANNUAL PER CAPITA PHYSICIAN VISITS BY SOCIAL CLASS AND ETHNICITY
(Rates for highest class compared to rates for lowest class)

| | Social Class or Proxy Thereof | | | | |
	Lowest	Highest	1964	1970s	1980
USA	Income Below $7,000	Income Above $25,000	1.3 (5.2:3.9)	.84[a] (5.0:5.9)	.83 (4.6:5.5)
	Black	White	1.3 (4.7:3.6)	.96[a] (4.9:5.1)	
France	Manual Laborers	Professionals/ Executives		1.16 (3.6:3.1)	1.08 (5.1:4.7)
	North African Immigrants	French			1.6 (5.3:3.3)
Canada					
Quebec	Income Below $3,000	Income Above $15,000	.8 (5.3:6.6)	.61 (4.8:7.8)	
Saskatchewan	Zero Income	Income Above $15,000	.21[b] (10%:47%)		
Britain	Class V	Class I		.5[c] (69:138)	

Sources: U.S. data: National Health Interview Survey, cited in U.S. Department of Health and Human Services, Health Resources and Services Administration, National Center for Health Statistics, *Health Status of Minorities and Low Income Groups* (Washington, D.C.: U.S. Government Printing Office, Pub. No. (HRSA) HRS-DV85-1, 1985), p. 239, Table 1.
French data: INSEE-CREDOC Survey (1970), cited in J. Devouassoux, B. Morel and D. Polton, "Recours aux Soins et Inegalités de Santé," *Santé Securité Sociale—Statistiques et Commentaires* 3 (Mai-Juin 1982), Tableau 9; INSEE Survey (1980), in A. Charraud and P. Mormiche, "Disparitiés de Consommation Médicale," in *Enquête Santé 1980-1981*, Les Collections de l'INSEE, Séries M, No. 118 (1981), Tableau 5.13 and Tableau 5.19.
Quebec data: Philip E. Enterline, Vera Salter, Alison D. McDonald and J. Corbett McDonald, "The Distribution of Medical Services Before and After 'Free' Medical Care— The Quebec Experience," *New England Journal of Medicine* 289: 22 (November 29, 1973), Table 2: 1174-1178 at 1175.
Saskatchewan data: R. G. Beck, "Economic Class and Access to Physicians' Services and Public Medical Care Insurance," *International Journal of Health Services* 3: 3 (Spring 1973): 341-355.
British data: Sir Douglas Black, et al., and Peter Townsend and Nick Davidson, eds., *Inequalities in Health: The Black Report* (New York: Penguin, 1982), p. 96.

[a]These data are for 1975.

[b]For the period 1963-1968. Data are not visits but percentage of highest and lowest income classes who received no physician visits.

[c]These figures represent physician consultations per 1000 population over a two-week period.

developed its own unique national taxonomy. For example, in Great Britain the General Household Survey uses five occupational groupings: Class I consists of high-level professional and administrative occupations—5 percent of the population; Class II consists of employers in industry and retail trades and the lower-level professions—18 percent of the population; Class III is comprised of skilled workers—50 percent of the population; Class IV is made up of partially skilled workers—18 percent of the population; and Class V encompasses unskilled workers—9 percent of the population. In France, the Institut National de Statistiques et Études Economiques (INSEE) classifies socioeconomic status according to ten categories: high-level professionals and executives; middle-level managers; business and commercial proprietors; skilled workers; specialized workers; manual workers; employees; agricultural workers; salaried agricultural workers; and miners. What is important to observe here is that some nation's studies rely on occupational groupings; others on educational attainment; and still others on income categories such as "poor" and "nonpoor."

Given these differences in socioeconomic groupings, even after measuring health inequalities, for example, by calculating the ratio of the lowest to the highest group, it would be misleading to draw any conclusions on the relative degrees of inequality at any given point. It would also be misleading to draw any inferences about the relative rates of progress toward equality, which are shown in Tables 3 and 4. The reason is that the relative size of each socioeconomic grouping has changed at different rates within each country, and calculating these rates gets very problematic due to different rates of inflation and different methods of calculating real income.

With regard to the stronger equity criterion, one of the more promising areas for comparison would be to examine the extent of inequality among socioeconomic groups in physician visits adjusted for health status. Yet, once again, there are not only the methodological problems related to cross-national and longitudinal analysis, but also the problem of developing valid indicators of need. Each country has relied on different data and methods for adjusting their figures on physician visits. This means that the British "use/need" ratios are really not comparable to the various American calculations of adjusted physician visits and to the limited number of French and Canadian studies.[63] This explains why Table 4 displays only physician visits with no adjustments for health status.

Concluding Observations

On the basis of the weak equity criterion, the United States is the least equitable health care system in comparison to France, Canada and Great Britain, because it is the only country where a significant portion of the population is uninsured. This status, which unquestionably affects the patient's ability to pay, means that providers are at risk for what has come to be known as "bad debt" or "uncompensated care."

From a private, office-based physician's perspective, there is no obligation to serve such patients. From a private hospital's perspective, as a general rule it is best to minimize such risk and ration costly resources either by transferring patients or by providing fewer services to them.

In France, Canada and Great Britain, since almost all hospitals are reimbursed on the basis of global budgets, there is also an incentive to ration costly resources, and problems of patient dumping do occur. This affects the elderly, the mentally ill, alcoholics and other, less desired patients. British consultants, for example, refer to "bed blocking" when such patients take up badly needed space. The United States, however, is the only country in this comparison where there exist systematic inequalities, based on ability to pay, in the health services received by the uninsured as compared to the insured. Although the uninsured usually receive some basic minimum care, as noted earlier, the evidence suggests that what they receive is *less* than adequate.

Regarding the stronger equity criterion, the extent of inequalities— both in relation to health outcomes as well as to the use of medical care—is clearly significant and pervasive. It appears to make little difference whether a health system is public or private or, for that matter, anywhere between the two ends of this continuum. In an insightful book which compares the health systems in the United States and Britain, J. Rogers Hollingsworth compares a number of measures of inequality and asserts that "if class inequalities in access to care still exist in England and Wales, they are substantially less than in the United States or at earlier times." [64]

However, the methodological problems of comparing inequalities in health make it extremely difficult to compare the degree of inequality between different health care systems. Indeed, in his concluding observations, Hollingsworth admits that "[t]he data here do not permit any definitive conclusions about the relationships between changes in the organization and technology of medical care services and changes in health across social classes and regions. . . ."[65]

What, then, may one conclude from this analysis of inequalities in public versus private health systems? Certainly, evaluating health systems on the basis of the stronger equity criterion appears to resemble what Odin Anderson called "an endless search for the dream." In this sense, this criterion is an elusive goal, which makes it a "weak test" of a health system's capacity to achieve equitable access to medical care services. In contrast, the weak concept of equity is a "strong test"—at least with regard to the health care system in the United States—because it has been achieved in France, Canada and Great Britain.

NOTES

[1]Odin W. Anderson, *Health Care: Can There Be Equity?* (New York: Wiley & Sons, 1972), Part IV, p. 161.

[2]For a review of this literature, see Diana B. Dutton, "Social Class, Health and Illness," in Linda Aiken and David Mechanic, eds., *Applications of Social Science to Clinical Medicine and Health Policy* (New Brunswick, NJ: Rutgers University Press, 1986), pp. 31-62.

[3]See, for example, Norman Daniels, "Equity of Access to Health Care: Some Conceptual and Ethical Issues," *Milbank Memorial Fund Quarterly* 60: 1 (Winter 1982): 51-81.

[4]See, for example, LuAnn Aday and Ronald Andersen, "Equity of Access to Medical Care: A Conceptual and Empirical Overview," *Medical Care* 19: 12 (Supplement 1981): 4-27.

[5]The only other attempts to study these issues in a cross-national perspective of which I am aware are: Pranlal Manga and Geoffrey R. Weller, "The Failure of the Equity Objective in Health: A Comparative Analysis of Canada, Britain and the United States," *Comparative Social Research* 3 (1980): 229-267; and Sir Douglas Black, et al., and Peter Townsend and Nick Davidson, eds., *Inequalities in Health: The Black Report* (New York: Penguin, 1982), chapter 5 (hereinafter, *The Black Report*). I have benefited greatly from both studies.

[6]A comprehensive survey of recent thinking on this issue may be found in the three volumes of the President's Commission for the Study of Ethical Problems in Medicine: Biomedical and Behavioral Research, *Securing Access to Health Care: A Report on the Ethical Implications of Differences in the Availability of Health Care Services* (Washington, D.C.: U.S. Government Printing Office, 1983).

[7]George Orwell, *Animal Farm* (New York: Harcourt, Brace & Co., 1946).

[8]For a helpful conceptual framework in analyzing equity in school financing, see Robert Berne and Leanna Stiefel, *The Measurement of Equity in School Finance* (Baltimore: The Johns Hopkins University Press, 1984).

[9]Daniels, op. cit. note 3; and Alain Enthoven, *Health Plan: The Only Practical Choice to the Soaring Cost of Medical Care* (Reading, MA: Addison-Wesley, 1980). See Enthoven's description of the Consumer Choice Health Plan at pp. 114-144.

[10]President's Commission, op. cit. note 6, Vol. 1, p. 4.

[11]LuAnn Aday, Ronald Andersen and Gretchen V. Fleming, *Health Care in the U.S.: Equitable for Whom?* (Beverly Hills, CA: Sage Publications, 1980), p. 41.

[12]See, for example, Vicente Navarro, "The Public/Private Mix in the Funding and Delivery of Health Services: An International Survey," *American Journal of Public Health* 75: 11 (November 1985): 1318-1320; or Gordon McLachlan and Alan Maynard, eds., *The Public/Private Mix for Health* (London: The Nuffield Provincial Hospitals Trust, 1982).

[13]Victor Rodwin, "American Exceptionalism in the Health Sector: The Advantages of 'Backwardness' in Learning from Abroad," *Medical Care Review* 44: 1 (Spring 1987): 41.

[14]Alan Maynard and Alan Williams, "Privatization and the National Welfare State," in Julian LeGrand and Ray Robinson, eds., *Privatisation and the Welfare State* (London: George Allen and Unwin, 1984), pp. 95-110.

[15]Estimates of the number of the uninsured range from 15 to 20 percent of the population. In 1984, the *Current Population Survey* of the U.S. Bureau of the Census estimated that 35.1 million people, 17.1 percent of the population under age sixty-five, were without insurance. The percentage increases if one broadens the definition to include the underinsured and those otherwise medically disadvantaged. See Margaret B. Sulvetta and Katherine Swartz, *The Uninsured and Uncompensated Care: A Chartbook* (Washington, D.C.: National Health Policy Forum, George Washington University, 1986).

[16]For an overview of the French NHI system, see Victor Rodwin, "The Marriage of National Health Insurance and *La Medécine Libérale*: A Costly Union," *Milbank Memorial Fund Quarterly* 59: 1 (Winter 1981): 16-43.

[17]For an overview of Canadian national health insurance, see Spyros Andreopoulos, ed., *National Health Insurance: Can We Learn From Canada?* Sun Valley Forum on National Health (New York: John Wiley & Sons, 1975).

[18]*A National Health Service* (London: HMSO, 1944, Cmnd. 6502).

[19]President's Commission, op. cit. note 6, Vol. 1, p. 1.

[20]Henry J. Aaron and William B. Schwartz, *The Painful Prescription: Rationing Health Care* (Washington, D.C.: Brookings Institute, 1984).

[21]Dumping patients has become a major public issue; at the time of this writing, a congressional committee is investigating allegations that some hospitals engage in this practice.

[22]Robert J. Blendon, Linda Aiken, Howard Freeman, Bradford L. Kirkman-Liff and John W. Murphy, "Uncompensated Care by Hospitals or Public Insurance for the Poor: Does It Make A Difference?" *New England Journal of Medicine* 314: 18 (May 1, 1986): 1160-1163.

[23]Karen Davis and Diane Rowland, "Uninsured and Underserved: Inequities in Health Care in the United States," *Milbank Memorial Fund Quarterly* 61: 2 (Spring 1983): 149-176.

[24]Gail R. Wilensky and Marc L. Berk, "The Health Care of the Poor and the Role of Medicaid," *Health Affairs* 1: 4 (Fall 1982): 93-100.

[25]Kenneth Thorpe and Charles Brecher, "Improved Access to Care for the Uninsured Poor in Large Cities: Do Public Hospitals Make A Difference?" *Journal of Health Politics, Policy and the Law* 12: 2 (Summer 1987): 313-324.

[26]Blendon, et al., op. cit. note 22.

[27]Howard E. Freeman, Robert J. Blendon, Linda Aiken, Seymour Sudman, Connie Mullinix and Christopher R. Corey, "Americans Report on Their Access to Health Care," *Health Affairs* 6: 1 (Spring 1987): 6-18.

[28]Ronald Andersen, Meei-Shia Chen, LuAnn Aday and Llewellyn Cornelius, "Health Status and Medical Care Utilitization," *Health Affairs* 6: 1 (Spring 1987): 136-156.

[29]Evelyn M. Kitagawa and Philip M. Hauser, *Differential Mortality in the United States: A Study in Socioeconomic Epidemiology* (Cambridge, MA: Harvard University Press, 1973).

[30]U.S. Department of Health, Education and Welfare, *Health of the Disadvantaged: Chartbook* (Washington, D.C.: U.S. Government Printing Office, Pub. No. (HRA) 77-628, 1977).

[31]U.S. Department of Health and Human Services, Public Health Service, National Center for Health Statistics, *Health: United States 1985* (Washington, D.C.: U.S. Government Printing Office, Pub. No. (PHS) 85-1232, 1985), p. 54.

[32]Marcel Crozé, "Mortalité infantile des générations 1950-1951 et 1955 à 1960 suivant le milieu social et la résidence," *Études et Documents Demographiques*, No. 9 (Paris: INSEE, 1965); and Solange Héméry and Marie-Claude Gérard, "Mortalité infantile en France selon le milieu social," in International Union for the Scientific Study of Population, *Proceedings, International Population Conference 1973*(Liege: IUSSP, 1973), Vol. 3, pp. 171-184.

[33]Data are based on a survey of eleven thousand births published by INSERM in 1980. See *Systéme de Soins et Solidarité: Les Inegalités Sociales et Géographiques et Quelques Contradictions dans le Fonctionnement Actuel du Systeme* (Paris: Documentation Française, 1981), p. 23.

[34]Ibid.

[35]Ursula M. Anderson, "Infant Survival Differentials in the City of Toronto: A Challenge to Health Planning and Research," *Canadian Family Physician* 16 (1970): 45-50.

[36]Russell Wilkins, *L'Espérance de Vie Par Quartier À Montreal, 1976: Un Indicateur Social pour la Planification* (Montreal: Institute for Research on Public Policy, April 1979).

[37]Robert Pampalon, *Géographie de la Santé au Quebec* (Quebec: Government of Quebec, Ministry of Health and Social Services, 1985), pp. 287, 361 and 369.

[38]See Avedis Donabedian, Soloman J. Axelrod and Leon Wyszewianski, eds., *Medical Care Chartbook*, 7th ed. (Washington, D.C.: AUPHA Press, 1980).

[39]*The Black Report*, op. cit. note 5, p. 52.

[40]Ibid., Table 10, p. 71.

[41]Data on the United States are routinely collected in the National Health Interview Surveys. For a thorough analysis of these data, see Paul Newachek, Lewis Batler, Aileen K. Harper, Dyan Piontkowski and Patricia Franks, "Income and Illness," *Medical Care* 18: 12 (December 1980): 1165-1176. Data for Great Britain are routinely collected in the General Household Survey. See *The Black Report*, op. cit. note 5, Table 12, p. 73. For an analysis of similar data from Canada, see Russell Wilkins and O. Adams, *Healthfulness of Life: A Uni-*

fied View of Mortality, Institutionalization, and Noninstitutionalized Disability in Canada (Montreal: Institute for Research on Public Policy, 1978).

[42]See Donabedian, et al., op. cit. note 38, for data on the United States (p. 35), England and Wales (p. 51) and Quebec (p. 53).

[43]There is a wide range of methods for adjusting data on physician visits for differential health status. Each country has relied on its own. For example, in Great Britain, data from the General Household Survey on rates per thousand people of general practitioner consultations in a two-week period are divided by the prevalence rate per thousand people of chronic handicapping illness. In the United States, the National Center for Health Statistics collects data for a use-disability index that summarizes the ratio of mean physician visits to mean disability days for respective age and income groups.

[44]Karen Davis, "Medicaid Payments and Utilization of Medical Services by the Poor," *Inquiry* 13: 2 (June 1976): 122-135.

[45]Joel C. Kleinman, Marsha Gold and Diane Makuc, "Use of Ambulatory Care by the Poor: Another Look at Equity," *Medical Care* 19: 10 (October 1981): 1011-1029.

[46]The survey was conducted in 1965 and 1966. See J. Devouassoux, B. Morel and D. Polton, "Recours Aux Soins et Inegalités de Santé," *Santé Securité Sociale—Statistiques et Commentaires* 3 (Mai-Juin 1982): 27-48; see especially Tableau 11, p. 39. Also see Michel Magdelaine, Andree and Arié Mizrahi, and George Rösch, "Un indicateur de la Morbidité appliqué aux données d'une enquête sur la consommation médicale," *Consommation* 14: 2 (Avirl-Juin 1967): 3-41 (Centre des Recherches et de Documentation sur la Consommation).

[47]Devouassoux, et al., op. cit. note 46, Tableau 9, p. 37.

[48]Marc Gentilini, Gilles Brücker and Robert de Montvalon, *Le santé des migrants: rapport au ministre de Affaires sociales et de la Solidarité nationale, et au secretaire d'Etat chargé de la Santé* (Paris: La documentation française, 1986), p. 42.

[49]Robin B. Badgley, Robert W. Hetherington, V. L. Matthews and Marjorie Schulte, "The Impact of Medicare in Wheatville, Saskatchewan, 1960-1965," *Canadian Journal of Public Health* 58: 3 (March 1967): 101-108.

[50]R. G. Beck, "Economic Class and Access to Physicians' Services and Public Medical Care Insurance," *International Journal of Health Services, Planning, Administration, Evaluation* 3: 3 (Spring 1973): 341-355.

[51]Philip E. Enterline, Vera Salter, Alison D. McDonald and J. Corbett McDonald, "The Distribution of Medical Services Before and After 'Free' Medical Care—The Quebec Experience," *New England Journal of Medicine* 289: 22 (November 29, 1973): 1174-1178.

[52]Statistics Canada, *Distributional Effects of Health and Educational Benefits in Canada, 1974* (Ottawa: Queen's Printer, 1977).

[53]Jack Siemiatycki, Lesley Richardson and Ivan Barry Pless, "Equality in Medical Care under National Health Insurance in Montreal," *New England Journal of Medicine* 303: 1 (July 3, 1980): 10-14.

[54]Even after Medicare, the emergency room remains the usual source of care for a disproportionate share of the lower social classes in Montreal. See Nicholas Steinmetz and John R. Hoey, "Hospital Emergency Room Utilization in Montreal Before and After Medicare," *Medical Care* 16: 2 (February 1978): 133-199.

[55]*The Black Report*, op. cit. note 5, p. 96.

[56]Elizabeth Collins and Rudolf Klein, "Equity and the NHS: Self-Reported Morbidity, Access and Primary Care," *British Journal of Medicine* 281 (October 25, 1980): 1111-1115. The other studies include J. Brotherston, "Inequality: Is It Inevitable?," in C. O. Carter and John Peel, eds., *Equalities and Inequalities in Health: Proceedings of the 12th Annual Symposium of the Eugenics Society* (London and New York: Academic Press, 1976); and D. P. Forster, "Social Class Differences in Sickness and General Practitioner Consultations," *Health Trends* 8: 2 (May 1976): 29-32. See also *The Black Report*, op. cit. note 5, Table 13, "Use/Need Ratios by Social Group," p. 77.

[57]Richard Morris Titmuss, *Commitment to Welfare*, 2nd ed. (London: Allen & Unwin, 1968).

[58]*The Black Report*, op. cit. note 5, pp. 81-84; and Margaret Bone, *Family Planning Services in England and Wales: An Inquiry Carried Out on Behalf of the Department of Health and Social Security* (London: HMSO, 1973).

[59]Ann Cartwright, *Parents and Family Planning Services* (London: Routledge & Kegan Paul, 1970).

[60]See John S. Bulman, et al., *Demand and Need for Dental Care* (Oxford, England: Oxford University Press, 1968); and P. G. Gray and the Department of Health and Social Security, *Adult Dental Health in England and Wales in 1968* (London: HMSO, 1970).

[61]Ann Cartwright, *Human Relations and Hospital Care* (London: Routledge and Kegan Paul, 1964); Ann Cartwright and Maureen O'Brien, "Social Class Variations in Health Care and in the Nature of General Practitioner Consultations," in Margaret Stacey, ed., *The Sociology of the National Health Service*, Sociological Review Monograph No. 22 (Keele, England: University of Keele Press, 1976), pp. 77-98.

[62]For data on the United States, see Joel Kleinman, "Medical Care Use in Nonmetropolitan Areas," in U.S. Department of Health and Human Services, Public Health Service, National Center for Health Statistics, *Health: United States 1981* (Washington, D.C.: U.S. Government Printing Office, Pub. No. (PHS) 82-1232, 1981), pp. 55-61.

[63]See endnote 43.

[64]J. Rogers Hollingsworth, *A Political Economy of Medicine: Great Britain and the United States* (Baltimore: The Johns Hopkins University Press, 1986), p. 191.

[65]Ibid., p. 215.

CULTURAL DIVERSITY IN HEALTH CARE: THE EDUCATION OF FUTURE PRACTITIONERS

Eugene S. Farley, Jr.

University of Wisconsin-Madison

We are a diverse and mixed society. This is a simple statement of our past, present and future reality. It is also a testimony to our strength. This fact makes it imperative for all primary care providers to be aware of, and responsive to, our diverse cultural heritage.

All health care providers deal with facts, uncertainties and ambiguities. They are taught and must learn "facts," many of which change rapidly. They deal with individuals and groups, and with their associated ambiguities and uncertainties. Providers vary tremendously: Some are personally warm and caring; others are cold and detached. A caring provider with personal sensitivity to patients might fail to recognize that the bruises on a Hmong child are from "coining" or "cupping" as part of a treatment belief system, and thus may report it as child abuse. A cold, detached provider who recognizes the same findings as a culturally related healing system may respond differently and appropriately. This brief illustration points to the fact that all doctors, whether sensitive and caring or cold and detached, need to be aware of their patients' cultural realities.

Doctors and other health care providers care for people with diverse sociocultural backgrounds and belief systems. The role of the provider in healing depends upon his/her own belief system, training and experience, and upon the belief system, experience and expectations of the patient; i.e., the role of the healer is determined by the healer's cultural expectations and professional training and by the patient's cultural expectations and experiences. Therefore, in order to understand and interpret some of the patient's symptoms and concepts of health, illness, prevention and cure, all providers must know something of their own and their patient's belief systems.

This chapter describes some issues important in preparing providers, particularly nurses and physicians, to care for the diverse populations they serve in a culturally sensitive and informed manner. This starts with the education of the physician or nurse in the bio-psychosocial model of medical education and practice, rather than the straight biological model that often dominates.[1] It requires teaching "the care of the patient in the context of family and community."[2]

The following educational concepts are important to the preparation of both undifferentiated general physicians (medical school graduates) and specialty clinicians (graduates of residency programs).

Definitions, Goals and General Statements

Preparation of a physician or health care provider must emphasize understanding and caring for the patient, in both health and disease, in the context of both family and community. Although frequently omitted or rushed over, general definitions of health and disease, general statements of goals for the practice and teaching of medicine, and general definitions of the populations served are required.

The definitions of health and disease vary among cultures. For example, the Navajo definition of health is inclusive enough, regardless of culture or traditions, to be acceptable to most people and providers. The Navajos define disease as being "out of harmony with one's environment;" conversely, health exists when one is "in harmony with the environment."[3] These concepts require definitions of "environment" and of "harmony." The definition of "environment" includes both micro and macro levels and biological, psychological and sociological factors. The definition of "harmony" includes a balance of these same factors. They are consistent with the biopsychosocial determinants of health and disease, and are therefore acceptable to "modern medicine."

If realizing and acting in accordance with the above definitions are valid goals of the practice of medicine and other health care professions, then the teacher of these professions must impart to students something of the philosophy consistent with these goals. Students must be taught to recognize disharmony when it exists, to be able to help the patient see harmony when not present, and/or to help the patient accept any inevitable disharmony.

To communicate this, the teacher has to know that such harmony is possible and must be able to envision that those without it may obtain it to a greater or lesser degree. One must be able to convey this vision to those students who lack it, and be able to give those with the vision the tools with which to make it a reality.

No one can practice medicine or the other health care disciplines without a sound basis in clinical knowledge relevant to the profession, but the health care disciplines must go further than merely teaching clinical knowledge and the techniques of applying it. They must also develop an awareness in the student of the disharmonies that exist in the society of which both the provider and patient are a part. In doing this, a vision must be shared—a vision of what society can be. Development of this vision requires the use of sociologists, anthropologists, psychologists, other social scientists, psychiatrists and the insights of people with wisdom gained from experience.

Knowledge of the society, by itself, is inadequate if full health requires one to be in harmony with the environment. What if one's environment is sick? To be in harmony with a sick environment, the individual must be sick and conform; yet one cannot demand conformity as a definition of health. It must be recognized that the one out of step with the society may be in greater harmony with the environment than is the society. If the provider does not understand what the society is, or have a vision of what it can be, he/she has no way to evaluate the disharmonies that exist. This may cause one to mistakenly interpret conformity with society as synonymous with harmony with one's environment, and call the sick well and the well sick.

People of all sociocultural groups need and use health care providers of various types, including practitioners of "modern medicine." The health status, need and use of health care resources vary widely among ethnic, cultural and socioeconomic groups. This variation may be caused by culturally determined beliefs and practices, discrimination by the dominant culture, self-imposed isolation, physical environment, resources available, socioeconomic and political factors, limitations of health care (including provider ignorance of the sociocultural determinants of health and disease), and/or genetic factors.

Education for life is a continuum, beginning at birth and ending at death. The education of those entering the healing professions is part of this continuum. Such education must build on the student's basic life and educational experiences. The people and institutions committed to educating health professionals must facilitate the integration of experiences, knowledge, skills and attitudes the students bring to their professional education with the new material (knowledge, skills and attitudes) needed to practice their chosen healing profession. They must help their students understand themselves in order to understand others better, aid them to find the best in themselves and develop that as part of what they have to offer in their healing role, and foster in them the technical knowledge, skills and attitudes necessary to provide care to those needing their services. Education must help the providers to make the best use of their experiences for the care of the patient and their own continuing education.

All physicians and health care providers are participating observers or observing participants. The patient comes to them with a problem or concern and asks them to observe (listen, look and feel) in order to understand or define the problem and to participate in its resolution (treatment). Therefore, the education of doctors and other health care providers must help students develop and refine certain skills:

- Observation/Data Collection
  -listening and questioning (history taking)
  -examination of the patient and his/her tissues, fluids and shadows (x-rays, MRI, etc.)
  -laboratory studies
  -special studies (x-rays, biopsies, CT scan, etc.)

- Integration and Analysis
  a. Data organization
     -the chart
     -the family folder
     -the filing or retrieval system
     - filing of folder by area of residence for epidemiologic studies and outreach
     - an age-sex registry for patient care, outreach and practice management
     - a morbidity problem or diagnostic index for patient care, outreach and research
  b. Data analysis to understand the pathophysiology and to identify the problem or diagnosis

- Participation
  a. Treatment
     -prevention
     -cure
     -amelioration
     -rehabilitation
  b. Sharing in the life of the patient and community.[4]

The words of Donald Ranson demonstrate this approach:

The physician is not a neutral observer and the patient is no gold-fish in a bowl. The signs and symptoms of disease can be embodiments of social relations, disguised as natural things. Every medical act is a political and economic act as well. The behavioral scientist's chief role is one of epistemological provocateur. . . . What we must all remember is Howard Stein's word to the wise, that we are working together to construct a world view of interrelatedness which can eventually benefit all of medicine and all patients.[5]

Medical schools provide undifferentiated physicians with a basic understanding of the biological, psychological and sociological determinants of human development and behavior in health and illness. These physicians then enter a graduate training program in the specialty of their choice. The graduate training program builds on the physician's basic preparation, while expanding his/her knowledge and skills in the specific specialty area.

To be able to function well at the primary care level, all such providers need to be prepared to recognize and respond to the cultural and social diversity represented by the population served. This means the providers must *understand* the sociocultural background of their patients and *care* for them in the context of family and community. This is particularly important for family physicians, who care for the individual regardless of age or sex, and who can, and often do, care for the entire family. Care of the whole family provides opportunities for added insights into the health and functions of the individual and family.

Families are important pragmatically because of their effect on the health process. No moral definition is attached to who comprises the family. Thus, the "family" consists of those individuals who have an impact on the health process. The traditional nuclear family typically has this kind of impact, but there are other intimate relationship groups in society which rival the nuclear family in intensity and impact. Any such group is of concern to the family systems thinker. Thus this model leads to the definition of family as a group of intimates with a history and future. There is no universal and absolute norm of what a family ought to be.

> The family is only one of a number of systems of which individuals are members and which influence health and health behavior. Strong arguments have been made by other advocates for the importance of the workplace, the community, ethnic and cultural factors and broad economic forces in determining individual health. There is substantial truth in all these arguments and the family physician is well placed to observe and study the effects of a number of these factors.[6]

Additional knowledge and skills are required to enhance the therapeutic potential of these insights.

Since all people have health care needs regardless of culture, socioeconomic status or education, providers are exposed to, and should be aware of, the social and economic problems of all levels of society. This should lead them to be agents for social change. In reality this often is not the case, because some providers settle among the affluent and/or elect to serve only those with the resources to pay them accordingly.

The modern health care provider must know how to help modify and change behavior. New knowledge about health maintenance and disease prevention often identifies the need to change lifestyles and habits. Increased emphasis on prevention and the increased involvement of most health care providers in the education of patients make it important for the providers to recognize behavior patterns and belief systems that affect health. This recognition, plus the acquisition of basic knowledge and skills needed for helping to change behavior, is necessary if providers are to know how to work with patients to facilitate modification of their behavior within the context of their habits and basic belief systems.

Insights and Understandings Helpful for Culturally Sensitive Health Care

Diversity of Our Own Society: What It Wants, Needs, Believes and Does

In preparing a chapter such as this, it is difficult to limit what one should examine—medicine, education, history, religion, political science, economics, sociology, anthropology. All seem to have a common theme: man's relationship to man and to his environment—physical, psychological (spiritual) and social— all of which contribute to the education and knowledge of health care providers.

Healing, whether based on religion, with good spirits (God?) and evil spirits (the devil?), on psychology, on sociology or on an organic medical viewpoint, involves belief of some sort by both the patient and the practitioner. Often practitioners of modern medicine assume they know the answer. They have knowledge, skills and tools never before available to facilitate healing. However, these same practitioners of modern medicine consciously or unconsciously depend upon rituals, beliefs and magic, just as have all healers over the millennia. "Scientific" doctors do not deny this last statement—they recognize it, use it, wonder about it, and try to understand it in the light of "modern science." This requires them to be participating observers who always question, wonder, and try to develop theories that may provide answers or at least further understanding. New knowledge about endorphins may provide a partial understanding of some of the results one observes. Endorphins (naturally occurring, body-produced painkillers similar to morphine) are released in the body in increased quantities by exercise, by placebos and, one assumes (but does not know for certain), by faith, belief, meditation, the mystical experiences associated with many types of healing and, possibly, laughter, according to Norman Cousins.

Examples of Our Own Ethnicity

All of us are ethnics of one sort to one group or another. Thus all health care providers should be sensitive to sociocultural differences between those who are superficially alike as well as to those who are superficially different. Continuing contact with a population of people with undifferentiated problems requires primary care providers in particular to be aware of the sociocultural determinants of health and disease. They need to understand that the patient may define disease in a way different from that of the doctor, and may have beliefs regarding the causes of disease that the doctor's "cure" may not "treat." These causes may include such concepts as: it's punishment for some real or imagined failure; it's predetermined; it's my fate; it's written in The Book; it's God's will (as expressed by many Christians, Hindus, Muslims and others); it's in the stars; or it's a response to a past event or a mistakenly incompleted act or ritual. This last belief refers to something which happened in the past: a snake crossed my mother's path when she was pregnant with me; my mother threw a snake in the fire by mistake, thinking it was a piece of wood; I walked under a ladder; a black cat crossed my path; I am possessed by an evil spirit (devil?); or a curse or sign was placed on me without my knowing it. Many people would consider these concepts of the causes of disease to be something from the past, and thus give them no credence. In reality, individuals all over the world hold one or more of these beliefs. With the return of a very primitive form of religious fundamentalism, people with some variations of these beliefs are being seen in increasing numbers, even among the educated.

All health care providers bring to the care of their patients beliefs and attitudes derived from their own cultures, lives and background.[7] Providers must be aware of these beliefs and attitudes and learn to understand them, just as they learn to understand the beliefs and attitudes of their patients. These differing belief systems within a society may generate debate and, at times, conflict. They often come to public attention in the political arena when one group tries to impose its belief system on others. Belief systems need to be discussed in medical and other health care education in order to give the provider a better understanding of diverse cultures that, at first glance, may seem totally foreign. Outstanding examples of differences in belief systems that affect health and health policy in this country at the present time include disagreements about when life "begins," abortion and whether a woman can have a choice or not; about war and ways to maintain peace; about increased nuclear weaponry and the medical consequences of nuclear war or disaster; about how the government should spend our money (for health and social welfare programs or for military buildup?); about the right to die at the end stages of illness or life; and about the death penalty and the right to live. When these issues, which cause intense feelings and concern in American society, are contrasted with some of the issues of seemingly foreign cultures and beliefs, it becomes apparent why ethnicity can be defined as those beliefs or behaviors held by others that we are unaware we also hold.

We may be unaware because we have not looked at our own beliefs critically, or because we fail to recognize similarities if the format is different. Commonly seen and heard examples of similarities include: Navajo religion is based on fear and superstition—we will help them become God-fearing people;[8] their healing rituals are based on mumbo jumbo and magic, our healings come from God or Christ and are helped by incantations, prayers and other religious rites, sometimes strengthened by a trip to Lourdes or to one of our faith-healing gospel preachers; they don't believe in or use modern medicine—their witch doctors use rituals and other magic rites; Christian Scientists do not believe in the need for medical treatment or help from the medical profession since God is the ultimate healer; they believe in large families as a sign of manhood and refuse to control the size of their families regardless of general environmental, economic and social realities; they believe birth control of any type is against the wishes of God and therefore seek to deny public support of it or information about it; they perform witchcraft or magical rituals over the dying patient, while our priest or minister will pray, perform a religious ritual or give him last rites; they give certain artifacts attributes of a god, a spirit or a great healer, while we may take communion to renew faith, hope and strength; they use worthless herbs and potions which may or may not be pharmacologically active, while we recognize the placebo effect of medications and find placebos may increase the endorphins and thereby relieve pain or symptoms; they are stupid because spitting on the floor, where people sit and children play, is socially acceptable (they know nothing of the germ theory or of contagion). To us, the smoking of cigarettes is socially acceptable, even though we know it causes health problems for which we have no cure.[9]

These comparisons are just a few of those one observes every day. They are not made to denigrate the customs and beliefs of any group.

On the contrary, they are made to help increase people's awareness of the similarities of their own cultural beliefs and practices to other cultural beliefs and practices that seem very different.

The above examples demonstrate that "American" is a mix of many cultures. The blending or amalgam of these cultures has resulted in a broad, loosely defined, open culture with many old and new subcultures. Practitioners often assume, without further inquiry, that a patient represents the general culture; therefore, even though they probably care for those from several subcultures, they may fail to recognize the variety and strength of these subcultures.

All cultures have many types of healers. Understanding the variety and role of these healers in the many American subcultures derived from Western European, Judaeo-Christian traditions makes it easier to understand the role of various healers in other cultures and belief systems. The various healers or healing rites with which most Americans are familiar include those that are:

- Religiously based: ministers, rabbis, priests, etc.; groups organized for prayer, meditation or fasting; Christian Science readers; charismatic faith healers such as Oral Roberts and other healers believed to have "divine" power;

- Professionally based: medical doctors, osteopaths, nurses, social workers, psychologists and other trained counselors; various allied health professions, including physician's assistants, physiotherapists, occupational therapists, various technicians and others such as chiropractors, who are professionally licensed, but are often considered "fringe" by some other providers;

- Individually or idiosyncratically developed: naturopaths, masseuses, spiritualists and others; and

- Non-person-dependent: amulets, charms, religious medals and other items that have a protective, healing and/or good luck function, including copper bracelets for arthritis, St. Christopher medals to protect travelers, crosses worn as symbols of good luck or for protection from evil, rabbits' feet, horseshoes, and the small medallions placed by the doors in many Jewish homes.

Two or more of these approaches are used by most people in their daily lives and in their response to illness.

Reasons to Be Aware of Sociocultural Diversity and Change

Individuals have differing attitudes toward illness, life and death. These attitudes are based on the individual's culture or belief system, life experiences, "mind set" or psychological state, state of health and/or stage of life or development.[10] These are part of the sociocultural determinants of health and disease. The provider must be aware of these different attitudes and beliefs as he/she works with the patient to diagnose (identify the problems) and treat (prevent, cure, maintain and/or ameliorate).

For instance, the provider must be aware of the role of diet in many cultures and religions such as Hinduism, Islam, Judaism, The Latter-Day Saints, Seventh-Day Adventists and others, and for many others unrelated to religious belief such as elective vegetarians and others with dietary beliefs or customs derived from past need or availability.

Health care providers must also recognize the symbolic healing and/or religious significance of certain actions, e.g., understanding that the number four has religious and healing significance to some Navajos, so that prescribing a medication four times a day, rather than two or three, improves compliance. Understanding the relationship between hot/cold concepts of food, illness and healing in many Hispanic and some Eastern cultures is important when helping these patients to accept needed treatment. Good health, they believe, requires a balance between hot and cold elements.[11] Some hot foods are chicken, duck and squash; some cold foods are beef, goat, cucumber and eggplant; some regular foods are cabbage and rice. Some cold illnesses are beriberi and stomachache; some hot ones are fever, malaria and tuberculosis. Boils, influenza and earaches may be either hot or cold. Only cold foods are acceptable to counteract hot illnesses, and vice versa. Understanding the role of prayer and other religious healing rituals may be important in the care of patients from all backgrounds, particularly those from a Judaeo-Christian tradition.

The healer should also be aware of social, family and individual belief systems. For instance, beliefs and customs (religious, moral, ethical and otherwise) about pregnancy, family development and function, the role of a baby's father, the role of children, life in utero and children out of marriage are of great importance in caring for pregnant women and families. Not all nonmarital pregnancies are unwanted, and some seemingly "unwanted" pregnancies are actually wanted. Counseling regarding family planning, abortion and family development must take into account the religious beliefs and traditions of those involved and the individual's attitudes towards them. Many nonmarital pregnancies are wanted, whether or not the individual is economically, emotionally or physically prepared to care for the offspring. The pregnancy and the baby are seen as something special that can improve the mother's self-esteem and provide her with someone she can love and who can, in turn, love her. It can also provide the grandmother with an additional child to replace one who has died or left home. While delivering or caring for babies in inner city and rural areas and in some Third World nations, a subset of the population clearly states, "This baby is for my mother."

Western medicine is placing increased emphasis on mind/body relationships as it finds out more about them. In the past it has often explained away or denied observed facts, but now laboratory work is providing biochemical explanations for what has been observed. The validity of the observations is therefore being accepted. Traditional folk healers in all cultures have at one time or another observed the same mind/body relationships and incorporated them into their healing rites or belief systems. The same is true of "mind sets." Primitive or folk healers have recognized that a spell or curse can be placed on individuals that will cause them to die, if they know it has been placed. We recognize that some individuals with anorexia nervosa or depression will starve themselves to death in the belief that they are overweight. The questions raised include: Are these mind sets culturally, genetically or individually determined? How are they turned on? What is their chemical basis? Neither modern nor traditional medicine can answer these questions yet, but at least the folk healers have recognized the phenomenon, incorporated it into their belief systems, and developed explanations as to what it means and what causes it.

Modern medicine, with its improved ability to save lives and prevent illnesses, affects the ecological balance of man with his environment much more than was ever possible with traditional healers and medical practices. This is particularly apparent in many Third World countries, where cultures have evolved in response to other problems and where educational systems for the transfer of knowledge have not been fully developed. Medical education and practice must be increasingly aware of and responsive to this fact. The improved health of populations can either follow or precede improved social, economic and political conditions. Improved social, economic and political conditions are essential, though, if the improved health conditions are to be maintained. These improvements are necessary to prevent severe disruption of a fragile ecosystem caused by population growth beyond the ability of the political, socioeconomic and agricultural systems to adapt, with resultant destruction of the carrying capacity of the land and inevitable starvation. Increasingly, medical education must stress some of the untoward results of improved health care in ecologically fragile environments. Medical educators and students will have to work more closely with social scientists, agronomists and others if they are to understand how to facilitate the sociocultural developments needed for improved health for all. This will require some changes in the "subculture" of medical education.

Educational Programs that Facilitate Development of Cultural Awareness and Sensitivity

Because of the number and diversity of cultures and belief systems, we cannot expect to prepare physicians and other health care providers to be knowledgeable in them all. However, we do have to prepare people who are sensitive to these issues and can learn about them "on the job" as they become involved with their patients. This exposure to the problem is the essence of problem-based learning.[12]

Medical education must help students to learn to solve problems, and problem-based learning (PBL) is a recognized approach. It requires exposure of the learner and the teacher to real issues, problems and persons. Books, literature, seminars, demonstrations, lectures, the laboratory, discussions and creative thinking are the resources used to help understand, in depth, the issues, the problems and their origins. This type of teaching relies heavily on preceptorial and experiential learning. A hands-on approach can facilitate the integration of bio-psychosocial concepts into the function, not just the test scores, of the provider.

Problem-based learning is just one of many approaches to helping students at all levels to be aware of, and sensitive to, ethnic and sociocultural issues of health care. Most approaches help the students to understand themselves and to know how to "listen" so as to understand the patient, as an individual, in the context of his/her life experiences and cultural experiences. The multiple approaches are taught by faculty from various medical school departments with such names as Community Health and Social Medicine, Behavioral Medicine, Community Medicine, Community Psychiatry and Family Medicine, reflecting social orientation along with the traditional departments. The courses have such titles as "The Doctor-Patient Relationship," "Interviewing and Obtaining the Patient's History," "Patient, Physician and Society," "Growth and Development," "Health Care Issues," "Psychosocial and Community Medicine," "Community Medicine," "Family Care Program," "Behavioral Science," "Social Issues in Medicine," "Community Science," "Human Values in Medicine," "Cross-cultural Issues in Medical Care" and "Medical Anthropology for Clinicians." The specific content of these courses cannot always be determined from their name, but most do discuss the biopsychosocial models of health care, and some also place considerable emphasis on the sociocultural aspects of health and disease.

Specific seminar courses held for residents in the University of Wisconsin-Madison Department of Family Medicine and Practice have included: "The Family—Focus and Function Around the World, Changes, Mythology, Relation to Medicine;" "Race in America—Biology, Culture, Misconceptions, Relation to Medicine;" "Our Multicultural Society;" "A Cross-cultural Look at Affective Disorders;"[13] and "Southeast Asians: Cultural Implications for Medical Care."[14] The teaching methods and sites for these courses vary. Most use a small-group seminar approach with some field experience in the community. There is more apt to be experimentation in teaching approaches in some of these courses than in the traditional medical school preclinical courses. Such approaches include:

- Assigning students to a preceptor in the first semester of medical school, and giving them a family to follow throughout their four years in medical school.[15]

- Requiring first-year students to spend two to three hours a week in the office of a practicing physician to begin to see how a physician practices and cares for a diverse population of patients, and to identify some of the psychosocial problems encountered.[16]

- Small-group seminars on specific selected topics chosen and presented by the students and/or faculty.[17]

- Assigning each student to work with a senior in a local inner-city high school to identify needs and to develop and present a health education program appropriate to the needs of the students.[18]

- Requiring each student to fill out a family genogram for his/her own family, with attention give to family structure, relationships and functions.[19] This can involve a look at the family's belief systems in healing, religion, politics, behavior and ethics. Such an approach increases student awareness of the diversity of those who seem to be the same, and of the similarity of those who seem to be different. It helps the student to understand better other families and belief systems by better understanding his/her own family, belief system, history and relationships.

- Requiring the student to relate the life development of each patient to the sociopolitical events of the time, i.e., to place each patient in the context of the time and place of his or her development.[20] This gives an important perspective to the historical context, above and beyond family and community, that may have influenced the individual's development and outlook. This works on all patients. Typical examples seen in teaching include: a) two seventy-two-year-old women in a Jewish hospital. The first had a German accent and was raised, through adolescence, in Germany as Hitler was coming to power. She escaped in 1939, with all possessions lost and much of her family killed. The second, with a midwestern twang, grew up in the Midwest and spent her adolescence on farms in eastern Colorado and Wyoming. Her family lost all their possessions in the Great Depression and the Dust Bowl, but maintained life and family. Students may have only a vague understanding of these historical events and need reminding to understand their impact on the development of these two women and how their present health and viewpoints are affected by these experiences; b) Two fifty-five-year-old, American-born, -raised and -educated physicians, both active leaders in their communities; one white, one black. The black had a limited choice of colleges, medical schools and residencies. Because he was black, he was denied use of the Tulane University School of Medicine Library to study for his specialty boards, he was unable to sit where he wanted in public transportation in the South, to eat in many restaurants, and to stay in most hotels prior to 1964. The white was of a racial and ethnic background that had experienced no discrimination. Therefore, even though on the surface these men seem very much alike, their life experiences are very different. This difference needs to be understood by medical students and others if they are to understand these men and their lives in America; c) Two thirty-four-year-old men, one a veteran of the Vietnam War, the other an active resister. The one fought in Vietnam and lost an arm, the other actively protested the war and finally left the country to avoid the draft. Both lost many friends in the war. Do medical students and other providers involved in their care understand each in the light of the history of the times?; d) Two midlife professionals, one a physician, the other a former teacher. The doctor was born, educated and raised in Germany. He had been part of the Hitler Youth during his adolescence, had fought with the Germans in World War II as a pilot, and had emigrated to this country after receiving his M.D. degree. The former teacher was a graduate of Columbia, and born, raised and educated in the United States. He was a volunteer in the Lincoln Brigade in the Spanish Civil War, "to protect the world from fascism," and later taught in New York state public schools. The doctor is now accepted into American society, whereas the former teacher lost his job during the McCarthy era as a supposed communist because of his involvement in the Lincoln Brigade, and has never been fully accepted into teaching or other professional work since. How many students know anything of the history of those times, of McCarthyism and of the impact these events have had on each man's development?

• Having students participate in interviews of families of different generations and backgrounds.[21]

• Having students spend time in inner-city, migrant worker or other health clinics and make house calls with the doctor, nurse or social worker.[22]

• Regularly scheduled discussions, lectures or seminars with and by members of various ethnic groups in the community served.[23]

• Elective work in a Third World nation, preceded by a seminar series on cross-cultural medicine.[24]

• Use of Community-Oriented Primary Care (COPC) clinics and practices as a place for student education.[25] These centers emphasize community involvement and outreach, identification of community problems, response to these problems at the level possible, and ongoing patient care in the context of family and community. Some of the Indian Health Service and Neighborhood Health Center Practices, as well as select individual group practices, fulfill these functions.

• Development of field training areas, ecologic units in which health care providers, agronomists, sociologists, anthropologists and others provide services, teach, do studies and receive training in cooperation with the population in the area served and other medical schools and health care provider programs.[26] This concept is being developed as an extension of the COPC model.

Public hospitals such as Denver General, Bellevue, King County (in New York City), Montefiore, Charity, Cook County and the former

Philadelphia General have in the past offered, and sometimes still do offer, access to large populations with diverse cultural backgrounds and significant social and economic problems. For those students and graduates who do not receive some of their training in such facilities, special efforts may be needed to make them aware of the obvious: Cultural diversity, poverty and social deprivation abound. Even in Jamaica, where approximately 85 percent of the population lives below the poverty level, there are medical students unaware of what poverty means. In the United States, with only 14 percent of the population below the poverty line, there are surely many students with such ignorance. Just as many Filipinos, Guatemalans, Hondurans, Colombians and Brazilians are oblivious to poverty in their own countries, many Americans fail to see or understand poverty in theirs.

Recognition of, and response to, ethnic and cultural aspects of health care require a historical perspective. The health care provider brings his/her own culture and set of beliefs to the treatment of the patient, who also has a culture and set of beliefs that may or may not be congruent with those of the provider. The cultural histories of both the patient and provider antedate the history of either individual. These cultural histories and belief systems are not fixed, but are constantly evolving in response to the pressures of the greater society. An interchange and adaptation of the cultures and belief systems[27] occur in the context of the doctor-patient (provider-patient) interaction. If this does not occur, effective interaction may be blocked.

An excellent example of this interchange and adaptation of the doctors' and patients' belief systems occurred early in the development of a new practice.[28] Approximately 10 percent of the deliveries in this practice each year were to young, unmarried women. To try to reduce this number, the physicians started sex education classes in cooperation with one of the churches and the American Legion (the subject could not be discussed in the schools in those days). The emphasis of the presentations was on abstinence and "traditional" morality. Contraceptive information was offered reluctantly to those who were unmarried, unless they had parental permission. Even though the "sexual revolution" had begun, the physicians were unaware of its full extent and had not as yet adapted their own beliefs and behavior so they could counsel more appropriately for the needs of the patients. Instead, they counseled conformity to the physicians' behavior and expectations, rather than to the changing society of which they were a part. Gradually (over a period of two to three years), the physicians became fully aware of the change and adapted to it. This adaptation allowed them to meet more nearly the counseling and care needs of those served, and (they hoped) to prevent many more unwanted pregnancies than they had with their previous approach.

The Physician's Role in Public Policy

Individuals may be slow to change, but institutions are often slower. Several questions must be considered as public policy is developed to facilitate needed changes in the provision of health care, including:

- How can we strengthen individual, family, social and community support systems for all people, particularly for those who presently have weak or dysfunctional support systems?

- How can we improve accessibility, availability and acceptability of care for the diverse populations served?

- How can we develop a health care system that facilitates appropriate health care for all?

- Most relevant to this chapter, how can we assure the education of practitioners appropriate for our culturally diverse population? Policy issues related to this include the need for:

  —identification and recruitment of culturally sensitive students;
  —recruitment and retention of ethnic minorities in the health professions;
  —the encouragement of those we educate and train to practice in areas of need and to serve ethnically diverse populations;
  —changing institutions;
  —reducing the fragmentation of medical education;
  —integrating the biopsychosocial aspects of health and illness into the function of all health care providers;
  —assuring the availability of funds needed to prepare students in the psychosocial aspects of health care, while also assuring that the physician is becoming an excellent clinical technician as well. Without solid clinical skills and knowledge, the physician is not fully functional in trying to meet patients' needs, is less needed, and as a result may have less need for cultural sensitivity and awareness; and
  —assuring the availability of funds needed to enable those from families without large incomes to pursue medical education.

The specialty of family medicine and practice was established to train doctors who would practice in areas of need and care for broad populations of patients. It succeeds in leading a larger percentage of practitioners into rural and other areas of need than any other specialty. Efforts are now underway to get more graduates into urban areas of need and into Third World countries. Increased federal funds are necessary to support programs that enable doctors and other health care providers to work in areas with need, but limited resources.

In summary, all medical and health care education must prepare physicians and other providers to be astute observers, sensitive to the needs of the patient in the context of family and community, able to collect the needed biopsychosocial data and, from these data, formulate appropriate questions. The appropriate questions asked may mean important answers found.

NOTES

[1] I am indebted to George L. Engel, M.D., for the genesis of this idea.

[2] The following is the definition of family practice that I wrote for a brochure developed in 1967 while on the medical school faculty of the University of Rochester: "It is a clinical specialty which provides continuity of care to an individual, regardless of age, sex or disease (organic, psychologic, sociologic), in the context of family and community."

[3] Clyde Kluckhohn and Dorothea Leighton, *The Navajo* (Garden City, NY: Doubleday & Co., Inc., 1962), pp. 178-179.

In white society too, religion has its social and economic aspects. Marriage rites of the church are commonly used to set up a new social and economic unit, the family. Prayers often begin sessions of legislative bodies, and the oath on the Bible usually establishes the integrity of witnesses in courts. Many other instances from daily life could be cited to demonstrate that the divisions between religious, social, and economic life in white society are not nearly so clearcut as people often unthinkingly assume. Because Western thought is so much influenced by the sup-

posedly watertight categories into which Aristotle and the scholastic phi-
losophers believed they could separate all reality, white persons tend to
forget that abstractions are just a convenience and that really everything in human life blends into everything else. They talk as if "a thing is
either black or white," forgetting that it may be both or neither. Pure
black and white are both rare; what we have mostly is an infinite variety
of shades of gray, separated from each other by almost imperceptible
gradations.

[4]Adapted from Eugene S. Farley, Jr., "New Directions in Medical Education: Family Medicine," in Edith F. Purell, ed., *Recent Trends in Medical Education* (New York: Josiah Macy, Jr. Foundation, 1976), pp. 180-192.

[5]Donald C. Ranson, "A Quiet Revolution Going On," *Family Medicine*
XVII: 3 (May-June 1985): 120.

[6]Charles E. Christianson, "Making the Family the Unit of Care: What
Does It Mean?," *Family Medicine* XV: 6 (November-December 1983): 208.

[7]Peter Morley and Roy Wallis, eds., *Culture and Curing: Anthropological
Perspectives on Traditional Medical Beliefs and Practices* (Pittsburgh: University of Pittsburgh Press, 1979, original copyright 1978). In Chapter 1, the authors state (pp. 14-15):

> . . . [M]odern Western medicine, blinded by the success of the germ the-
> ory of disease, has for a long time ignored the relationship between social
> disturbance and individual affliction. Of course, contemporary allopathy
> is now more fully aware of the nexus between social disturbance and ill-
> ness, and this growing interest is reflected in the development of psycho-
> somatic medicine. Certainly, when juxtaposed to the notions of psycho-
> somatic medicine and other dimensions of post-Cartesian thought, the
> ancestor-spirit/witchcraft theory of illness causations, emphasizing the
> quality of the patient's social relations, does not appear as fatuous as at
> first glance. Even at the level of disease caused by infecting micro-organ-
> isms, "bad social relations could well tip the scales one way or the other."
> [Citation omitted.]

> . . . [W]hile industrial man may be well informed as to the existence of
> such pathogenic factors as bacteria, germs, and viruses, it is doubtful if
> many individuals are that well informed that they fully comprehend the
> structure, function, and general physiologic effects of such pathogenic
> organisms. . . . In essence, the allopath's patient is, like the Zande, a
> participant in a belief system. Perhaps the essential difference is that the
> Zande are more involved in, and less mystified by, both the belief system
> itself and the diagnostic utterances of its practitioners than are the pa-
> tients within the Western allopathic medical context.

[8]From a book written about Dr. Salsbury, founder of the Ganado Mission
in Arizona. I could not find the book, but easily recall the statement.

[9]Walsh McDermott, M.D., a heavy smoker, always pointed this fact out to
medical students and others visiting the Navajo-Cornell Clinic at Many

Farms, Arizona. He emphasized looking at your own behavior and beliefs before criticizing those of others.

[10]See Don J. Levinson, *The Seasons of a Man's Life* (New York: Ballantine Books, 1979) and George E. Vaillant, *Adaptation to Life: How the Best and the Brightest Came of Age* (Boston: Little, Brown and Co., 1977).

[11]Margaret Clark, *Health in the Mexican American Culture: A Community Study*, 2d ed. (Berkeley, CA: University of California Press, 1970).

[12]Howard S. Barrows and Robyn M. Tamblyn, *Problem Based Learning: An Approach to Medical Education* (New York: Springer Publishing Co., 1980).

[13]These seminars were developed and are led by Lorraine Zimmerman, Ph.D., Medical Anthropology, at the University of Wisconsin-Madison's Department of Family Medicine and Practice, Wausau Residency Program.

[14]Janet West, M.D., and David Silver, M.D., used this conference topic at the University of Wisconsin-Madison's Department of Family Medicine and Practice, Madison Residency Program and St. Mary's Hospital Medical Center.

[15]Since the early 1950s, students at Case Western Reserve University have been assigned a family with a pregnant member to follow through their four years in medical school.

[16]The new curriculum at the University of Rochester is experimenting with this in the first year of medical school. It has been doing a similar thing in the fourth year for the past twenty-five years.

[17]An example of such a seminar is "Patient, Physician and Society," a first-year course at the University of Rochester.

[18]This idea is taken from Stephen J. Kunitz, ed., *The Training of Primary Physicians* (Lanham, MD: University Press of America, 1986).

[19]This is done at SUNY Medical School at Stony Brook.

[20]The Universities of Colorado and Wisconsin-Madison have experimented with this plan.

[21]A large number of medical schools have required this, but it is particularly well developed at the University of New Mexico.

[22]Several medical schools have done this as well; again, the University of New Mexico has an exemplary program.

[23]An elective course in holistic medicine and alternative-type healers has been developed by Jack Cobb, M.D., at the University of Colorado.

[24]Many schools, especially the medical schools at the Universities of Arizona and Minnesota, have well-organized, formal programs.

[25]The University of New Mexico has a strong COPC program.

[26]This idea has been partially implemented at some schools. The Department of Family Medicine and Practice and the Center for International Health

Resources and Services at the University of Wisconsin-Madison are hoping to develop a model site.

[27]Ann McElroy and Patricia K. Townsend, *Medical Anthropology in Ecological Perspectives* (North Scituate, MA: Duxbury Press, 1979). Chapter 8, "Health Repercussions of Culture Contact," provides these definitions of degrees of contact (pp. 334-338):

Diffusion: The process of people "borrowing" an idea, a piece of equipment, or a type of food from another people and incorporating it into their way of life is called diffusion. Diffusion involves selective borrowing on the basis of the perceived usefulness and acceptability of the idea or item borrowed.

. . . Incorporating foreign tools and foods into the Eskimos' way of life did not bring rapid changes, but each new item, especially those used in hunting, had ecological and health repercussions over the long run. . . . An example of the health repercussions of diffusion comes from the wide acceptance of tobacco all over the world since its introduction into Spain from the New World in 1558.

Acculturation: Acculturation involves continuous and intense contact between two previously autonomous cultural traditions, usually leading to extensive changes in one or both systems. . . . It entails large scale reorganization of a society to accommodate the presence of another cultural group. The health problems of acculturation are many, ranging from poor nutrition because of change in diet to the emotional stress of political or economic subordination, and to exposure to new hazards in the environment.

Assimilation: Assimilation occurs when one group changes so completely that it becomes fully integrated into the dominant society or when two groups merge into a new cultural system. Assimilation is a long-range process and is more easily accomplished by individuals motivated to change than by total groups. Generally speaking, assimilated people face health problems similar to those of the dominant group. The new lifestyle they take on poses new disease risks as well as occupational and recreational hazards.

Ethnic Revitalization: When racial or class barriers to assimilation deter total change in lifestyle, or when people become disillusioned and frustrated in accommodating to a powerful foreign culture, attempts to revitalize the old system may emerge. Actually at each stage of contact and acculturation, some individuals do look to ritual or political mechanisms to regain a sense of control, to revitalize their culture, and to attempt to restore equilibrium. In reaffirming ethnic identity, these movements reduce the psychological stress of rapid change. They may also encourage people to reject unhealthy behaviors, foods and stimulants that have diffused from the intrusive society.

Although for some purposes it is useful to think of diffusion, assimilation and ethnic revitalization as stages of cultural change, whole societies do not pass through one stage at a time. In reality there is much intra-cultural diversity in how people respond to contact. Some families modernize easily, and others resist change. Some people try out modern practices, but later reject them. It is difficult for groups to reverse the direction of change, however . . . .

[28]This was my wife's and my experience shortly after entering practice in the late 1950s and early 1960s.

POVERTY, STRESS AND MENTAL HEALTH: PERSPECTIVES FROM THE BLACK COMMUNITY

Lawrence E. Gary

Howard University

Introduction

The aim of this chapter is to examine the relationship between poverty, stress and mental health within the black community. The following questions will be addressed: What is the extent of poverty among blacks? What factors influence the distribution of poverty among black people? What function does poverty perform in our society? How are stressful life events defined and measured? What is the extent of stressful life events among black people? What impact does stress have on mental health, especially depression? What is the general mental health status of blacks? And most important, what is the relationship between poverty and mental health?

An extensive review of the literature will be used to answer the aforementioned questions. Although secondary data sources for assessing these relationships will be relied upon primarily, much attention will be devoted to identifying research studies which used primary data collection procedures. In general the discussion will focus on black people, even though some data sets used the less precise "nonwhite" category for analytic purposes. Moreover, a racial comparative approach will not be emphasized, although some racial comparisons are made. It is imperative to move beyond the assumption that the black community is homogeneous, thus researchers and policymakers should spend more time examining and calling attention to differences within the black community. The chapter will conclude with a discussion of the policy implications of developing a better understanding of the impact of poverty on stress and mental health within the black community.

Defining Poverty

From an historical perspective, poverty has always been an issue in American society. According to Ronald Federico, "[p]overty has moved from one group to another and has been associated with different social conditions at different times, but it has always existed."[1] In their book, *Long Memory: The Black Experience in America*, Mary Berry and John Blassingame detail the various strategies that black individuals and families have used in their attempt to deal with the problems of poverty, racism and violence.[2] Even though the United States has always had an impoverished "underclass," poverty was first viewed as a major social problem during the depression years of the 1930s. World War II and the prosperous postwar years, however, diverted public attention to other issues. During the 1940s and '50s, American society experienced rapid economic growth and prosperity, reflected in the growth of suburbs, the upward mobility of a large group of Americans, the expansion of educational resources, improvements in technology and automation, and high levels of consumption. In fact, John Kenneth Galbraith, a liberal economist, defined the nation's major problem as coping with growing affluence rather than poverty;[3] it was assumed that economic deprivation would no longer be a factor in the United States. In 1962, however, Michael Harrington, in *The Other America: Poverty in the United States*, jarred the consciousness of many civic and political leaders and citizens regarding the extent of poverty in our society.[4] Harrington provided considerable evidence of severe deprivation and malnutrition among a large segment of the population. Moreover, his book was widely read by governmental officials, including President John Kennedy. The presidencies of Kennedy and Lyndon Johnson developed social programs designed to eradicate poverty as a way of life for millions of Americans. As a result of their leadership, poverty in the midst of wealth was publicly recognized as a social problem and government intervention was accepted as an appropriate means to solve it.[5]

There are numerous ways of defining poverty, and each definition has different policy or political implications. Commenting on how poverty is defined, Diane DiNitto and Thomas Dye observed:

> The very first obstacle to a rational approach to poverty in America lies in conflict over the definition of the problem. Defining poverty is a political activity. . . . Political conflict over poverty, then, begins with contending definitions of the problem of poverty. In an attempt to influence policymaking, various political interests try to win acceptance for their own definitions of the problem.[6]

One definition of poverty is absolute deprivation—a lack of basic necessities.[7] This definition assumes that a family needs a certain amount of income to secure basic needs; if its income is less than a specific amount, the family is poor. As one would expect, there are conflicting opinions about exactly how much income a family or person needs to live above the poverty line. Although defining poverty as absolute deprivation has some serious limitations, social services professionals and social welfare agencies have traditionally used this definition. In addition, officials at various levels of our government and social scientists have also used this definition of poverty. The federal government has established what is called the poverty index or line. Ian Robertson concluded:

> In some respects, then, the federal government's method of measuring poverty provides an unrealistically low minimum income. The method does have the advantage, however, of determining with some precision the number of Americans who are unquestionably without the means to enjoy the basic necessities of life.[8]

Another approach to defining poverty is looking at relative deprivation— that is, the failure to attain living standards that are customary in the society.[9] This approach views poverty not only in terms of material goods, but also in terms of the psychological effects on an individual of not having certain resources that people around him or her have. As Lee Rainwater has stated:

> What causes the various lower-class pathologies that disturb us— "apathy," "poor educational performances," "crime and delinquency," the various forms of striking out at those around you and those who are better off—is not the *absolute deprivation* of living below some minimum standard, but the *relative deprivation* of being so far removed from the average American standard that one cannot feel himself part of his society.[10]

The basic principle underlying this approach is that poor people see affluence all around them and assess their situation or position in relation to both their basic needs and the wealth in society as a whole. In this sense, then, poverty is defined as inequality in the distribution of income. Under the relative deprivation approach, Robertson argued,

> The poor are arbitrarily defined as some proportion of the lowest earners in the society, say, the bottom tenth or the bottom fifth. Improvement in the status of the poor is then measured by how much their income rises in relation to the rest of the population.[11]

There are other approaches to defining poverty, including viewing poverty as culture or as exploitation, but a discussion of these approaches is beyond the scope of this chapter. For purposes of analysis, both the absolute and relative criteria have been used widely in defining poverty. Personal judgments, that is, the values of the researchers, usually determine which approach is used. The particular approach used, however, will determine the number of persons classified as poor and their social correlates.

Extent of Poverty

One can examine the extent of poverty in America by focusing on inequality in the distribution of income. As is well known, wealth and income are not evenly distributed in most societies, including those in North America. Measuring differences in income and in wealth provides two means of determining the extent of economic inequality in a given society. These two concepts—wealth and income—are closely related but are not the same. For example, income refers to the amount of money a person makes in a given year, and wealth may be defined as a person's total assets—real estate and personal property, stocks, bonds, cash and so forth.[12]

It is believed that wealth is distributed much more unevenly than is income in the United States. Data from the 1960s indicate, for instance, that the richest 20 percent of the American population had three times as much wealth as did all the rest of the people combined.[13] It has been estimated that there are over 210,000 millionaires, 155 families worth $10 million and 60 families worth more than $100 million in the United States. These individuals and families control more than half of all stock in this country.[14] It should be noted that most of this wealth is not the result of hard work by those who have it, but rather has been accumulated through inheritance.

Since the government publishes figures on income, more current and accurate information is available regarding its distribution within the nation, communities and various groups in our society. One way to determine the extent of income inequality is to divide American families into five numerically equal groups, or quintiles, and show the distribution of personal income among these groups. As shown in Table 1, personal income in America is distributed unequally. For example, in 1985 the poorest one-fifth of all American families received only 4.6 percent of all personal family income; at the same time, the highest one-fifth of Americans (defined as the wealthy) received 43.5 percent of all family income. During this same period, the top 5 percent received 16.7 percent of all family income.

TABLE 1

INCOME DISTRIBUTION BY QUINTILE OF FAMILIES
AND BY RACE: 1985

Quintile Distribution of Aggregate Income	Percent of Total Income All Families	Percent of Total Income by Race		
		White Families	Non-White Families	
			Total	Black
Lowest Fifth	4.6	5.0	3.6	3.7
Second Fifth	10.9	11.2	9.1	9.1
Third Fifth	16.9	16.9	15.7	15.7
Fourth Fifth	24.2	23.9	25.1	25.2
Highest Fifth	43.5	42.9	46.4	46.3
Top 5 Percent	16.7	16.5	17.1	16.7

Source: U.S. Bureau of the Census, *Statistical Abstract of the United States: 1987*, 107th ed. (Washington, D.C.: U.S. Government Printing Office, 1986), p. 437.

TABLE 2

INCOME DISTRIBUTION BY QUINTILE
OF FAMILIES: 1960 TO 1980

Quintile Distribution of Aggregate Income	1960	1965	1970	1975	1980
Lowest Fifth	4.8%	5.2%	5.4%	5.4%	5.0%
Second Fifth	12.2	12.2	12.2	11.8	11.3
Third Fifth	17.8	17.8	17.6	17.6	17.4
Fourth Fifth	24.0	23.9	23.8	24.1	24.4
Highest Fifth	41.2	40.9	40.9	41.1	41.9
Top 5 Percent	15.9	15.5	15.6	15.5	15.4

Source: U.S. Bureau of the Census, *Statistical Abstract of the United States: 1982-83*, 103rd ed. (Washington, D.C.: U.S. Government Printing Office, 1982), p. 435.

During the 1930s and the years of World War II, income inequality among Americans was reduced. For example, the share of income received by the top 5 percent decreased from 26.5 percent in 1936 to 24 percent in 1941.[15] Since the 1960s, as can be observed in Table 2, the income share of the low-, middle- and high-income groups has re-

mained somewhat constant. It is interesting to note that in comparison
to the white community, there is more income inequality within the
black community. As indicated in Table 1, the highest one-fifth of
black Americans received 46.3 percent of all personal family income in
1985, compared to 42.9 percent for white families. Moreover, there
seems to be a trend toward greater income inequality within the black
community. For example, in 1981 the top 5 percent of black families
received 15.3 percent of income compared to 16.7 percent in 1985.[16]
Also in 1981, the poorest one-fifth of black families received only 4.1
percent of all black personal family income, but in 1985 the correspond-
ing figure was 3.7 percent.

One can also measure the extent of poverty by using the absolute
approach. Through the Social Security Administration, the federal
government establishes the official poverty line. It is based on estimates of the cash income required for families to maintain minimum
food, housing, clothing and medical care needs. Consideration is given
to family size, sex, the age of the family head and residence. Cash income is estimated for each family type and for persons living alone.
Based on the official poverty line, over 7 million families—or 11.4 percent of all families—lived in poverty in 1985. Moreover, it is estimated
that about 33.1 million people in the United States—or 14 percent of
the population—are living at or below the official poverty line. [17] Since
the Social Security Administration's definition of poverty excludes "in
kind" (nonmonetary) benefits given to the poor, it is important to examine the extent of poverty when these benefits are calculated as cash
income. When these nonmonetary benefits are considered, the poverty
rate is reduced, but the extent of the reduction depends on the methods
used to determine the value of these benefits. As can be seen in Table 3,
the poverty rate using the market value approach (including food and
housing) was 12.5 percent for all persons in 1985, but it was 12.8 percent for the same period using the recipient and/or cash equivalent approach (including food and housing).

The incidence of poverty is not equally distributed among the various segments of our society. Age, family structure, residence and ra-
cial/ethnic background influence the distribution of poor people in a
given community. The young and the old are much more likely to be
poor than are people in their middle years. For example, the poverty
rate was 44.5 percent for blacks under sixteen years of age in 1985, but
it was only 23.6 percent for those between the ages of twenty-two and
forty-four. On the other hand, 31.5 percent of blacks sixty-five years of
age and older lived in poverty in 1985, compared to 22.2 percent of
blacks between the ages of forty-five and sixty-four.[18] Families headed

TABLE 3

POVERTY RATE USING ALTERNATIVE METHODS
OF VALUING NONCASH BENEFITS: 1985

Poverty Rate Methods	All Persons	Race or Ethnicity		
		Black	White	Spanish[b]
Market Value Approach				
Including food and housing	12.5%	27.5%	10.2%	25.5%
Including food, housing and medical benefits[a]	9.3	19.4	7.8	19.1
Including food, housing and all medical care	9.1	18.7	7.7	18.9
Recipient and/or Cash Equivalent Approach				
Including food and housing	12.8	28.6	10.5	26.2
Including food, housing and medical benefits[a]	12.0	26.8	9.7	24.6
Including food, housing and all medical care	11.8	26.4	9.7	24.5
Poverty Budget Share Value Approach				
Including food and housing	12.6	27.9	10.3	25.7
Including food, housing and medical benefits[a]	11.6	25.7	9.5	23.9
Including food, housing and all medical care	11.6	25.7	9.5	23.9
Current Poverty Definition	14.0	31.3	11.4	29.0

Source: U.S. Bureau of the Census, *Statistical Abstract of the United States: 1987*, 107th ed. (Washington, D.C.: U.S. Government Printing Office, 1986), p. 446.

[a]All institutional expenditures are excluded.

[b]Persons of Spanish origin may be of any race.

by women are more likely to be below the poverty line than are other families. In 1985 the poverty rate for all black families was 28.7 percent, but for female-headed households (no husband present) the rate was 51.7 percent. The poverty rate was 13.8 percent for black married-couple families and 23.8 percent for black male-headed households (no wife present) during the same period.[19]

Table 4 shows that the age of the householder also influences the distribution of poverty. As the age of the householder increases up to a threshold in late middle age, the incidence of poverty decreases. Table 4 also indicates that large families are more likely to be poor than are small families. For example, in 1985 49.7 percent of black families with seven or more persons were poor, compared to only 24.8 percent of black families with two people. Black families who live in the Midwest were more likely to be poor than black families in other regions of the country. Householders who work (particularly those who work full-time) tend to have a much lower incidence of poverty than those who do not work.

Contrary to popular stereotypes, the majority of poor people in the United States are white, not black. Census data indicate that 68 percent of all poor people are white.[20] However, the proportion of blacks below the poverty line is considerably higher than the proportion of whites below that line. In 1985 about 11.4 percent of all whites were poor, compared to 31.3 percent of all blacks.

The black poor do not form a homogeneous group, and a variety of factors (economic, cultural, political and behavioral) can push a person or a family into poverty. To a large extent there are many prejudices against the poor in general, and black welfare recipients in particular. The poor are blamed for their condition, when in many instances they are victims of society. In *Blaming the Victim*, William Ryan advances the provocative argument that social problems—especially poverty—are caused by society; lower-class people thus are not offenders against society but rather the victims.[21]

Herbert Gans argues that poverty plays useful functions in our society for those who are not poor.[22] He identifies these functions of poverty: 1) ensuring that dirty work gets done; 2) creating jobs for some of those who are not poor; 3) making an affluent lifestyle easier; 4) providing a market for inferior goods and services; 5) guaranteeing the status of those who are not poor; 6) legitimating American values; and 7) providing a group that can be made to bear the political and economic costs of change. All this implies that many powerful groups do not want poverty eliminated. If poverty were eliminated, groups that are not poor might suffer in certain respects.

TABLE 4

SELECTED CHARACTERISTICS OF FAMILIES
BELOW THE POVERTY LEVEL (PERCENT)
BY RACE AND SPANISH ORIGIN: 1985

Characteristics	Percent Below Poverty Level			
	All Races	Black	White	Spanish[a]
Total Families	11.4	28.7	9.1	25.5
Northeastern families	9.7	26.3	8.0	36.9
Midwestern families	11.7	32.9	9.0	20.4
Southern families	13.0	29.3	9.5	23.4
Western families	10.4	19.5	9.6	22.8
Age of Householder				
15 to 24 years	30.2	62.1	24.7	40.2
25 to 44 years	13.1	30.3	10.5	28.5
45 to 54 years	7.9	20.3	6.1	16.3
55 to 64 years	8.2	22.5	6.8	17.1
65 years and over	7.0	22.0	5.6	16.6
Size of Family				
2 persons	9.1	24.8	7.6	18.8
3 persons	11.1	27.5	8.9	26.0
4 persons	11.3	29.0	9.1	24.2
5 persons	14.9	30.0	11.9	28.7
6 persons	19.0	35.6	15.2	30.3
7 persons or more	32.1	49.7	25.0	46.2
Education of Householder[b]				
Less than 8 years elementary	26.2	33.8	24.1	36.2
8 years elementary	15.9	32.7	13.9	34.7
Less than 3 years high school	19.4	39.4	15.0	30.2
4 years high school	9.9	25.0	7.9	15.0
1 year or more college	4.0	13.7	3.1	8.6
Employment Status of Householder[c]				
Worked	7.5	16.9	6.4	16.9
Worked full-time	3.9	8.6	3.4	9.9
Worked part-time	21.1	40.1	18.3	34.0
Unemployed	24.6	55.9	18.6	55.0

Source: U.S. Bureau of the Census, *Statistical Abstract of the United States: 1987*
107th ed. (Washington, D.C.: U.S. Government Printing Office, 1986), p. 445.

[a]Persons of Spanish origin may be of any race.

[b]Householders 25 years of age or older.

[c]These figures restricted to families with civilian workers.

Some of the major consequences of being poor are reflected in such aspects of life as longevity, health and family stability. Among the disadvantages of being poor are a shorter life span, higher rates of divorce and desertion, less access to high quality medical care, inferior schooling, inadequate housing, a higher incidence and increased severity of mental illness, and exposure to more stressful life events than others.[23] The emphasis here will be primarily on the mental health consequences of being poor and black.

Stress and Stressful Life Events

In the past decade, the amount of research concerning stress and mental health in the black community has increased. We live in a stress-ridden society, one in which survival itself means experiencing varying degrees of stress. The notion of stress implies excessive exposure to environmental forces that can harm a person's well-being. There are many definitions and uses of the concept of stress. Some social scientists have defined stress as environmental events that make demands on the person, while others have defined stress as the individual's responses to events.[24] Stress has also been defined as "any unpleasant and disturbing emotional experience due to frustration."[25] Raymond Fleming and others conceptualized stress as "a process that involves recognition of and response to a threat or danger."[26] Underlying these definitions is the notion that stress results from an alteration of, or interference with, an individual's usual pattern of behavior. Glen Hughes, Mark Pearson and George Reinhart concluded:

> Stress plays a key role in daily life influencing, if not governing, happiness, productivity, and health. Estimates of medical problems directly attributable to stress range to 75% of all medical disorders.[27]

It is assumed that too many stressful life events (pleasant and unpleasant) will increase the probability of one's susceptibility to illness. According to Thomas Holmes and Richard Rahe, stressful life events are those whose advent is either indicative of, or requires a significant change in, the ongoing life pattern of an individual.[28] Research has shown that stressful life events contribute to the development of many physical and psychological disorders, including heart disease, cancer, chronic asthma, respiratory illness and mental illness.[29] In examining the link between stress and health, researchers have developed a variety of scales by which to measure stress, including the Schedule of Recent Experiences, the Life Experience Survey, Daily Hassles, the Social Readjustment Rating Scale and the PERI Life

Events Scale. From a psychometric perspective, these instruments have a number of methodological and conceptual problems which have implications for policy, planning, clinical practice and the interpretation of results.[30] For example, normative data have not been systematically presented for some of these scales. Moreover, the researchers have used a variety of operational definitions of stress which creates problems of comparability. Also, the selection of specific events for inclusion in the life event inventories has been somewhat arbitrary, with an emphasis on very stressful and very infrequently occurring events. Finally, the field of stressful life events research has given little attention to cultural or racial/ethnic issues. [31] Some researchers do not seem to understand that certain life events such as marriage and the death of close family members have different meanings and significance among the various racial/ethnic groups. For example, Emily Rosenberg and Barbara Dohrenwend concluded that certain questionnaires, such as the Holmes and Rahe Social Readjustment Rating Scale, which use a marriage item with a preassigned value to assist the respondents in rating other life events, may not be appropriate for all racial/ethnic groups.[32] In comparing blacks and Mexican Americans with middle-class whites, Anthony Komaroff and others found some similarities among the three groups, but the two minority subgroups were more similar to each other than they were to the white middle-class groups.[33] According to Charles Pine, Amado Padilla and Margarita Maldonado:

> . . . Ethnic or cultural influences exist that affect the cognitive appraisals of the stressfulness of life events. However, because information is limited, it may be premature to base any conclusions on existing data. Research that focuses on the relationship between life events and disorders needs to consider whether ethnic or cultural factors are involved. The first step in this direction is to explore possible differences among ethnic groups on a traditional life events measure in order to identify which, if any, items are perceived differently by any of the groups.[34]

As suggested earlier, mental illnesses are associated with stress. One of the more common types of mental illness associated with stress is depression. Previous research indicates a positive relationship between the onset of depression and one or more stressful life events.[35] Stress theories in particular have been used to explain the onset of depressive symptoms in blacks. Community and clinical studies suggest that the stressful life conditions of poverty and discrimination faced by many blacks increase their risk for depressive symptoms.[36] When one looks at items on the Holmes and Rahe Scale such as the death of a family member or spouse, divorce, imprisonment or arrest, or job loss, it is clear that black people are exposed to a large number of stressful life events. For example, in 1983 the age-adjusted death rate per 100,000 population for the white male was 701.8; it was 1024.7 for black males. During the same period the age-adjusted death rate for white women was 391.5 and 571.5 for black women.[37] Thus, death as a stressor is much more prevalent in the black community than it is in the white community. Social class also has been shown to influence how a person perceives and handles stress.[38] It is argued that poor people will be both more highly exposed to stressful life events and more highly affected by them than will middle-class or high-income persons. In a study of depressive symptoms among black men, this author found that two stressful events—unemployment and conflict between the sexes—were significantly correlated with depressive symptoms.[39]

Overall, few studies have examined systematically the relationship of stressful life events to depressive symptoms among relatively large black samples. Many studies that are available simply link stressful life events to low economic status among blacks, without serious consideration for the array of chronic stressful conditions which affects blacks on a daily basis. While stressful life events are occurrences that require a significant change in the ongoing pattern of the individual's behavior, daily stressors or hassles may require continued adjustment to chronic sources of stress. In recent years, researchers have started to focus more on minor events and their relationship to mental health. Allen Kanner and his colleagues, for instance, compared major life events to minor events in predicting psychological symptoms. [40] They defined hassles as "irritating, frustrating, distressing demands that to some degree characterize everyday transactions with the environment."[41] Examples of daily hassles are status incongruity between the spouses, sex role conflict, work overload and underload, and role ambiguity. The researchers discovered that daily hassles were better predictors of psychological symptoms than were major life events. These findings suggest that in studying stress and depression, it is important to not underestimate minor life events.

Mental Health and Illness

Many professionals, such as those in psychiatry, social work, psychology and nursing, and interested individuals, from the bartender or beauty salon operator to the teacher or minister, are involved in the complex field of mental health and illness. For many years social and behavioral scientists have been trying to provide a definition for these two concepts, but there is little agreement on their meaning because the definition of each varies with the perspectives of the definers, the points of reference used, and the values considered important. Several questions may be asked when defining mental health concepts: What is mental health? What is a mentally healthy person? What is a normal person? What is normal behavior under oppression? What is mental illness? What constitutes a mental disorder? These are important research, policy and practice questions for which we do not have immediate answers.

In *The Sociology of Mental Disorder*, William Cockerham reviewed in some detail the various perspectives and arguments regarding the definitions of mental illness.[42] Among the ways of classifying mental illness are the following: 1) according to its cause (demon theory; imbalance of body fluids; physiological interaction; unresolved conflicts of early development; etc.); 2) according to the degree of disability (deviant behavior requiring hospitalization versus home care); 3) according to its legal implications (insanity defense; involuntary hospitalization; the concept of danger; legal certification for business contracts; estate management; education; etc.); and 4) according to its effect on an individual's behavior (the degree of deviation from what is considered normal behavior and the frequency and intensity with which deviation occurs).[43] A focus on deviant behavior has been a central concern for many social scientists. William Eaton, for example, approached the concept of mental illness from the perspective of bizarre behavior, which he defined as "human activities that are rare, culturally deviant and inexplicable."[44]

It appears that the various mental health professionals view mental illness either as a disease, as a disturbance in the the functioning of the personality, or as a problem in living. Furthermore, it seems that most definitions of mental illness are based on symptoms which are related to the concept of normality.[45] In this regard it is important to note that who determines the criteria for establishing the norm is a critical ethical problem for both researchers and practitioners. Perhaps this is why Thomas Szasz has suggested that the term "mental illness" should be expunged from our vocabulary.[46] Several writers have commented on the fact that concepts or definitions of mental disorder often change over time.[47] For example, homosexuality is no longer considered a mental disorder, and terms such as melancholia, amentia hysteria, moral insanity and neurosis are no longer referred to as disease categories. These changes are reflected in the third edition of the *Diagnostic and Statistical Manual of Mental Disorder* published by the American Psychiatric Association in 1980.[48] It is hoped that this new manual will bring some clarity to the concept of mental illness.

In recent years, greater emphasis has been placed on the concept of mental health—rather than on mental illness—primarily because it has positive connotations. In their discussion of the concept of mental health, Morris and Charlotte Schwartz observed that this emphasis is an outgrowth of the mental hygiene movement in the United States and the development of psychotherapy and personality research.[49] Rather than focusing exclusively on the care and treatment of the emotionally disturbed, this movement gives special attention to the prevention of mental disorder and social and psychological maladjustment.

In arriving at a definition of mental health, Paul Insel and Walton Roth have taken a different approach by analyzing what mental health is *not*.[50] They argue that normality, a statistical concept, is not the same as mental health. What is normal is related to "whatever state most of the people in a population are in at a given time." Moreover, they suggest that the absence of symptoms of a mental disorder or the absence of problems does not necessarily mean that a person is mentally healthy. In other words, some "healthy" people may have problems and some "unhealthy" people may not have any significant symptoms of mental illness. "Everlasting happiness" is not a criterion for a mentally health person simply because "no one is happy all the time; healthy people have ups and downs." The ability to function in areas of life should not be taken as the standard for mental health. Again, according to Insel and Roth, "never having had help to make adjustments to society or reality is not a sure sign of a healthy person."[51]

Although there are different theoretical approaches to the definition of mental health, there is some agreement as to the basic elements of the concept. For example, Donald Miller observed:

Positive mental health suggests that an individual has a realistic or nondistortive orientation toward his social and physical environment, that he has (and is able to exercise) social skills in interpersonal relations, that his emotional life is personally satisfying, and that he meets reasonable role expectations of others who know him, as for example, fellow workers or members of a family.[52]

In his article, "Toward a Working Definition of Mental Health," Bert Kaplan reached this conclusion:

Mental health is a sequence of states of mind that unfold when the emergence, functioning, and integration of mental processes become differentiated from and integrated with the emergence, functioning, and integration of physical maturational processes as both sets of phenomena fit with each other and, taken together, are in keeping with the individual's adaptation to the environment.[53]

Both of these constructions afford black social scientists sound conceptual grounding for scrutinizing problems and issues pertaining to
mental health.

In developing alternative parameters for studying the mental health
of blacks, black scholars are especially cognizant of the functional significance of physical, social, political, economic and other environmental forces which influence the mental health of individuals in particular
and, thus, their community in general. In developing a working definition of mental health, Claudewell Thomas and James Comer stated:

> ... [M]ental health includes people's feelings of worth in the con-
> text of the total cultural and societal system as well as within the
> identifiable groups to which they belong. . . . Mental health en-
> compasses the issue of the availability of the good life within a
> given social, political and economic context.[54]

Thomas and Comer also view positive mental health as the ability "to
cope or function within society in an adaptive way."[55] They define positive adaptation as "the results of everyday endeavors to cope which
produce in turn a heightened capacity to cope and increased willingness
to engage in society."[56]

In order to understand positive mental health in the black community, Preston Wilcox identified several factors which influence mental
health-related behavior: 1) a conscious awareness that this society is
hostile to one's existence; 2) a constant state of dynamic tension; 3) an
ability to deal with superordinated power; 4) a lack of desire to oppress
or to be oppressed; 5) a need to be involved in shaping and/or controlling one's own destiny; 6) a steady involvement in self-confrontation;
7) a sense of being steeped in an identity of one's own culture; 8) a basic
knowledge of society's destructive characteristics; and 9) an ability to
perceive the humanity of oppressed people.[57] While these factors are
important, they are difficult to measure and implement from a policy or
practice perspective. Wilcox's analysis is useful in that he suggests that
the promotion of mental health in the black community rests in its
ability to utilize its resources to fight the debilitating effects of racism.
This implies that behavior in the white community should not be the
normal standard for black people.

Mental Health Status of Black People

Despite the absence of a settled definition of mental health, a major
industry has developed in the mental health field in terms of physical
facilities (public and private mental hospitals and clinics, community
mental health centers, etc.) and the work force (psychiatrists, psychol-

ogists, nurses, social workers, paraprofessionals and others). It has been estimated that about 15 percent of the nation's population needs some type of mental health services.[58]

Both treatment data and field surveys are good sources of information when examining the mental health status of black people. The most recent national treatment data are somewhat outdated but are the best available; one must be aware of other limitations as well. In addition to the problem of defining mental health, data are often not collected by race and by social class. Labels such as "white" and "other" are used, so one is forced to use data on "others" or "nonwhites" as a proxy for using data specifically regarding black people. Although blacks account for about 90 percent of the nonwhite groups included in the treatment data, using this category to determine the mental health characteristics of the black population can be misleading. In using secondary data sources on mental health services, one has to be aware of both sampling and nonsampling errors. Since certain mental health status rates are based on population data, the reader should be conscious of the problem of the census undercount of black people, especially black men. There are other limitations in making cross-group comparisons. For example, when looking at the pattern of institutionalization by different classes and by racial/ethnic groups, one has to be aware that the types of behavior which are considered to be abnormal by one socioeconomic or racial/ethnic group are not always considered abnormal by members of another. Also, some evidence shows that blacks and whites are diagnosed differentially for similar behavioral problems.[59]

Given these limitations, one can draw some conclusions in relation to the mental health status of black people. This assessment will be made on treatment data, that is, admission rates to state and county mental hospital inpatient units, private mental hospitals, non-federal general hospitals, and outpatient psychiatric facilities. These data show that blacks are more likely than whites to be admitted to all types of mental health facilities except private hospitals. For example, as shown in Table 5, in 1975 the age-adjusted admission rate per 100,000 population for outpatient psychiatric services was 814.0 for blacks, compared to 639.2 for whites and 528.0 for Hispanics. Of all racial/ethnic and sex groups, black men tend to have the highest admission rate to state and county inpatient psychiatric services. In 1975, for example, the inpatient psychiatric admission rate to county and state hospitals was 213.2 for white men compared to 509.8 for black men. Black women had the highest admission rates to outpatient psychiatric facilities in 1975. Their rate of admission to such facilities was 865.9, compared to 682.7 for white women, 587.7 for white men and 729.7 for black men. As revealed in Table 6, nonwhite people—especially non-

TABLE 5

**AGE-ADJUSTED ADMISSION RATES PER 100,000
POPULATION BY RACE/ETHNICITY AND SEX:
SELECTED MENTAL HEALTH FACILITIES, UNITED STATES, 1975**

Type of Facility	White	Black	Hispanic Origin
	Both Sexes		
Outpatient Psychiatric Services[a]	639.2	814.0 (1.27)[b]	528.0 (0.83)[b]
Inpatient Psychiatric Services			
State and county mental hospitals	159.2	367.5 (2.30)	123.9 (1.78)
Private mental hospitals	64.4	40.6 (0.63)	37.4 (0.58)
Non-federal general hospitals	243.3	258.9 (1.06)	271.6 (1.12)
Public	60.9	110.6 (1.82)	133.6 (2.19)
Nonpublic	182.4	148.3 (0.81)	138.1 (0.76)
	Male		
Outpatient Psychiatric Services[a]	587.7	729.7 (1.24)[b]	499.7 (0.85)[b]
Inpatient Psychiatric Services			
State and county mental hospitals	213.2	509.8 (2.39)	193.6 (0.91)
Private mental hospitals	56.9	41.3 (0.73)	39.2 (0.69)
Non-federal general hospitals	206.4	237.3 (1.15)	256.4 (1.24)
Public	64.0	122.1 (1.91)	148.0 (2.31)
Nonpublic	142.4	156.2 (1.10)	108.4 (0.76)
	Female		
Outpatient Psychiatric Services[a]	682.7	865.9 (1.27)[b]	553.2 (0.81)[b]
Inpatient Psychiatric Services			
State and county mental hospitals	110.0	248.4 (2.59)	60.8 (0.55)
Private mental hospitals	71.3	40.0 (0.56)	35.9 (0.50)
Non-federal general hospitals	277.9	277.5 (1.00)	283.4 (1.02)
Public	57.7	101.2 (1.75)	118.6 (2.06)
Nonpublic	220.1	176.3 (0.80)	164.8 (0.75)

Source: U.S. Department of Health and Human Services, Public Health Service, Health Resources and Services Administration, *Health Status of Minorities and Low Income Groups* (Washington, D.C.: U.S. Government Printing Office, Pub. No. (HRSA) HRS-P-DV85-1, 1985), p. 171.

[a]Affiliated and freestanding outpatient psychiatric services.

[b]Entries in parentheses are ratios of minority facility usage to white facility usage.

TABLE 6

MEDIAN AGE OF ADMISSIONS BY RACE/ETHNICITY AND SEX: SELECTED MENTAL HEALTH FACILITIES, UNITED STATES, 1975

Type of Facility	White	Black	Hispanic Origin
	Both Sexes		
Outpatient Psychiatric Services[a]	28.5	25.9	28.7
Inpatient Psychiatric Services			
State and county mental hospitals	35.8	32.2	31.2
Private mental hospitals	38.3	29.9	32.6
Non-federal general hospitals	36.3	28.6	28.3
Public	33.5	27.5	28.6
Nonpublic	37.5	29.3	27.7
	Male		
Outpatient Psychiatric Services[a]	24.7	17.5	24.9
Inpatient Psychiatric Services			
State and county mental hospitals	34.6	30.0	31.9
Private mental hospitals	36.2	28.6	30.8
Non-federal general hospitals	34.2	27.7	25.7
Public	32.4	25.7	25.2
Nonpublic	35.4	29.2	26.6
	Female		
Outpatient Psychiatric Services[a]	30.7	30.0	31.2
Inpatient Psychiatric Services			
State and county mental hospitals	37.9	38.0	29.3
Private mental hospitals	39.7	31.0	34.9
Non-federal general hospitals	37.6	29.2	30.7
Public	34.6	29.0	32.8
Nonpublic	38.4	29.3	28.5

Source: U.S. Department of Health and Human Services, Public Health Service, Health Resources and Services Administration, *Health Status of Minorities and Low Income Groups* (Washington, D.C.: U.S. Government Printing Office, Pub. No. (HRSA) HRS-P-DV85-1, 1985), p. 172.

[a]Affiliated and freestanding outpatient psychiatric services.

white men—are generally admitted to mental health facilities at a younger age than are white people. In 1975 the median age of white men admitted to outpatient psychiatric facilities was 24.7 years, while the median age of black men was 17.5 years. In contrast, the median age of white women admitted to such facilities in 1975 was 30.7 years, about the same as the 30.0 years for black women.

Once admitted to mental health facilities, nonwhite and white people have significantly different experiences in terms of their primary diagnosis at the time of admission. Figures showing the primary diagnoses of patients admitted to state and county mental health inpatient units in 1975 (Table 7) call out that nonwhite people were more likely than were white people to be diagnosed as having alcohol disorders, drug disorders, organic brain syndromes, schizophrenia, personality disorders, childhood disorders and transient situational disorders. Concerning the primary diagnoses of outpatients in 1975, the data in Table 8 show that nonwhites were more likely than were whites to be diagnosed as having depressive disorders, alcohol disorders, drug disorders, organic brain syndromes, schizophrenia, childhood disorders, transient situational disorders and social maladjustment. It is interesting to note the outpatient admission rates for patients who were diagnosed as having no mental disorder. In 1975 this admission rate was the highest of all for nonwhite males—222.1, compared to 57.4 for white males, 64.5 for nonwhite females and 71.5 for white females.

Using treatment data, Judith Rabkin examined the relationship between ethnic density (the relative size of a given ethnic group in a multiethnic neighborhood) and risk for psychiatric hospitalization.[60] Exploring black, white and Puerto Rican residents of New York City in 388 health areas, she found that the smaller the concentration of a particular ethnic group, the higher its hospitalization rate in comparison to both the rate of other residents in the same area and that of members of the same ethnic group living in areas where they constituted a numerical majority. The author controlled for poverty, family cohesiveness and population mobility in making this finding. Gerald Klee and his colleagues also showed that very small black populations living in predominantly white areas of Baltimore experienced high rates of mental illness compared to those living in predominantly black areas of that city.[61] These findings have some important implications for clinical practice and public policy. For example, what do these findings mean in terms of the integration of neighborhoods, schools, colleges and treatment facilities? Social service providers and mental health planners need to be alert to the unique mental health needs of nonwhites, especially blacks who live in predominantly white communities.

TABLE 7

ADMISSION RATES TO STATE AND COUNTY MENTAL HEALTH HOSPITAL INPATIENT UNITS BY PRIMARY DIAGNOSIS, RACE AND SEX: UNITED STATES, 1975

(Rates per 100,000 population)

Mental Disorders	All Races Total	Male	Female	White Total	Male	Female	All Other Races Total	Male	Female
All Mental Disorders	182.2	243.7	124.7	161.1	214.2	111.2	321.9	444.5	212.0
Alcohol disorders	50.4	86.1	17.1	45.0	79.5	12.4	86.7	131.1	47.0
Drug disorders	6.8	10.9	3.0	6.4	10.0	3.0	9.6	17.0	3.0
Organic brain syndromes	9.6	10.6	8.7	8.2	8.6	7.8	19.2	23.8	15.2
Depressive disorders	21.3	21.3	21.2	22.4	21.7	23.1	13.7	18.5	9.4
Schizophrenia	61.2	71.9	51.2	49.0	56.3	42.8	140.2	178.5	105.8
Neuroses	2.8	2.1	3.4	3.1	2.3	3.8	1.0	*	*
Personality disorders	12.5	19.1	6.3	11.6	16.9	6.6	18.4	33.6	*
Childhood disorders	2.8	4.7	1.1	1.8	2.4	1.2	9.8	19.9	*
Transient situational disorders of adolescent, adult and late life	6.2	6.5	5.8	5.9	6.6	5.4	7.5	*	8.6
Social maladjustment	0.5	0.6	0.5	0.5	0.6	0.4	*	*	*
No mental disorder	2.4	3.6	1.3	2.5	3.7	1.5	1.8	3.4	*
All others	5.6	6.2	5.0	4.5	5.5	3.5	13.2	10.9	15.2

Source: U.S. Department of Health and Human Services, Public Health Service, Health Resources Administration, Office of Health Resources Opportunity, *Health of the Disadvantaged—Chart Book II* (Washington, D.C.: U.S. Government Printing Office, 1980), p. 8.

*Five or fewer sample cases. Estimate not shown because it does not meet standards of reliability.

Epidemiological field surveys are useful in assessing the mental health status of black people. Both the Health and Nutrition Examination Survey (HANES) and the Health Interview Survey (HIS) are important resources for such an assessment, because these surveys consist of multi-stage, stratified probability samples of over thirty thousand adults, including a large sample of black people. In the 1981 HIS study, 11.8 percent of the population rated their health as "fair" or "poor," but a different pattern emerged when controlling for race/ethnicity. Nearly 20 percent of blacks rated their health as "fair" or "poor" compared to 10.8 percent of whites.[62] As income decreased, the percentage of people who rated their health as "fair" or "poor" increased. In one HANES study, the data showed significant sex and race differences regarding general psychological well-being:

TABLE 8
ADMISSION RATES TO OUTPATIENT SERVICES
BY PRIMARY DIAGNOSIS, RACE AND SEX:
UNITED STATES, 1975[a]

(Rates per 100,000 population)

Mental Disorders	All Races			White			All Other Races		
	Total	Male	Female	Total	Male	Female	Total	Male	Female
All Mental Disorders	665.0	621.1	706.0	637.3	593.8	678.2	848.8	806.9	886.3
Alcohol disorders	25.1	39.5	11.6	22.9	35.8	10.8	39.8	65.1	17.1
Drug disorders	10.4	13.5	7.6	7.1	7.7	6.5	32.7	53.0	*
Organic brain syndromes	14.6	15.0	14.2	13.7	14.2	13.3	20.1	20.5	19.7
Depressive disorders	85.5	50.3	118.3	84.2	54.6	112.0	93.9	21.0	159.2
Schizophrenia	70.1	67.9	72.3	62.7	64.6	60.9	119.7	90.2	146.1
Neuroses	54.8	34.9	73.4	56.1	36.2	74.7	46.1	25.8	64.4
Personality disorders	65.9	69.4	62.5	70.0	73.0	67.1	38.5	44.8	32.8
Childhood disorders	67.8	96.1	41.5	65.9	94.6	38.8	81.0	106.0	58.6
Transient situational disorders of adolescent, adult and late life	94.6	80.9	107.5	92.1	81.4	102.2	111.5	77.6	141.8
Social maladjustment	67.8	42.0	91.9	65.1	42.9	85.9	85.8	35.6	130.7
No mental disorder	74.4	78.5	70.6	64.7	57.4	71.5	139.0	222.1	64.5
All others	33.9	33.1	34.7	32.9	31.3	34.4	40.8	45.2	36.9

Source: U.S. Department of Health and Human Services, Public Health Service, Health Resources Administration, Office of Health Resources Opportunity, *Health of the Disadvantaged—Chart Book II* (Washington, D.C.: U.S. Government Printing Office, 1980), p. 84.

[a]Excludes all admissions to federally funded OMHCs, VA psychiatric services and private mental health practitioners.

*Five or fewer sample cases. Estimate not shown because it does not meet standards of reliability.

White males reported the highest level of well-being, with 70 percent having "positive" well-being. Black males and white females reported about the same level, with 54 percent and 58 percent respectively, having positive scores. Black females reported not only the lowest level of positive well-being, with 37 percent having positive scores, but more than half reported moderate to severe levels of distress. Almost a third of the black females showed a level of distress comparable to that reported by three-fourths of an independent sample of mental health patients. [63]

Other studies have shown a strong relationship between race and psychiatric impairment, but recently this assumed association has been questioned, especially in regard to depressive symptoms.[64] Instead of using hospital admissions as the data source, these recent studies have utilized community survey data and multivariate statistical techniques. For the most part, these studies have found that when the effects of socioeconomic status are controlled, black subjects tended to be no more psychologically impaired than did white subjects. For example, studies comparing the psychosocial adjustment of black elderly and white elderly have found that racial/ethnic differences were decreased or erased when economic status or social class was held constant.[65]

Poverty and Mental Health

Innumerable researchers have found that lower-class status is associated with higher rates of mental disorders.[66] In the 1850s, Edward Jarvis, a physician and epidemiologist, established the link between social class and mental illness. The classic studies by Robert Faris and H. Warren Dunham, August Hollingshead and Frederick Redlik, Leo Srole and his associates, and Alexander Leighton and his colleagues have also provided extensive support for the finding of an inverse relationship between social class and mental disorders.[67] Some writers—such as S. M. Miller and Elliot Mishler and Ramsey and Joan Liem—have suggested that this tie between social class and mental illness may indeed exist, but that it is a complex relationship and thus some caution must be exercised in interpreting results from studies showing the connection.[68] First, most of these studies have been based on treatment data. Caution must be taken when studying treatment data groups because they represent only those persons seeking help, and as discussed earlier, differential treatment of patients is a function of class and race in many mental health facilities. Second, some of these studies of social class and mental illness have found a linear relationship and others have shown a curvilinear relationship. This implies that a variety of socioeconomic factors influences the link between social class and psychiatric outcomes. Furthermore, as suggested by Liem and Liem, social class does not necessarily imply a "rigid, narrowly circumscribed life context shared equally by all members of the same class."[69] The lower class consists of a diverse group of people and not all of them suffer from high levels of mental disorders.

The literature on the impact of social class on mental illness has not been totally consistent, particularly in regard to specific diagnostic categories. Research has consistently shown that members of the lower class have the highest prevalence rates for schizophrenia and personality disorders. However, some data indicate that affective disorders with psychotic symptoms (especially manic depression) and anxiety disorders tend to be more common among the upper classes.[70] Depression is a mental disorder often ignored when discussing black people. There is confusion—as well as contradictory findings—regarding the existence and rate of depressive illness among blacks.[71] For example, regarding the 1975 treatment data mentioned earlier, whites were more likely than were nonwhites to be admitted to state and county mental hospital inpatient units for depressive disorders. (See Table 7.) For outpatient services, however, nonwhites had higher admission rates for depressive disorders than did whites.

When one examines nontreatment data, a different picture emerges. In their study of 1,645 adults, of whom 366 were black, George Warheit, Charles Holzer and John Schwab found that race had no effect upon depressive symptomatology when socioeconomic status, age and sex were controlled. [72] In a study of 713 respondents, of whom 67 were black, James Neff and Baqar Husaini discovered that a significant relationship between race and depression existed, but that it disappeared when controls were instituted for age, sex, marital status, income, occupational status and education. [73]

In contrast, George Comstock and Knud Helsing's examination of depressive symptoms showed a slightly higher percentage of impaired white subjects, as compared to black respondents, when adjustments were made for variables related to socioeconomic status.[74] What is interesting about the latter study is that, contrary to other studies which showed that women tend to have higher rates of depression than men, it found that black females had lower depression scores than black men when adjustments were made. Similarly, in a nationwide sample of adults, William Eaton and Larry Kessler found that black men had a slightly higher rate of depression than did black women. [75] In addition, Robert Roberts and his colleagues' study of 4,209 adults, of whom 382 were black, discovered that black men had a higher adjusted depression score than did black women.[76]

In general, the literature shows an inverse relationship between social class and depressive illness. Although different measures of socioeconomic status and depression have been utilized, research, for the most part, shows that low-income groups tend to report more depressive symptoms than do higher income groups.[77] The findings have been the same in studies which focused specifically on blacks. For example, in our 1984 study of depressive symptoms among 450 black adults, we found a significant relationship between family income and depressive symptoms.[78] Members of the lowest income group (those families earning less than $6000 a year) had the highest number of depressive symptoms in comparison to persons from other income groups. In another study of depressive symptoms among black men, this author discovered that members of the lowest income group scored the highest on a depression scale when compared to members of the other income categories.[79] Using multiple regression techniques, of the four variables measured (family income, conflict between the sexes, household size and employment status), family income was the best predictor of depressive symptoms among the black men.

Conclusion

Through the data presented in this chapter, some important conclusions become apparent. The first is that poverty is a fact of life for a large percentage of blacks in the United States—33.8 percent. Regardless of the poverty measures used, black people are much more likely to live in poverty than are white people. Even though a variety of strategies have been implemented to reduce poverty in general, and black/white disparity in particular, the data demonstrate that the problem of poverty among black people continues to be a major domestic policy question. The reduction of economic inequality between blacks and whites is central to policy in such other arenas as welfare, where the inadequacy of benefits is related to black poverty; education, where progress pertaining to educational equity with whites has decelerated; and economics, where increased productivity cannot become a reality because of the failure of our society to employ more people, especially blacks. Finally, the black labor force represents a wasteful underutilization of human capital. The national and local levels of government must make a stronger policy commitment to reduce poverty and to provide equal opportunity for black people in all aspects of American life. Without such a commitment, one can expect the current income inequality within the black community and between blacks and whites to increase. One can observe that these events are already occurring. If they continue, further harm will be done to the black community from a mental health perspective.

The research findings regarding poverty, stress and mental health have not been consistent. In fact, one can characterize much of the research which focuses on blacks as confusing and contradictory. The policy implication for solving this problem is clear—greater support for mental health research. It is important for these funds to be allocated to scholars who have an interest in increasing our knowledge of human behavior within the black community.

As more research support is sought, researchers should be mindful of the major criticisms of mental health research pertaining to black people. For example, many of the scales and measures used to study mental health problems have not been validated on black subjects. In too many studies, the researchers have not used adequate controls for social class or for sex within the context of the black community. Too often, these researchers have ended up comparing middle-class whites to lower-class blacks. They also generally assumed a uniform black experience, treating the black community as if it were monolithic. It should be stated that the black poor are not a homogeneous group and that being black and poor does not necessarily mean that an individual has poor mental health. There is diversity within black communities just as there is in other communities.

Although the research paradigm where blacks and whites are compared has some utility, there is a need to examine mental health functioning and not just mental disorders within black communities. An important research question centers on the balance between universal and cultural considerations in dealing with the mental health problems of black people. Greater emphasis should be placed on comparisons of subgroups within black communities.

Social science research does not consist of scientific methodology alone, but involves politics, funding, values and philosophical perspectives. Individual social scientists make certain assumptions and hold certain attitudes. Because of this, it is important for blacks and other minorities to be involved in all aspects of the mental health research industry. New perspectives—especially those from a diversified sociocultural frame of reference—are needed in mental health research. When we examine critically studies regarding rates of mental disorders in black communities, most do not identify the adaptive characteristics of African-American culture and social structure. More research questions should be presented concerning the reasons why black people do not show yet higher rates of psychosocial pathology, given the greater amount of stress to which they are exposed. Part and parcel to this would be to explore the factors in black culture which serve to buffer the effects of environmental stress. As indicated earlier, researchers have tended to ignore cultural diversity within black communities. In the mental health field, the value of cultural frames of reference in assisting one to develop appropriate service and policy strategies for solving mental health problems confronting blacks must be appreciated more fully. A sociocultural approach to examining the relationships between poverty, stress and mental health in the heterogeneous black community would provide us with better data for designing programs to assist various segments of our society in dealing with the problems of life.

NOTES

[1]Ronald C. Federico, *The Social Welfare Institution*, 4th ed. (Lexington, MA: D. C. Heath & Co., 1983), p. 242.

[2]Mary Frances Berry and John Blassingame, *Long Memory: The Black Experience in America* (New York: Oxford University Press, 1982).

[3]John Kenneth Galbraith, *The Affluent Society*(New York: Houghton Mifflin, 1958).

[4]Michael Harrington, *The Other America: Poverty in the United States* (New York: The Macmillan Company, 1962).

[5]Federico, op. cit. note 1, p. 242.

[6]Diana M. DiNitto and Thomas R. Dye, *Social Welfare: Politics and Public Policy* (Englewood Cliffs, NJ: Prentice-Hall, 1983), pp. 45-46.

[7]Ibid., pp. 46-47.

[8]Ian Robertson, *Social Problems*, 2nd ed. (New York: Random House, 1980), p. 182.

[9]DiNitto and Dye, op. cit. note 6, p. 50.

[10]Lee Rainwater, "The Problems of Lower-Class Culture and Poverty-War Strategy," in Daniel P. Moynihan, ed., *On Understanding Poverty* (New York: Basic Books, 1969), p. 254.

[11]Robertson, op. cit. note 8, p. 183.

[12]James Coleman and Donald Cressey, *Social Problems*, 2nd ed. (San Francisco: Harper & Row, 1984), p. 159.

[13]Ibid.

[14]For a discussion of stock ownership and class in American society, see Daniel W. Rossides, *The American Class System* (Boston: Houghton Mifflin, 1976); Robert A. Rothman, *Inequality and Stratification in the United States* (Englewood Cliffs, NJ: Prentice-Hall, 1978); and Marshall E. Blume, Jean Crockett and Irwin Friend, "Stock Ownership in the United States: Characteristics and Trends," *Survey of Current Business* 54: 11 (November 1974): 16-40.

[15]DiNitto and Dye, op. cit. note 6, p. 52.

[16]U.S. Bureau of the Census, *Statistical Abstract of the United States: 1982-83*, 103rd ed. (Washington, D.C.: U.S. Government Printing Office, 1982), p. 435.

[17]U.S. Bureau of the Census, *Statistical Abstract of the United States: 1987*, 107th ed. (Washington, D.C.: U.S. Government Printing Office, 1986), pp. 437 and 444.

[18]Ibid., p. 444.

[19]U.S. Bureau of the Census, *Money Income and Poverty Status of Families and Persons in the United States, 1984,* CPR Series P-60 No. 149 (Washington, D.C.: U.S. Government Printing Office, March 1985), p. 20.

[20]Ibid.

[21]William Ryan, *Blaming the Victim* (New York: Random House, 1971).

[22]Herbert J. Gans, "The Uses of Poverty: The Poor Pay All," *Social Policy* 2: 2 (July-August 1971): 20-24, and "The Positive Functions of Poverty," *American Journal of Sociology* 78: 2 (September 1972): 275-279.

[23]See Coleman and Cressey, op. cit. note 12, p. 186; and Robertson, op. cit. note 8, pp. 175-203.

[24]Raymond Fleming, Andrew Baum and Jerome E. Singer, "Toward an Integrated Approach to the Study of Stress," *Journal of Personality and Social Psychology* 46: 4 (April 1984): 939-949.

[25]George A. Theodorson and Achilles G. Theodorson, *Modern Dictionary of Sociology* (New York: Thomas Y. Crowell, 1969), p. 422.

[26]Fleming, Baum and Singer, op. cit. note 24, p. 939.

[27]Glen H. Hughes, Mark Pearson and George R. Reinhart, "Stess: Sources, Effects, and Management," *Family and Community Health* 7: 1 (May 1984): 47-58.

[28]Thomas H. Holmes and Richard H. Rahe, "The Social Readjustment Rating Scale," *Journal of Psychosomatic Research* 11: 2 (October 1967): 213-218. See also Thomas H. Holmes and Minora Masuda, "Life Changes and Illness Susceptibility," in Barbara S. Dohrenwend and Bruce P. Dohrenwend, eds., *Stressful Life Events: Their Nature and Effects* (New York: John Wiley and Sons, 1974), pp. 45-72.

[29]Holmes and Masuda, ibid.; Hughes, Pearson and Reinhart, op. cit. note 27; Richard Rahe and Juhani Paasikiri, "Psychosocial Factors and Myocardial Infarction, II: An Outpatient Study in Sweden," *Journal of Psychosomatic Research* 15: 1 (March 1971): 33-40; Gilberto de Araujo, Paul P. Van Arsdel, Jr., Thomas H. Holmes and Donald Dudley, "Life Change, Coping Ability, and Chronic Intrinsic Asthma," *Journal of Psychosomatic Research* 17: 5/6 (December 1973): 359-363; and Martin A. Jacobs, Aron Z. Spilken, Martin M. Norman and Luleen S. Anderson, "Life Stress and Respiratory Illness," *Psychosomatic Medicine* 32: 3 (May-June 1970): 233-242.

[30]Judith G. Rabkin and Elmer L. Struening, Jr., "Life Events, Stress, and Illness," *Science* 194: 4269 (December 3, 1976): 1013-1020.

[31]Charles J. Pine, Amado M. Padilla and Margarita Maldonado, "Ethnicity and Life Event Cognitive Appraisals and Experience," *Journal of Clinical Psychology* 41: 3 (July 1985): 460-465.

[32]Emily J. Rosenberg and Barbara S. Dohrenwend, "Effects of Experience and Ethnicity on Rating Life Events as Stressors," *Journal of Health and Social Behavior* 16: 1 (March 1975): 127-129.

[33]Anthony L. Kamaroff, Minora Masuda and Thomas H. Holmes, "The Social Readjustment Rating Scale: A Comparative Study of Negro, Mexican, and White Americans," *Journal of Psychosomatic Research* 12: 2 (June 1968): 121-128.

[34]Pine, Padilla and Maldonado, op. cit. note 31, p. 460.

[35]George W. Brown, Máire Ni Bhrolchaim and Tirril Harris, "Social Class and Psychiatric Disturbance Among Women in an Urban Population," *Sociology* 9 (1975): 225-259; Hughes, Pearson and Reinhart, op. cit. note 27; Peter M. Lewinsohn and Christopher S. Amenson, "Some Relations Between Pleasant and Unpleasant Mood-Related Events and Depression," *Journal of Abnormal Psychology* 87: 6 (December 1978): 644-654; and George J. Warheit, "Life Events, Coping, Stress, and Depressive Symptomatology," *American Journal of Psychiatry* 136: 48 (April 1979): 502-507.

[36]James E. Blackwell, *The Black Community: Diversity and Unity*, 2nd ed. (New York: Harper & Row, 1985); DiNitto and Dye, op. cit. note 6; and Robertson, op. cit. note 8.

[37]U.S. Department of Health and Human Services, Public Health Service, National Center for Health Statistics, *Health: United States 1984* (Washington, D.C.: U.S. Government Printing Office, Pub. No. (PHS) 85-1232), pp. 51-52.

[38]Barbara S. Dohrenwend, "Life Events as Stressors: A Methodological Inquiry," *Journal of Health and Social Behavior* 14: 2 (June 1973): 167-175.

[39]Lawrence E. Gary, "Correlates of Depressive Symptoms Among A Select Population of Black Men," *American Journal of Public Health* 75: 10 (October 1985): 1220-1222.

[40]Allen D. Kanner, James C. Coyne, Catherine Schaefer and Richard S. Lazarus, "Comparison of Two Modes of Stress Measurement: Daily Hassles and Uplifts Versus Major Life Events," *Journal of Behavioral Medicine* 4: 1 (March 1981): 1-39.

[41]Ibid., p. 3.

[42]William C. Cockerham, *The Sociology of Mental Disorder* (Englewood Cliffs, NJ: Prentice-Hall, 1981).

[43]Ralph Minear, "Mental Illness," in Jean Mayer, ed., *Health* (New York: D. Van Nostrand Co., 1974), pp. 294-299.

[44]William W. Eaton, *The Sociology of Mental Disorders* (New York: Praeger Publishers, 1980), p. 1.

[45]Donald H. Miller, *Community Mental Health: A Study of Services and Clients* (Lexington, MA: Lexington Books, 1974); Minear, op. cit. note 43; and Daniel Offer and Melvin Sabshin, *Normality: Theoretical and Clinical Concepts of Mental Health*, rev'd. ed. (New York: Basic Books, 1974).

[46]See Thomas S. Szasz's *The Myth of Mental Illness: Foundations of a Theory of Personal Conduct* (New York: Hoeber-Harper, 1961).

[47]Cockerham, op. cit. note 42; Eaton, op. cit. note 44; and David Mechanic, *Mental Health and Social Policy*, 2nd ed. (Englewood Cliffs, NJ: Prentice-Hall, 1980).

[48]American Psychiatric Association, Task Force on Nomenclature and Statistics, *Diagnostic and Statistical Manual of Mental Disorder*, DSM-III (Washington, D.C.: American Psychiatric Association, 1980).

[49]Morris S. Schwartz and Charlotte Green Schwartz, "Mental Health: The Concept," in David L. Sills, ed., *International Encyclopedia of the Social Sciences*, Vol. 10 (New York: Macmillan & Co. and The Free Press, 1968), pp. 215-221.

[50]Paul M. Insel and Walton T. Roth, *Core Concepts: Health in a Changing Society* (Palo Alto, CA: Mayfield Publishing Co., 1977), pp. 56-57.

[51]Ibid.

[52]Miller, op. cit. note 45, p. 31.

[53]Bert L. Kaplan, "Toward a Working Definition of Mental Health," *Community Mental Health Review* 1: 2 (1976): 1 and 4-9.

[54]Claudewell S. Thomas and James P. Comer, "Racism and Mental Health Services," in Charles V. Willie, Bernard M. Kramer and Bertram S. Brown, eds., *Racism and Mental Health: Essays* (Pittsburgh, PA: University of Pittsburgh Press, 1973), pp. 165-181 at 165-166.

[55]Ibid., p. 166.

[56]Ibid.

[57]Preston Wilcox, "Positive Mental Health in the Black Community: The Black Liberation Movement," in Charles V. Willie, et al., op. cit. note 54, pp. 467-468.

[58]President's Commission on Mental Health, *Report to the President from the President's Commission on Mental Health*, Vol. 1 (Washington, D.C.: U.S. Government Printing Office, 1978), p. 8.

[59]U.S. Department of Health and Human Services, Health Resources and Services Administration, National Center for Health Statistics, *Health Status of Minorities and Low Income Groups* (Washington, D.C.: U.S. Government Printing Office, Doc. No. (HRSA) HRS-P-DV85-1, 1985), p. 159.

[60]Judith G. Rabkin, "Ethnic Density and Psychiatric Hospitalization: Hazards of Minority Status," *American Journal of Psychiatry* 136: 12 (December 1979): 1562-1566.

[61]Gerald D. Klee, Evelyn Spiro, Anita K. Bahn and Kurt Gorwitz, "An Ecological Analysis of Diagnosed Mental Illness in Baltimore," in Russell R. Monroe, Gerald D. Klee and Eugene Brody, eds., *Psychiatric Epidemiology and Mental Health Planning*, Psychiatric Research Reports of the American Psychiatric Association, Report No. 22 (Washington, D.C.: American Psychiatric Association, 1967).

[62]U.S. Department of Health and Human Services, op. cit. note 59, p. 84.

[63]U.S. Department of Health, Education and Welfare, Public Health Service, National Center for Health Statistics, *Health: United States 1979* (Washington, D.C.: U.S. Government Printing Office, Pub. No. (PHS) 80-1232, 1980), p. 12.

[64]See the studies reported in James Alan Neff and Baqar A. Husaini, "Race, Socioeconomic Status, and Psychiatric Impairment: A Research Note," *Journal of Community Psychology* 8: 1 (January 1980): 16-19; Robert E. Roberts, John M. Stevenson and Lester Breslow, "Symptoms of Depression Among Blacks and Whites in an Urban Community," *The Journal of Nervous and Mental Disease* 169: 12 (December 1981): 774-779; and George Warheit, Charles E. Holzer III and John J. Schwab, "An Analysis of Social and Racial Differences in Depressive Symptomatology: A Community Survey," *Journal of Health and Social Behavior* 14: 4 (December 1973): 291-299.

[65]Jacquelyne Johnson Jackson, "Negro Aged: Toward Needed Research in Social Gerontology," *Gerontologist* 11: 1, part II (Spring 1971): 52-57.

[66]For a review of these studies see Evelyn J. Broment, "Epidemiology," in Alan S. Bellock and Michael Hersen, eds., *Research Methods in Clinical Psychology* (New York: Pergamon Press, 1984), pp. 266-282; Cockerham, op. cit. note 42, pp. 172-190; Minako K. Maykovich, *Medical Sociology* (Sherman Oaks, CA: Alfred Publishing Co., 1980), pp. 125-129; David Mechanic, *Medical Sociology*, 2nd ed. (New York: The Free Press, 1978), pp. 435-492; and Frederic D. Wolinsky, *The Sociology of Health* (Boston, MA: Little, Brown & Co., 1980), pp. 225-232.

[67]Robert Faris and H. Warren Dunham, *Mental Disorders in Urban Areas* (Chicago: The University of Chicago Press, 1939); August Hollingshead and Frederick C. Redlick, *Social Class and Mental Illness* (New York: Wiley, 1958); Leo Srole, Thomas Langer, Stanley T. Michael, Marvin Oppler and Thomas A. C. Rennie, *Mental Health in the Metropolis: The Midtown Manhattan Study*, 2 vols. (New York: McGraw-Hill, 1962); and Dorothea C. Leighton, John S. Harding, David B. Mackin, Allister M. Macmillan and Alexander H. Leighton, *The Character of Danger: Psychiatric Symptoms in Selected Communities*, The Stirling County Study of Psychiatric Disorder and Sociocultural Environment, Vol. III (New York: Basic Books, 1963).

[68]S. M. Miller and Elliot G. Mishler, "Social Class, Mental Illness, and American Psychiatry: An Expository Review," in Frank Reissman, Jerome Cohen and Arthur Pearl, eds., *Mental Health of the Poor* (London: The Free Press, 1964), pp. 11-15; and Ramsey Liem and Joan Liem, "Social Class and Mental Illness Reconsidered: The Role of Economic Stress and Social Support," *Journal of Health and Social Behavior* 19: 2 (June 1979): 139-156.

[69]Liem and Liem, ibid., p. 141.

[70]Cockerham, op. cit. note 42, p. 173; and Maykovich, op. cit. note 66, p. 141.

[71]Billy E. Jones, Beverly A. Gray and Elvin B. Parson, "Manic Depressive Illness Among Poor Urban Blacks," *American Journal of Psychiatry* 138: 5 (May 1981): 654-657.

[72]Warheit, et al., op. cit. note 64, pp. 291-299.

[73]Neff and Husaini, op. cit. note 64, pp. 16-19.

[74]George W. Comstock and Knud J. Helsing, "Symptoms of Depression in Two Communities," *Psychological Medicine* 6: 4 (November 1976): 561-563.

[75]William W. Eaton and Larry G. Kessler, "Rates of Symptoms of Depression in a National Sample," *American Journal of Epidemiology* 114: 4 (October 1981): 528-538.

[76]Roberts, et al., op. cit. note 64, pp. 774-779.

[77]Eaton and Kessler, op. cit. note 75; Warheit, et al., op. cit. note 64; and Roberts, et al., op. cit. note 64.

[78]Lawrence E. Gary, Diane R. Brown, Norweeta G. Milburn, Veronica G. Thomas and Donald S. Lockley, *Pathway: A Study of Black Informal Networks* (Washington, D.C.: Institute for Urban Affairs and Research, Howard University, 1984).

[79]Ibid., pp. 1220-1222.

INFANT MORTALITY AND RISK FACTORS AMONG AMERICAN INDIANS COMPARED TO BLACK AND WHITE RATES: IMPLICATIONS FOR POLICY CHANGE

Joyce M. Kramer

University of Minnesota, Duluth

Introduction

It has been said that there is great sorrow in heaven at the death of infants and children. In this chapter, I should like to analyze the processes which contribute to ethnic differentials in infant mortality rates and propose policies that would improve the relatively high rates experienced by most minorities within the United States. The demographic perspective assumed is that the study of births and deaths, as well as migrations of populations, is best understood within a human ecology framework.[1] In particular, the explanations provided are grounded in an examination of the social and physical environments that sustain life and provide the context in which human beings are born, migrate and die. These contexts differ dramatically across ethnic and racial boundaries within the United States. The analysis focuses particularly on the circumstances of American Indians, which are compared to those of blacks and whites in this country.

The overall strategy is first to examine very briefly variations in infant mortality from a global perspective. Comparisons and contrasts are then made between American Indians, blacks and whites in the United States. The underlying objective of this approach is to advance our epidemiological understanding of infant mortality by analyzing ethnic similarities and differences in the prevalence of risk factors.

From a global perspective, the principal differences observed in infant mortality rates are between Third World countries as compared to urban industrial nations. Rates of infant mortality range from highs up to 175 per 1,000 live births in the least developed countries[2] to as low as 6 per 1,000 live births, which was Finland's rate in 1985.[3] The principal

explanations for these drastic differences are (a) the scarcity of basic
resources in the Third World which are required to sustain life—especially, the global maldistribution of food which affects the Third World
particularly severely—and (b) the presence of contagious diseases cor-
responding with an absence of public health measures (such as adequate supplies of potable water and universal immunization programs)
to control them.

Comparing the urban-industrial nations of the world, the United
States, despite its relative wealth as a nation, ranked seventeenth in
1982 with 11.5 infant deaths per 1,000 live births. Finland and Japan
ranked first and second with rates of 6.0 and 6.6 respectively during the
same year.[4] Closer examination of the rates within the United States
by ethnicity—focusing on the two lowest income groups—helps to explain why its overall rate compares so unfavorably in relation to the
other industrialized nations.

TABLE 1

INFANT MORTALITY RATES FOR AMERICAN INDIANS, ALASKAN NATIVES AND SELECTED U.S. POPULATIONS

Calendar Year	American Indian and Alaskan Native	U.S. Black	U.S. All Races
1982	11.0[a]	19.6	11.5
1955	62.7[a]	43.1	26.4

Source: Indian Health Service, Vital Events Staff, "Infant Mortality Rates
for American Indians and Alaskan Natives and Selected U.S. Populations, 1954-1983" (Rockville, MD: Health Resources and Services
Administration, January 18, 1985).

[a]Three-year rate centered in the year specified.

Since 1955, the earliest date for which there are comparable data,
infant mortality has declined for all populations. The overall rate of
decline has been similar for blacks as for the United States population
as a whole over this period, with a 55 percent decline for blacks as compared to a national average of 56 percent. Despite universal improvements, however, the gap between white and black infant mortality
rates remains. Measured as the ratio of black rates to the national average, black infants were 1.63 times more likely to die in 1955. By 1982
the ratio of risk had increased to 1.70. The data for American Indians
and Alaskan Natives have dramatically improved by comparison. In
1955, American Indian infants were 2.38 times as likely to die as the
average infant in the United States, whereas by 1982 the American Indian rate was below the national rate.

One of the purposes of this chapter is to explore the factors contributing to the dramatic improvements in American Indian infant mortality rates and to discuss their potential applicability for accelerating the progress of blacks and other low-income populations within the United States. A second related objective is to document what is being done correctly within American Indian and Alaskan Native communities so that the current progress will not be jeopardized by negative policy changes. A third objective is to examine critically the American Indian experience with an eye towards making further progress. Finally, it is hoped that this comparative analysis will be of value in informing policy that fosters the ultimate objective of minimizing infant mortality for all populations within the United States. The United States has the material resources to be in the global vanguard with regard to the health status of its population. What is needed is the understanding and the will to implement changes which will advance that goal.

The Human Ecology of Infant Mortality within the United States

For the United States as a whole, infant mortality rates have been dropping steadily during the twentieth century from 125 per 1,000 births in 1910 to a low of 10.6 per 1,000 births in 1984.[5] The declines in death rates over this period are principally attributed to large reductions in deaths due to infectious causes: diarrhea and enteritis, tuberculosis and diptheria. These, in turn, are attributable to improvements in public health sanitation, better nutrition and living conditions, widespread immunization and improved access to medical care.[6]

An average decline of 4.6 per year persisted until 1982 when the decline began to level off.[7] Also in 1982, the gap between black infant and white infant mortality rates began widening; it is presently the largest it has been within the last forty years. The finding that in 1983, "[a] black infant in Chicago, Cleveland, or Detroit was more likely to die in the first year of life than an infant born in Costa Rica"[8] is indicative that the environment in which many black people in the United States are attempting to produce and rear children more closely resembles that of Third World countries than the affluent nation in which they actually reside.

The relative success of American Indians and Alaskan Natives in lowering infant mortality rates is remarkable given that their demographic profile is very similar to that of blacks in most dimensions.

TABLE 2

SOCIAL AND ECONOMIC CHARACTERISTICS, 1980

	American Indian and Alaskan Native	U.S. Black	U.S. All Races
Median Age	22.6	24.9	30.0
Median Family Income	$13,700	$12,600	$19,900
Mean Family Income	$16,500	$15,700	$23,100
Median Per Capita Income of Persons with Income:			
Female.............	$ 4263	$ 4674	$ 5263
Male	$ 8077	$ 7827	$12,192
Percent of Persons below Poverty Level..........	28.2	29.9	12.4
Percent High School Graduates............	55.3	49.6	66.5
Percent College Graduates...	7.4	6.5	16.2
Percent in Labor Force, 16 years and older:			
Female.............	47.7	53.3	49.9
Male	68.5	66.7	75.1
Percent of Civilian Labor Force Unemployed, 16 years and older:			
Female.............	11.9	11.3	6.5
Male	14.5	12.3	6.5
Median Age at Death (1981)	55 years	65 years	72 years
Birth Rate per Thousand Population (1981)	27.9	21.9	15.9
Percent Rural	47.0	15.0	26.0
Percent of Total U.S. Population	0.6	11.7	100.0

Source: Adopted from U.S. Department of Health and Human Services, *Indian Health Service Chart Series Book: April 1985* (Rockville, MD: Health Resources and Services Administration, 1985), p. 14, and U.S. Bureau of the Census, *The United States 1980 Census of Population* (Washington, D.C.: U.S. Government Clearinghouse, 1980).

The progress that has been made in combatting American Indian infant mortality is particularly impressive given the relatively poor health status and high mortality rates for their population as a whole. Age-specific death rates of American Indians and Alaskan Natives between the ages of fourteen and forty-four were approximately twice the rate for the United States as a whole in 1981.[9]

A brief examination of the historical position of blacks as compared to American Indians within the economy and with respect to the federal government provides background for understanding the variations observed over time in American Indian and black infant mortality rates. Fundamental differences include the circumstances by which these two populations historically came under the control of the United States government, the degree to which the government assumes responsibility for their well-being, their roles within the economy and their numbers as a proportion of the total population.

American Indians are unique among minority groups within the United States in that most tribes have "trust" relationships with the federal government as the result of the treaties which were negotiated between the United States government and the sovereign Indian nations. These treaties, signed between 1778 and 1871, are agreements whereby the Indians relinquished their rights to land in exchange for the federal government's promises to provide food, clothing, shelter, health care and educational services. [10] (It is in reflection of this historical precedent that contemporary Indians boast of having the first "pre-paid health plan"—which was purchased with their land.)

While the quality of assistance provided by the federal government has usually been substandard, the ongoing obligation to provide services to American Indian people irrespective of income is unique. The significance of this is that, while the nation is still debating the concept of universal and comprehensive national health services, and while health and human services continue to operate on dualistic, "ability-to-pay" criteria, American Indians as compared to all other Americans are provided comprehensive health care as well as other life sustaining programs through agencies of the federal government such as the Indian Health Service and the Bureau of Indian Affairs.

Historically, American Indians have been obstacles to non-Indians' aspirations to acquire land, and the obligation to provide Indians with health, education and social services is often perceived grudgingly as a "burden upon the taxpayer." In contrast, black people were brought to North America and valued as laborers within the white-dominated economy. These historic differences in the way that black and American Indian populations are viewed economically have far-reaching policy implications which are operative to this day. For example, at the national as well as state levels of government, "assimilationist" legislation has, from time to time, been passed, and policies have been formulated to narrowly define who is "American Indian," thereby limiting the numbers of people entitled to publicly funded services. By way of contrast, it has been in the economic interests of many influential whites, particularly in the antebellum South, to foster very broad definitions of who is "black" (e.g., anyone with any known African ancestry) and to promote discriminatory practices, thereby assuring a large pool of people who are disadvantaged in the labor market and thus readily available to work at unpleasant tasks for minimal wages. (This system of assuring a cheap labor supply only functions if there is not a good alternative system of support available. North-South discrepancies in the amounts of assistance offered to low-income families suggest the possibility that this historic demand for cheap labor contributes significantly to the dearth of publicly funded health and other social services available in the South.)

For American Indians, there have been periodic attempts to reduce the federal government's trust responsibilities. For example, the Dawes (General Allotment) Act of 1887 undermined the integrity of tribally controlled lands. During the period from 1887 through 1934, when the policy of giving individual Indians legal title to an allotment was in effect, 140 million acres of American Indian land were reduced to under 50 million acres, and the health and welfare of Indian people declined markedly. [11] Similarly, in 1953 House Concurrent Resolution 108 of the 83rd Congress was passed to terminate trust status. Over one hundred tribes, bands and rancherias were terminated (affecting twelve thousand individuals and 2.5 million acres of land) between 1953 and 1968 when this termination policy was in effect. Like allotment, this "assimilation" and "urbanization" policy had devastating effects on the health and well-being of American Indian people. However, in 1968 President Lyndon Johnson launched a new self-determination policy which respected the integrity of tribal governments and encouraged them to administer their own health, education and social services. In 1975 the American Indian Self-Determination and Educational Assistance Act was passed by Congress to provide a contracting mechanism whereby tribal governments could elect to contract for Indian Health Service and Bureau of Indian Affairs dollars and manage their own services. [12] In 1976 the American Indian Health Care Assistance Act was passed to upgrade health care. [13] In practice as well as in theory, local control combined with increased resources has meant dramatic improvements in the quality and quantity of services within some American Indian communities.

In a case study of one reservation contracting for health, education and social services, [14] it was found that health services expanded from the presence of two community health representatives in 1976 (involving a total health care budget of $28,700) to a large outpatient clinic which the reservation operates at the present time. Over the period from 1976 to 1982, total resources of the reservation expanded from $162,451 to $3,396,472 (much of which was from sources other than the federal government). The number of health, education and social services offered to Indians by the reservation expanded from one in June

FIGURE 1

TRIBAL SERVICES

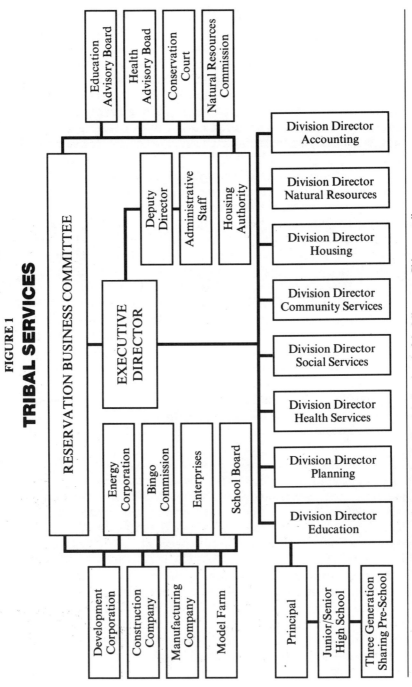

Source: The above is the organizational chart for the Fond du Lac band of the Minnesota Chippewa tribe.

1976 to twenty-nine by June 1983. Figure 1 provides a graphic representation of the services which were developed within tribal governance under self-determination provisions. Seventy-nine percent of the staff who run these services are enrollees of that particular reservation. They are thus personally knowledgeable about local conditions and service needs, and they have a vested interest in the success of the programs they provide. Every two years since 1976, a nearby university has assisted in conducting a health and social service needs assessment/ evaluation utilizing random sampling techniques of the service population. General satisfaction with the services provided has increased significantly each time the survey has been conducted.

A significant number of tribes, however, have been reluctant to contract for programs for fear that doing so will eventually result in "self-termination" rather than "self-determination." Reflecting upon the negative history, they believe that the federal government will eventually use the self-determination policy as a ploy to abdicate its responsibility and withdraw funding. It is noteworthy to observe that federal support for all health and social services has been in jeopardy under the Reagan administration, including those for American Indians.

Most Indian Health Service programs are partially protected from Gramm-Rudman by a 1 percent cutback limit in 1986 and 2 percent in later years. [15] However, Reagan's budget proposal for 1987 (independent of Gramm-Rudman) included a 16 percent cutback in the Indian Health Service, a 13 percent cutback in basic Indian education services and an 8 percent cutback in the Bureau of Indian Affairs. To absorb these changes, such drastic measures as elimination of $19.4 million to provide water and sanitation for federally built Indian homes was proposed. [16]

One reason that Indian programs have been able to avoid drastic cutbacks in funding is that American Indians constitute such a small proportion of the total United States population that continuation of health services to American Indians at current levels requires very little commitment in terms of the overall federal budget. In other words, legislators can salve their collective conscience at very little cost with regard to American Indians, while the same is not true for blacks and other poor populations within the United States.

It is these differences in the availability of health-related services which probably account for most, if not all, the differences observed between the infant mortality rates of blacks as compared to those of American Indians. At the same time that Indians have continued to benefit from the Self-Determination and Educational Assistance Act of 1975 and the American Indian Health Care Improvement Act of 1976, health and welfare services for other low-income populations in the

United States have been cut back drastically. A study by the Children's Defense Fund indicates that in 1985, Medicaid reached only 46 percent of poor and near-poor families compared to 65 percent in 1969. In 1985, forty-two states served fewer than half of all mothers, infants, and children eligible for WIC nutritional supplements. "Eight states served fewer than 30 percent of all eligible persons. . . . In 1985, forty-nine states defined 'need' in the AFDC program for a family of three with children at an amount less, and usually far less, than 100 percent of federal poverty level. Eighteen states. . . defined these families' needs at an amount less than 50 percent of the federal poverty level. [Fewer than half of all states paid] AFDC benefits in 1985 that were equal to 100 percent of their standards of need." [17]

These cutbacks, coupled with recession and the increasing stratification of the economy, have had a negative impact on the health of black children:

> The dramatic upswing in childhood poverty from 1979 to 1983 and downswing in vital public health, nutrition, and family support services from 1981 to 1983 have been accompanied by a marked slowdown in the decline of overall and neonatal infant mortality, a nationwide rise in postneonatal infant mortality, an increase in the percentage of low birthweight babies and in women receiving late or no prenatal care, and the widest disparity in more than four decades between the infant mortality rates of blacks and whites. [18]

The underlying reality is that there are a large number of people in the United States, a disproportionate number of whom are racial minorities, whose resources are so minimal as to place the lives of their offspring in jeopardy.

Factors Contributing to Infant Mortality Rates within American Indian and American Black Populations

An examination of the causes of infant deaths by race/ethnicity contributes to our understanding of the manner in which the availability of health-related resources is correlated with risk.

It is clear from Table 3 that the black population in the United States has a considerably higher overall infant mortality rate as compared to the rate for the United States as a whole (19.6 as compared to 11.5). With the exception of congenital anomalies, the rates for all the other causes listed are higher for blacks than the national averages. After congenital anomalies, the leading causes of death for blacks are sudden infant death syndrome and disorders relating to short gestation

TABLE 3

LEADING CAUSES OF INFANT DEATHS IN THE UNITED STATES
(Rates per 1,000 live births, 1982)

Specific Causes	American Indian and Alaskan Native[a]	Black	All Races
Sudden Infant Death Syndrome	2.5	2.5	1.4
Congenital Anomalies	1.9	2.5	2.5
Respiratory Distress Syndrome	0.8	1.7	1.1
Disorders Relating to Short Gestation and Unspecified Low Birthweight	0.5	2.4	1.0
Accidents and Adverse Effects	0.4	0.5	0.3
Pneumonia and Influenza	0.4	0.5	0.2
Meningitis	0.3	0.2	0.1
All Causes	11.0	19.6	11.5
Neonatal Deaths	5.0	13.1	7.7

Source: Indian Health Service, "Leading Causes of Infant Death by Age:
        American Indians and Alaska Natives in Reservation States (1981-
        1983) and U.S. All Races and Other than White Population (1982)"
        (Rockville, MD: Health Resources and Services Administration,
        April, 1986), p. 25.
[a]Three-year rate centered in 1982.

and unspecified low birthweight. The latter set of disorders is over
twice the rate among blacks as compared to the national average.

   The pattern for American Indians is somewhat different. The leading cause of death among Indians is sudden infant death syndrome (almost twice the national average), whereas congenital anomalies as well
as disorders related to short gestation and unspecified low birthweight
are well below the national averages. While most infant deaths occur
during the neonatal period within both the nation as a whole as well as
within its nonwhite subpopulation, Indian and Alaskan Natives' neonatal rates are well below the others.

   A note is in order here regarding terminology. "Infant mortality" is
conventionally defined as deaths occurring during the first year of life.
These are broken down analytically into "neonatal," that is deaths occurring from birth to twenty-eight days after birth, and "postneonatal," that is deaths occurring within twenty-eight days to one year
after birth.[19] While the cutoff date is somewhat arbitrary, it is generally understood that neonatal deaths are more likely to be the result of
prenatal factors and/or trauma at the time of birth, and consequently
they are indicative of the health status of the mother and/or the conditions in which the birth occurs. Deaths due to congenital anomalies,
low birthweight and respiratory distress syndrome are more likely to

occur during the neonatal period. By comparison, postneonatal deaths are more attributable to the environmental conditions in which the infant is being reared. High postneonatal mortality rates are an index of poverty, poor nutrition, inadequate shelter, sanitary problems and lack of basic health care. Sudden infant death syndrome, accidents and infectious diseases such as pneumonia, influenza and meningitis are the principal causes of death during the postneonatal period.[20]

Given that low socioeconomic status and its correlates—low birthweight, inadequate maternal nutrition, substandard clothing and shelter, vulnerability to infectious diseases, low educational attainment, adolescent maternity, nonmarried maternal status, high parity, inadequate reproductive and infant medical attention as well as tobacco, alcohol and other drug abuse—are factors contributing to infant mortality, many of these will be discussed, comparing Indians, blacks and whites within the United States. The focus will be on explaining those causes of infant deaths in Indians and blacks that are higher than the national average.

Sudden infant death syndrome (SIDS) is the highest among these, and its etiology is elusive. What epidemiological studies do reveal is that the risk is disproportionately high for infants of low-income households, those of unwed mothers, and those of low birthweight (LBW). Also, in the general population, males tend to be at greater risk than females, as are offspring of adolescent mothers, although the last two relationships have not been consistently found in American Indian and Alaskan Native populations.[21] Given that all of the factors mentioned tend to be present in most low-income groups, no single causal relationship is readily identifiable. Furthermore, SIDS appears to be on the increase in all populations. It is not clear whether this is an artifact of improved identification and recordkeeping or whether the increase in rates reflects an actual increase in risk.

Prematurity and low birthweight (LBW is usually defined as less than 2,500 grams or 5.5 pounds) are very clearly associated with low income in the general population.[22] LBW infants have more than twenty times the death rate of normal birthweight infants. It is a particularly salient cause of neonatal deaths when delivery occurs outside of a hospital setting. Black babies are more than twice as likely as white babies to be LBW,[23] and the risk of LBW is disproportionately high in black populations even when socioeconomic status is statistically controlled.[24] Interestingly, however, black LBW infants are more likely to survive than their white counterparts.[25] Some analysts are inclined to attribute the disproportionately high rates of LBW to a genetic predisposition among blacks, but others argue that such explanations are overly simplistic and fail to take into consideration the complexity of environmental factors which affect gestation.[26] Margaret Boone's in-depth, controlled study of low birthweight among economically disadvantaged black women concludes that

> [lack of] prenatal care, alcoholism, migrant status, smoking, hypertension history and previous poor pregnancy outcome distinguished women with very low birthweight infants. The medical record review also implicated violence, weak social support systems, poor social and psychological adjustments and ineffective contraception. Three-quarters of all women are unmarried at the time of delivery, and interviewed women (who had suffered infant deaths within one year after delivery) expressed bitterness and resentment toward the men in their lives for non-support. . . . These women feel powerless, hopeless and that life is somewhat meaningless.[27]

Boone proposes a number of innovative programs to train health professionals and improve services for low-income, inner-city women during pregnancy.

Studies of the effectiveness of routine prenatal care suggest that "prenatal care, as routinely practiced, does not reduce LBW rates, and that more aggressive treatments must be used . . . ."[28] However, controlled studies of the Women, Infants and Children (WIC) Program indicate that this particular nutritional supplement and clinical care program is effective in improving birthweight and reducing neonatal mortality rates, particularly among such high risk groups as ethnic minority infants and those born to adolescent and unwed mothers.[29]

As contrasted to the black population, low birthweight is less prevalent within the American Indian and Alaskan Native population than within the United States population as a whole. That is, 6.2 percent of all American Indian and Alaskan Native infants were of low birthweight in 1981 to 1983, as compared to 6.8 percent of all races in the United States in 1982.[30] While it is conceivable that genetic factors may contribute to some of the discrepancy between the American Indian and black experiences with regard to the prevalence of LBW, the fact that there has been a long history of providing surplus commodities to reservation Indians probably, at least in part, accounts for the better outcomes. In general, nutritional deficiency does not appear to be a problem among American Indians so much as malnutrition of another sort. Analysis of commodities distributed to Indian people indicates that there are sufficient nutrients in individual rations to meet the recommended daily allowance, provided that excessive calories in the form of carbohydrates and animal fats are consumed. Also, commodities are excessively high in salt. Obesity and diabetes mellitus are endemically high among American Indians: Age-adjusted diabetes mortality rates were 20.5 per 1000 for Indians and Alaskan Natives, 17.8 for American nonwhites and 9.6 for all races.[31]

In addition to undernourishment and lack of satisfactory social support, cigarette smoking and alcohol abuse have been found to have negative congenital impacts, contributing to low birthweight as well as producing other congenital anomalies.[32] Furthermore, involuntary passive smoking by the offspring of tobacco-smoking parents is known to increase the incidence of respiratory illness in infants.[33] Habitual cigarette use is higher among racial minorities than among white Americans and higher among American Indians than any other ethnic group—55 percent of all Indians aged seventeen and older smoke as compared to 37 percent for blacks and 35 percent for whites.[34]

One explanation for the high cigarette use among American Indians is that tobacco is considered a sacred substance within most Indian cultures. Tobacco smoke is believed to be pleasing to the ancestor spirits and is offered to them as a means of acquiring their blessings. Many Indians believe that Indian people are, therefore, protected from the detrimental health effects which tobacco has on non-Indian populations. However, Jim Jackson, a reknowned Ojibwe medicine man, advises that tobacco, like alcohol (which is also a sacred substance used ceremonially in the Christian communion), should be reserved for sacred purposes and that casual abuse can make people of all races ill.[35] Spiritual leaders like Jim Jackson, as well as many political leaders within tribal governments, are spearheading a national health and sobriety movement among American Indians.

As with tobacco use, there is little or no research linking alcohol abuse directly with infant mortality in American Indian populations. However, there is increasing evidence in one body of the literature that fetal alcohol syndrome tends to be high in subsets of the American Indian population,[36] and another body of this literature linking alcohol abuse to infant and child abuse and neglect in the general population.[37]

There is considerable variation across tribes concerning patterns of alcohol use and abuse.[38] For example, it has been found that the incidence of fetal alcohol syndrome ranges from 1.3 per 1000 live births in the Navajo to 10.3 in the Plains tribes.[39] Overall, the evidence is overwhelming that alcohol abuse poses a very serious health hazard within many American Indian communities.[40] Among American Indian women aged fifteen through thirty-four, one in twenty deaths is caused by alcoholic cirrhosis,[41] and cirrhosis of the liver is only one of the many ways that alcohol contributes to Indian morbidity and mortality rates. Accidents, homicides and suicides are much higher for Indians than for the white population. In 1983, the age-adjusted accident mortality rate per 100,000 population among Indians was 82.9, as com-

pared to 34.7 for the white population, and accidents were second only
to diseases of the heart as the principal cause of death among all Indians.[42] Given these statistics, it seems probable that alcohol-related neglect and violence contribute to some of the high mortality rates attributed to accidents.

While some cultures are more permissive than others, there are no
American Indian cultures which philosophically promote the consumption of alcohol. The differences in alcohol consumption between and
within groups, consequently, are probably much more indicative of the
profound malaise which occurs as a result of economic, political and
social powerlessness than they are a consequence of cultural factors per
se.[43] It may be no coincidence that the national sobriety movement
among American Indians corresponds with the community vigor which
self-determination brings. More research needs to be done on the new
"culture of sobriety" among American Indians so that its successes can
be enhanced.

In the meantime, alcohol treatment centers are providing services to
American Indians with mixed success. An evaluation of the Indian
Health Service's alcoholism treatment program indicates that a majority of the individual projects are successful when measured by recognized standards for efficiency, effectiveness, appropriateness and adequacy.[44] Most apply variations of the Alcoholics Anonymous
confrontational approach, although this probably needs adaptation to
be effective among those Indians who come from less confrontational
and individualistic cultures, and whose religious orientations are less
likely to include a personal god that takes interest in one's daily conduct.[45] At the same time, treatment programs serving the general public tend to be too narrowly focused on individual therapy rather than
on family services, and tend to neglect the implications of alcohol and
drug abuse on parenting. One outcome of this neglect is that mothers of
young children are sometimes reluctant to seek residential treatment
because they would have to leave their children and risk losing them.
This is a particularly salient concern for American Indian women, in
that the risk of losing one's children has historically been high. In 1978,
when the Indian Child Welfare Act was passed by Congress to address
this problem, one out of every four Indian children were living in a non-
Indian residence.[46] Another problem with current treatment programs
is that they are often physically and structurally isolated from other
health and social services. Ideally, programs providing maternal and
child services should be screening participants to identify and refer
parents who have alcohol and drug problems.

Focusing on accidents as a cause of infant deaths, Kristine
Wicklund, Shelia Moss and Floyd Frost found in the general popula-

tion that "maternal age and education are inversely related to infant accident mortality while mother's parity is directly related."[47] Again, the degree to which these correlates of low income are directly linked to infant deaths is speculative. It is easy to imagine that knowledge (as acquired through education) and experience (as acquired through age) would empower mothers to prevent life-threatening accidents more successfully. However, the relationships are probably far more complex, in that relatively educated and mature women are more likely to have the resources at their disposal to reduce risks by living in an environmentally safe home, by driving an automobile which is in good repair, and by hiring competent child care providers when not personally caring for their children.

Another important risk factor to infants is the age of the mother:

> Babies born to teen and unmarried mothers are at greater risk of poverty, late or no prenatal care, low birthweight, and infant death and poor health outcomes than those born to married and adult women. In 1983, one out of every nine white and one out of every five nonwhite babies was born to a teen mother. One of every two nonwhite [babies] and one of every eight white babies was born to an unmarried mother in 1983.[48]

For American Indian and Alaskan Native births in 1983, 21 percent were to teen mothers (approximately the same as the one out of five cited for nonwhites above). The consequences with respect to infant mortality are documented by Marie McCormick and her coauthors, who found in their sample of young mothers residing in four regions of the United States that infants born to women who had not yet reached their eighteenth birthday, and to multiparous women who were eighteen or nineteen years of age, were nearly twice as likely to die during infancy as compared to other infants. A greater propensity for low birthweights among young mothers is the principal explanation provided for the differences in neonatal mortality rates, while inexperience combined with socioeconomic disadvantage are offered to explain the higher postneonatal mortality rates among infants of young mothers.[49] Noting that low income, adolescent maternity, unmarried status, high parity and narrow spacing between births are all factors contributing to infant mortality, some policymakers propose enhancing family planning services as a primary prevention strategy. While fertility control information, technology and services should be readily accessible to all fecund people, it is important to understand that an unplanned pregnancy is not necessarily an unwanted pregnancy—particularly within a Third World context where the family is the primary source of social support as well as economic security. The relationships between socioeconomic state, fertility and infant mortality are more complex than immediately meet the eye.

Third World people (who usually lack alternative forms of economic security such as savings, unemployment compensation, health and life insurance, and old age pensions) tend to rely upon their large extended families to pool resources when any of their members need help.[50] Generally, the larger the pool of kin, the better this system works. Consequently, there is a strong impetus to have many children—not only because the children are expected eventually to become economically contributing members of the family, but also because the birth of a child is an event which is expected to bring two sets of kin (those of the infant's mother as well as the father—even if not married) together to support and nurture the child and the child's household. Despite American Indians' high fertility rates, their relatively low infant mortality rates suggest that any relationship between fertility and infant mortality is not necessarily direct or causal.

Focusing finally on infectious diseases such as pneumonia, influenza and meningitis, it is important to note that much of the progress in reducing infant deaths within American Indian communities is attributable to improvements in public health sanitation. Figure 2 gives a graphic representation of the correlations between postneonatal death rates and changes in the availability of home sanitation facilities.

One of the difficulties in promoting preventive programs is that it is often hard to demonstrate the health benefits. However, Figure 2, derived from the Indian Health Service, is certainly suggestive of a direct causal relationship between sanitation improvements and reductions in infant deaths. It is important to note that despite the impressive progress which has been made in sanitation, there is still considerable room for improvement. There are still many Indian households, particularly those in remote rural areas, which do not have an adequate supply of safe water or satisfactory waste disposal facilities. As noted earlier, the Indian Health Service budget proposed by the Reagan administration to Congress did not include provisions for plumbing in new houses.

When an infant is inflicted with a life-threatening illness such as pneumonia, influenza or meningitis, the probability that the illness will cause death is directly related to the general health status of the victim and to the promptness with which medical attention is obtained. Differentials in access to medical services can only be inferred from the discussion of the free universal and nearly comprehensive services provided to American Indians by the Indian Health Service, as contrasted to the much more limited services available to low-income non-Indians. For rural Indians, the principal barrier to access is the long distances which must be travelled on some reservations in order to reach clinical services. Sensitive to this problem, many reservations arrange

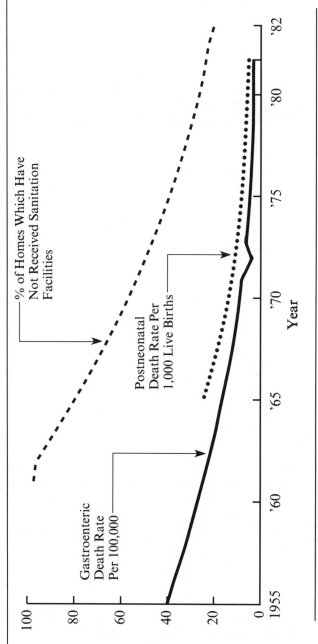

FIGURE 2

DEATH RATES VERSUS
LACK OF SANITATION FACILITIES (1984) [a]

% of Homes Which Have
Not Received Sanitation
Facilities

Postneonatal
Death Rate Per
1,000 Live Births

Gastroenteric
Death Rate
Per 100,000

Year

1955 '60 '65 '70 '75 '80 '82

100 80 60 40 20 0

[a] The above graph was prepared by the Indian Health Service, Division of Environmental Health, Office of Environmental Health
and Engineering.

for community health nurses and paraprofessionals to travel regularly to outlying areas to set up temporary ambulatory clinics and to make house calls. The 53 percent of all American Indian people who live in urban areas have a different problem. Unless they are among the fortunate who live within proximity of one of the thirty-seven Indian Health Service-supported urban projects, they must either travel back to the reservation on which they are enrolled, utilize alternative non-Indian services within their locale, or go without. Finally, another type of barrier is the one which differences in language and culture pose. Many health providers, even within the Indian Health Service, are non-Indians. Some Indians are reluctant to utilize available facilities because of doubts regarding the quality of care provided by those that are underfunded and staffed by non-Indians. Despite the shortcomings in Indian Health Service facilities, however, the utilization rates as well as the quality and quantity of services have improved. Table 4 provides pertinent data regarding changes in the quantity of hospitals and in utilization rates.

TABLE 4

INDIAN HEALTH SERVICE INCREASES IN MEDICAL CARE

	FY 1955	FY 1985	Percent Increase
Hospital Admissions	50,143	108,777	117
Outpatient Visits	455,000	4,411,597	870
	FY 1972	FY 1985	
Total IHS Hospitals	50	45	
Accredited Hospitals	22	37	
Hospitals Not Accredited	28	8	

Source: U.S. Department of Health and Human Services, *Indian Health Services Chart Series Book: April 1985* (Rockville, MD: Health Resources and Services Administration, 1985), pp. 9 and 39.

Improvements in utilization rates include significant ones in prenatal care to American Indian and Alaskan Native women. Of all the women for whom the month that prenatal care began was recorded (108,136 births) in 1981 to 1983, 12.9 percent (13,995 births) were to women receiving late (during the last trimester) or no prenatal care.[51] The importance of improvements in the coordination, comprehensiveness and overall quality of postnatal and antenatal care is underscored in a number of studies of changes in neonatal mortality rates within the United States and elsewhere.[52] Yet for the United States as a whole, "In 1983, for the third consecutive year, and after a decade of steady decline, the percentage of babies born to women receiving late . . . or no prenatal care increased."[53] The chief reasons for this deterioration in service delivery and utilization are that Medicaid has been cut and there is a growing proportion of women who have neither Medicaid eligibility nor coverage through a private health program. At the same time, growing numbers of private physicians, clinics and hospitals are refusing to accept Medicaid clients; some argue that reimbursement (which is much lower than under privatized schemes) is not sufficient and that the paperwork to obtain reimbursement is excessive. As a result of these forces, the spectacle of indigent women being denied access to hospitals to deliver their babies, and of the critically ill and injured being denied access to emergency room treatment and/or being transported prematurely to alternative facilities, is occurring.[54] Furthermore, the issue of access to crisis-oriented medical care does not even broach the critical need to provide effective preventive services such as early antenatal care and well-baby clinics.

Expanded community services to include primary prevention in such areas as substance abuse, and supportive services such as twenty-four-hour-drop-in child care centers, are greatly needed. To be effective, these programs need to maximize community involvement in their planning and implementation. This means acquiring input and endorsement from community leaders, organizing community advisory boards and consulting with them regularly on all major policy issues, and hiring minority personnel at all levels, especially management, to carry out the programs. Only in this manner can programs be responsive to cultural sensitivities and effectively mobilize primary community support systems.[55]

Enhanced antenatal and postnatal care are both needed, and are particularly effective if active outreach and services beyond routine clinical care are offered.[56] Culturally sensitive outreach to low-income minority families is crucial in facilitating access to needed services, and nutritional supplements appear to be critical in improving birthweights. In general, services should be as comprehensive and coordinated as possible. Physically concentrating all economic, health and social services in one easily accessible and centralized location can greatly facilitate the coordination of these services by providers. This is done in Indian communities through the multiple use of community centers. Particularly for low-income clients, who are often stressed and have transportation problems, one rather than multiple locations increases the probability that they will all be appropriately utilized and that coordinated case management will occur.

Some argue that offering discretionary resources directly to indigent people encourages irresponsibility. While it is not within the scope of this chapter to discuss this very complex issue at length, the report of the Children's Defense Fund challenges this assumption in relation to teen pregnancy by noting that "[t]he proportion of births to teens generally was lower in states with more generous public assistance payment levels and higher in states with lower public assistance levels."[57] This finding is consistent with the observation that among Third World people (who generally have marginal economic security), large families are preferred because they can more effectively pool their resources as a hedge against economic and social disaster. When public assistance is ample, the critical need for a large supportive family becomes less so.

The available data indicate that primary prevention, particularly that which is oriented toward expanding the resources which the poor have at their disposal to maintain health, is far more important in lowering infant mortality than is the amount of medical care that is available.[58] One implication of this is that, given alternatives with limited resources, primary and tertiary prevention should take priority over medical treatment in the development of programs. (This is the difficult choice which Everett Rhoades, M.D., Director of the Indian Health Service, selected when he decided not to offer expensive dialysis treatment in IHS facilities. Rhoades defends this controversial decision on the grounds that the money is more effectively spent on preventive services and that it is impossible to do both given the limitations of the IHS budget.[59])

Fundamentally, effective primary prevention focuses very broadly on all the factors affecting human health and well-being, such as ensuring that families have a sufficient income to afford basic necessities and that communities have quality water, effective waste disposal and universal immunization programs. Generally, American society has more readily provided community-based public health services than individual and family benefits. However, immunization programs have been jeopardized by Reagan administration cutbacks,[60] and there is still considerable room for improvement in inner city as well as rural areas in assuring that housing is safe, that waste disposal is not hazardous, and that there is an abundant supply of uncontaminated water.

Conclusions

It is clear that the discrepancies in infant mortality rates between blacks and American Indians and between the United States and the more socially progressive urban industrial nations are remediable provided that the required resources are made available. Unlike Third

World nations which lack the means to improve significantly the conditions contributing to high infant mortality rates, the United States has the requisite material resources. What appears to be lacking is sufficient public sentiment to mobilize these resources on behalf of those infants who are at disproportionately high risk principally because they are born to low-income parents.

The most apparent difference between blacks and American Indians is that Indians enrolled in federally recognized tribes and living within proximity of an Indian Health Service-supported facility have access to nearly comprehensive health services which are universally free (irrespective of income). This means that Indians can seek services within that system without the stigma of a financial means test and without the danger of being turned away because the provider does not want to serve indigents at lower-than-par reimbursement rates. While some Indian Health Service facilities do not provide all that is desired in terms of the quality of care, American Indians are much better off than their low-income, uninsured non-Indian counterparts, who often have difficulty receiving even emergency room entry, not to mention preventive services. The fact that American Indians and Alaskan Natives have a unique trust status which obligates the federal government to provide health, education and social services, and that this obligation has been a key contributory factor to dramatic improvements in their infant mortality rates, provides a model or glimpse of what is possible, absent trust status, for other low-income populations as well.

Unfortunately, current policy appears to be in a diametrically opposed direction. As a consequence of federal cutbacks, rates of infant mortality are actually increasing among most of the nation's other vulnerable poor and minority groups. Meanwhile, the budget for the Indian Health Service has remained constant (which actually, due to inflation, represents a reduction in real dollars), and has also been threatened by proposed cutbacks which would, of course, jeopardize the progress that has been made within Indian communities.

In fiscal year 1986, the estimated population eligible for care by the Indian Health Service was 989,204 American Indians and Alaskan Natives. The Indian Health Service's expenditures for health care for this population during the same year was a surprisingly low $763,989,204. This is an allocation of less than $100.00 per person, and is to be contrasted with health care expenditures of $360 billion for the United States resident population as a whole.[61]

Robert Maxwell makes some interesting observations on what urban industrial societies can learn from Third World nations that have had to make do with less medical technology and expertise. The principles he espouses articulate the ways in which the Indian Health Service has been able to do so much with so little in improving infant mortality. They are:

- "to give priority to the use of low-cost remedies of proven effectiveness;"

- to collaborate "with other agencies, such as water, sanitation, housing, and transport, as well as health-care providers;"

- "to link the first-line providers in these impoverished communities with the full back-up of referral services, even though these cannot be placed in every community;" and

- to foster "a partnership of mutual confidence between health-care workers and the community concerned. . . . In general, Third World experience shows that first-line health workers in deprived communities must belong to their community, in the sense of sharing its culture, being accountable to it, and living within it."[62]

There is indeed much which could be adapted from the American Indian experience and applied to services for other low-income communities within the United States.

Because of the resistance of private physicians, hospitals and the health insurance industry to "socialized" alternatives to the current medical system, Harold Leppink, a physician who directs the St. Louis County Public Health Department in northeastern Minnesota, proposes that universal and comprehensive coverage might be introduced by collaborating with current third-party payment systems. That is, public financing would be utilized to subsidize any plan which low-income people elected to use. A sliding scale based on ability to pay would be applied to assess the recipient's contribution.[63]

This proposal has the advantage of avoiding dualistic systems which are inherently unequal in that services offered to the indigent are often inferior. In fact, providers need not necessarily even know who among their clients are publicly subsidized. A further elaboration of this concept might be to promote health maintenance organizations (HMOs) as a preferred option, possibly by subsidizing them to accept all applicants and to base fees on a community rating, rather than to reject high risk groups or individuals and/or base fees on experience ratings, as is presently the practice. Given the built-in incentives of prepaid health plans to provide preventive services (so as to avoid having to offer more costly medical services later), HMOs could assume principal responsibility for providing comprehensive maternal and infant care as well as for administering supplemental feeding and other preventive programs. Basically, HMOs could function within non-Indian communities in ways quite similar to the ones that the Indian Health Service currently employs within the American Indian and Alaskan Native communities—with benefits to all.

NOTES

[1]Amos A. Hawley, "Ecology and Population," *Science* 179 (March 23, 1973): 1196-1201.

[2]UNICEF, *The State of the World's Children 1987* (New York: Oxford University Press for UNICEF, 1987), p. 128.

[3]C. Arden Miller, "Infant Mortality in the U.S.," *Scientific American* 253: 1 (July 1985): 31-37. Cf. C. Arden Miller, *Monitoring Children's Health: Key Indicators* (Washington, D.C.: American Public Health Association, 1986).

[4]Miller, "Infant Mortality," ibid.

[5]Ibid.

[6]Muin J. Khoury, J. David Erickson and Myron J. Adams, Jr., "Trends in Postneonatal Mortality in the United States, 1962 Through 1978," *Journal of the American Medical Association* 252: 3 (July 20, 1984): 367-372; and Barbara Starfield, "Giant Steps and Baby Steps: Toward Child Health," *American Journal of Public Health* 75: 6 (June 1985): 599-604.

[7]Miller, "Infant Mortality," op. cit. note 3.

[8]Children's Defense Fund, *Maternal and Child Health Data Book: The Health of America's Children* (Washington, D.C.: Children's Defense Fund, 1986), pp. xi and xiii.

[9]Indian Health Service, Vital Events Staff, *Infant Mortality Rates for American Indians and Alaskan Natives and Selected U.S. Populations, 1954-1983* (Rockville, MD: Health Resources and Services Administration, January 1985), p. 24.

[10]United States Commission on Civil Rights, *Indian Tribes: A Continuing Quest for Survival* (Washington, D.C.: U.S. Government Printing Office, 1981), pp. 17-20.

[11]Brookings Institute, "Meriam Report: The Problem of Indian Administration" (1928), reprinted in part in Francis Paul Prucha, ed., *Documents of United States Indian Policy* (Lincoln, NE: University of Nebraska Press, 1975), Document No. 136, pp. 219-221.

[12]Indian Self-Determination and Educational Assistance Act, P.L. 93-368, now codified as 25 U.S.C. Sec. 450 et seq.

[13]Vine Deloria, Jr. and Clifford M. Lytle, "American Indians in Historical Perspective," in *American Indians, American Justice* (Austin, TX: University of Texas Press, 1983), pp. 1-24.

[14]Joyce Kramer, Will Dodge and Phil Norrgard, "The Indian Self-Determination Act: A Case Study," unpublished paper presented at the International Conference on Social Development (Montreal, Quebec: August 3, 1984).

[15]National Indian Health Board, "IHS Slated for $10.8 Million Cut in '86 Under Gramm-Rudman," *NIHB Health Reporter* (Denver, CO) 4: 2 (August 3, 1986): 1-3.

[16]James McGregor, "Budget Cutbacks Will Hurt Program to Build Indian Homes, Says Senator," *News-Tribune and Herald* (Duluth, MN: February 19, 1986), p. 6B.

[17]Children's Defense Fund, op. cit. note 8, pp. 14, 53 and 14.

[18]Ibid., p. xi.

[19]Marie C. McCormick, Sam Shapiro and Barbara Starfield, "High-Risk Young Mothers: Infant Mortality and Morbidity in Four Areas in the United States, 1973-1978," *American Journal of Public Health* 74: 1 (January 1984): 18-23.

[20]Children's Defense Fund, op. cit. note 8, pp. 32, 33 and 35.

[21]Melissa M. Adams, "The Descriptive Epidemiology of Sudden Infant Deaths Among Natives and Whites in Alaska," *American Journal of Epidemiology* 122: 4 (January 1985): 637-643.

[22]Nigel Paneth, Sylvan Wallenstein, John L. Kiely and Mervyn Susser, "Social Class Indicators and Mortality in Low Birthweight Infants," *American Journal of Epidemiology* 116: 2 (August 1982): 364-375.

[23]Children's Defense Fund, op. cit. note 8, p. 35.

[24]Jon Van, "Low Birth-Weight Mystery: Doctors Probe Race Link to Risks for Newborns," *Chicago Tribune* (January 3, 1986), sec. 1, p. 3.

[25]Nancy L. Binkin, Ronald L. Williams, Carol J. Hogue and Peter M. Chen, "Reducing Black Neonatal Mortality: Will Improvement in Birth Weight Be Enough?," *Journal of the American Medical Association* 253: 3 (January 18, 1985): 372-375.

[26]Miller, "Infant Mortality," op. cit. note 3.

[27]Margaret S. Boone, "Social and Cultural Factors in the Etiology of Low Birthweight Among Disadvantaged Blacks," *Social Science and Medicine* 20: 10 (1985): 1001.

[28]Donna M. Strobino, Gary A. Chase, Young J. Kim, Barbara E. Crawley, Joan H. Salim and Gigliola Baruffi, "The Impact of the Mississippi Improved Child Health Project on Prenatal Care and Low Birthweight," *American Journal of Public Health* 76: 3 (March 1986): 277.

[29]Milton Kotelchuck, Janet B. Schwartz, Marlene T. Anderka and Karl S. Finison, "WIC Participation and Pregnancy Outcomes: Massachusetts Statewide Evaluation Project," *American Journal of Public Health* 74: 10 (October 1984): 1086-1092.

[30] U.S. Department of Health and Human Services, *Indian Health Service Chart Series Book: April 1985* (Rockville, MD: Health Resources and Services Administration, 1985), p. 16.

[31] Ibid., p. 37.

[32] Ernest L. Abel, "Smoking and Pregnancy," *Journal of Psychoactive Drugs* 16: 4 (October-December 1984): 327-338.

[33] Frank A. Padreira, Vincent L. Guandolo, Edward J. Feroli, Gordon W. Mella and Ira P. Weiss, "Involuntary Smoking and Incidence of Respiratory Illness During the First Year of Life," *Pediatrics* 75: 3 (March 1985): 594-597.

[34] National Center for Health Statistics, "Prevalence of Smoking," unpublished data from the 1980 National Health Interview Survey (Bethesda, MD: National Institute of Health).

[35] Jim Jackson, keynote address at the grand opening and dedication of the Fond du Lac Ojibway School (Cloquet, MN: January 5, 1981).

[36] Philip A. May, Karen J. Humbaugh, Jon M. Aase and Jonathan M. Samet, "Epidemiology of Fetal Alcohol Syndrome Among American Indians of the Southwest," *Social Biology* 30: 4 (Winter 1983): 374-387.

[37] Joseph L. Pursch, et al., "Alcohol and Substance Abuse," paper presented at the Fourth National Conference on Child Abuse and Neglect in Los Angeles, California, October 7-9, 1979 (Long Beach, CA: Alcohol Research Center, Navy Alcohol and Drug Abuse Prevention Program).

[38] Joy Leland, *Firewater Myths: North American Indian Drinking and Alcohol Addiction* (New Brunswick, NJ: Publications Division, Rutgers Center of Alcohol Studies, 1976).

[39] May, et al., op. cit. note 36.

[40] Personal communication with Aaron Handler, Vital Events Staff, Indian Health Service, U.S. Department of Health and Human Services (Rockville, MD: 1986).

[41] Henry J. Malin, Neil E. Munch and Loran P. Archer, "A National Surveillance System for Alcoholism and Alcohol Abuse," Report to the 32nd International Conference on Alcoholism and Drug Dependence (Rockville, MD: National Institute on Alcohol Abuse and Alcoholism, 1978).

[42] U.S. Department of Health and Human Services, op. cit. note 30, p. 23.

[43] Joseph Westermeyer, "Indian Powerlessness in Minnesota," *Society* (March/April 1973): 45-52.

[44] G. Mike Charleston, Jennifer G. Myers and Karen Charleston, *Indian "Alcoholism" Program Evaluation: Fiscal Year 1984 National Report* (Washington, D.C.: U.S. Department of Health and Human Services, Indian Health Service, 1985).

[45] Anthony E. Thomas, "The Rice Lake Center: An Observer's Account of an American Indian Drug Treatment Program," unpublished paper read post-

humously by Joyce Kramer at the American Anthropological Association Meetings (Washington, D.C.: December 8, 1985).

[46]Steven Unger, ed., *The Destruction of American Indian Families* (New York: Association on American Indian Affairs, 1977), p. 1.

[47]Kristine S. Wicklund, Sheila Moss and Floyd Frost, "Effects of Maternal Education, Age, and Parity on Fatal Infant Accidents," *American Journal of Public Health* 7: 10 (October 1984): 1150-1152.

[48]Children's Defense Fund, op. cit. note 8, p. xiv.

[49]McCormick, et al., op. cit. note 19.

[50]Carol Stack, *All My Kin: Strategies for Survival in a Black Community* (New York: Harper and Row, 1975, © 1974); and Joyce M. Kramer, "Production and Reproduction in the Modern World System," unpublished Ph.D. dissertation (Chapel Hill, NC: University of North Carolina, 1980).

[51]Personal communication with Aaron Handler, op. cit. note 40.

[52]Paula Piekkala, Risto Erkkola, Pentti Kero, Arja Tenovuo and Matti Sillanpää, "Declining Perinatal Mortality in a Region of Finland, 1968-1982," *American Journal of Public Health* 75: 2 (February 1985): 156-160; Ronald L. Williams and Peter M. Chen, "Identifying the Sources of the Recent Decline in Perinatal Mortality Rates in California," *New England Journal of Medicine* 306: 4 (January 28, 1982): 207-214; and Paneth, et al., op. cit. note 22.

[53]Children's Defense Fund, op. cit. note 8, p. 5.

[54]Edward Chen, "Emergency Room Doors Closing, ACLU Takes on Patient Dumping," *ACLU News* (San Francisco), American Civil Liberties Union of Northern California (March 1986), pp. 1-2; and Peter Aleshire, "Indigent Health Care Issues Take Spotlight," *Oakland Tribune* (Oakland, CA: December 29, 1985), pp. A1-A5.

[55]Joyce M. Kramer, Anthony E. Thomas and Tony L. Whitehead, "Primary Social Support and Helping Networks: Their Relationship to Health Care Delivery," in Charles Tilquin, ed., *Systems Science in Health Care* (Toronto and New York: Pergamon Press, 1981), Vol. 1, pp. 647-651.

[56]Loren P. Petersen, Gary Leonardson, Robert J. Wingert, Willis Stanage, Julie Gergen and Howard T. Gilmore, "Pregnancy Complications in Sioux Indians," *Obstetrics and Gynecology* 64: 4 (October 1984): 519-523; and F. Rahbar, J. Momeni, A. Fomufod and L. Westney, "Prenatal Care and Perinatal Mortality in a Black Population," *Obstetrics and Gynecology* 65: 3 (March 1985): 327-329.

[57]Children's Defense Fund, op. cit. note 8, p. xiv.

[58]Charles H. Brooks, "Path Analysis of Socioeconomic Correlates of County Infant Mortality Rates," *International Journal of Health Services* 5: 3 (1975): 499-514.

[59]Personal communication with Everett Rhoades, Assistant Surgeon General and Director, Indian Health Service, U.S. Department of Health and

Human Services (Anaheim, CA: American Public Health Association Annual Meetings, November 13, 1984).

[60]"The First Round of Gramm-Rudman Cuts Eliminated Money to Vaccinate Some 65,000 Children This Year," *News-Tribune and Herald* (Duluth, MN: March 11, 1986), p. 4A.

[61]Indian Health Service, "Table II—Estimated Indian and Alaskan Native Service Population by Area" (Rockville, MD: Health Services Administration, February 6, 1986); and Indian Health Service, "Health Care Expenditures of the Indian Health Service and the U.S. Resident Population, Fiscal Years 1977-87" (Rockville, MD: Health Services Administration, February 8, 1986).

[62]Robert J. Maxwell, "Health Care in Urban Areas: Learning from the Third World," *The Lancet* 8474 (January 25, 1986): 222-223.

[63]Personal communication with Harold Leppink, Executive Director, St. Louis County, Minnesota Health Department (Duluth, MN: 1986).

BIOLOGY VS MORALITY: TEENAGE PREGNANCY AND PUBLIC POLICY IN THE UNITED STATES*

Maria Luisa Urdaneta

The University of Texas at San Antonio

Tom Thompson

Social Science Research Association

Introduction

Physical anthropologists have been among the first to note that a biological revolution has been taking place in the more developed countries (MDCs). The average age at which puberty begins for MDC girls has been dropping about three months each decade since 1845.[1] (See Figure 1.) This fundamental biological transformation has been taking place at the same time that our society is endorsing a longer period of adolescence through prolonged schooling, delayed economic independence and delayed marriage. While sexual activity, sanctioned by marriage, occurs later in life, the potential for motherhood at an early age has increased greatly. In the United States, this has resulted in societal mismanagement of physical maturation and social adolescence, with deleterious repercussions in the areas of education, economics and health status, not only for the teenage mother but also her offspring.

Unlike other MDCs, the policy response to teenage pregnancy in the United States has been fraught with emotional concerns of sexual mo-

---

*The authors wish to acknowledge the assistance of Kay Scott Bard, Chair, National Executive Direction Council of Planned Parenthood; Janet Alyn, Director of Education, Planned Parenthood, San Antonio, Texas; Karen Glenney, Public Affairs Director, Planned Parenthood, San Antonio, Texas; Hector Gonzales, consultant to the Edgewood Independent School District, San Antonio, Texas; and M. Estellie Smith, Ph.D, State University of New York-Oswego.

rality rather than with the pragmatic concerns of preventing pregnancy among teenagers. A survey by the Alan Guttmacher Institute of
Sweden, the Netherlands, France, England and Wales, and Canada indicated that government-sponsored programs in sex education and
contraception information in their school systems were widely accepted by the public.[2] This, however, has not been the case in the
United States, with the result that it not only has the highest teenage
pregnancy rate of any developed country, but also the highest teenage
abortion rate. In this respect the United States fits the pattern of the
less developed countries (LDCs) more than that of the industrialized
West.[3]

FIGURE 1

MEDIAN AGES OF MENARCHE FROM 1845 TO 1969
IN SELECTED EUROPEAN COUNTRIES
AND THE UNITED STATES

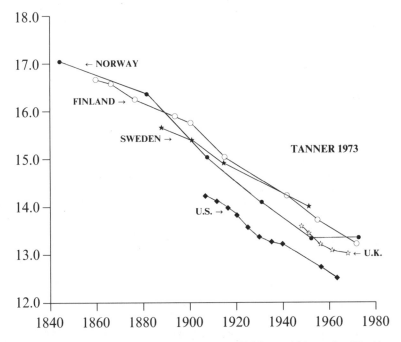

Source: Alex F. Roche, "Secular Trends in Stature, Weight , and Maturation," in Alex
F. Roche. ed., *Secular Trends in Human Growth, Maturation and Development,*
Vol. 44, nos. 3-4, Serial No. 179, Monograph of the Society for Research in
Child Development (Chicago: University of Chicago Press, 1979), p. 20. fig.11.

Mexican Americans make up the second largest minority population in the United States. It has been projected that by 2000, they will be the largest ethnic minority. Mexican Americans are a young population in that most of its members are under the age of twenty-five. The problem of teenage pregnancy among Mexican Americans can be said to be acute. For example, in 1984 in San Antonio, Texas, one predominantly Mexican-American school district which makes up 11 percent of the city's total population accounted for 21 percent of births to mothers under the age of eighteen.[4] This statistic portends all of the undesirable and deleterious effects of interrupting a young woman's life during her teenage years. An early pregnancy is likely to place her permanently into a lower socioeconomic status, where she will remain a candidate for social welfare services and all of the accompanying dismal features attributed to living in a cycle of poverty. In Arthur Campbell's words:

> The girl who has an illegitimate child at the age of 16 suddenly has 90 percent of her life's script written for her. She will probably drop out of school; even if someone else in her family helps to take care of the baby, she will probably not be able to find a steady job that pays enough to provide for herself and her child; she may feel impelled to marry someone she might not otherwise have chosen. Her life choices are few, and most of them are bad. Had she been able to delay the first child, her prospects might have been quite different . . . .[5]

We shall examine the problem of teenage pregnancy in the United States in general, and look specifically at statistics from San Antonio, Texas, an urban, predominantly Mexican-American area. Comparisons between the policies of agencies in the United States with those in other MDCs will be made where appropriate. Finally, suggestions and proposals for public policy strategies to address the problem of teenage pregnancy will be advanced.

The Biological Revolution and Social Norms and Mores

The sharp trend to earlier maturity and greater height that has been noted since the mid-1800s among populations of the developed world indicates that people had a potential for growth that was not previously being realized. What has changed? Technological improvements in transportation and in trade networks, plus new modes of preserving and distributing food, have decreased regional and seasonal variations in diet. This, in turn, has resulted in a markedly improved nutritional status among people in the developed world. In addition, outbreeding

seems to result in an increase in stature. In the last century, urbanization, transportation and communications have served to decrease the
amount of inbreeding in many parts of the world, and this may have
contributed to the increase in stature. All this has resulted not only in
teenagers who are physically larger than their parents and grandparents, but also to the earlier onset of puberty in teenage women. Among
anthropologists, this is known as a secular trend.

In the nineteenth century, a woman was likely to marry shortly after the onset of menses. Males were economically productive as part of
a family enterprise such as farming, or could otherwise be apprenticed
in the trades at least by their mid-teens. Postponing marriage or employment for increased schooling was not part of the process of becoming an adult. While sexual activity was sanctioned only within the marriage bond, neither females nor males experienced a prolonged period of
abstinence between puberty and marriage. Today, not only does the
female begin menstruating at an earlier age, but society has also imposed a longer period of adolescence for both sexes through prolonged
schooling and postponement of economic independence until after attaining a high school diploma or, preferably, a college degree.

Print and visual media in the United States place a high value on
youth and sexual attractiveness. Films, television, magazines and
novels romanticize sexual activity, but rarely indicate negative results
such as an unwanted pregnancy. The reality of raising a child as a single mother with little or no potential for economic independence is not
dealt with effectively in fact or fiction. At the same time that the media
promote sexual attractiveness, our cultural values contradictorily emphasize the point that "good" people, especially girls, do not indulge in
sexual activities. Although the "sexual revolution" of the '60s and '70s
loosened things somewhat (the recent AIDS crisis may be tightening
things up again), American culture continues to emphasize the immorality of sexual activity outside the marriage bond, thus trying to impose unrealistic expectations of sexual abstinence on a biological phenomenon which is not of the teenagers' making. In short, social norms
and mores vis-à-vis adolescence and adulthood are lagging behind biological changes.

The harmful effects of this cultural attitude can be illustrated quite
eloquently through the following examples. Brides of seventeen and
under tend to be poor marriage risks—their marriages are three times
more likely to break up than are those of their contemporaries who
wait until their twenties to marry.[6] Teenage couples who marry as a
result of pregnancy are more likely to be disadvantaged socioeconomically, thus placing further strains on the marriage and making it more
vulnerable to divorce, separation and family instability. Married

women who have their first child at age seventeen or younger can expect to have a larger family, whereas those who wait to have their first child between the ages of twenty to twenty-four can expect three or fewer children. Those having their first child at seventeen can expect at least four children before their family is completed. Girls who have their first child young tend also to bear their subsequent children in rapid succession. Since there is evidence to link large family size with the children's decreased physical growth and intelligence, as well as with increased child mortality, this is an especially sobering statistic.[7]

The fragility of teenage marriages has been widely documented, and perhaps media coverage has actually begun to influence teenagers to delay marriage even when there is the complication of pregnancy. While sexual activity among unmarried women aged fifteen to nineteen living in metropolitan areas rose by two-thirds in the 1970s, the teenage marriage rate dropped 4 percent for whites and 45 percent for blacks during the same period.[8] Sexual activity and teenage pregnancy, however, have been on the increase. In 1981 a report on teenage sexuality indicated that in 1978, eight in ten males and seven in ten females were sexually active by the age of nineteen. [9] About one-half of the teenagers (9.5 million males and 5 million females) in the fifteen-to-nineteen-year-old age group had had intercourse. Of over a million teen pregnancies in 1978, 22 percent were carried to term unmarried, 10 percent were eventually legitimated by marriage, 13 percent miscarried, and 38 percent were aborted. Only 17 percent of teen pregnancies were conceived after marriage. Of total teenage pregnancies that were carried to term, 69 percent of the teenage mothers remained unmarried. The social, economic and demographic consequences of this pattern are alarming.

The first and most immediate social consequence of adolescent pregnancy is the often permanent disruption of the young woman's education. Even though legislation and numerous court decisions confirm the rights of school-age mothers to an education, dropout statistics suggest that many school policies and personnel may "encourage" students who are pregnant and/or who are mothers to leave. Studies show that 80 percent of those who become mothers when they are seventeen and under never complete high school.[10] A factor compounding the problem is that very few states have day care centers that will accept infants under the age of two. By the time a young mother has interrupted her education for about two and one-half years (assuming that she keeps her child and cares for it herself), it is most unlikely that she will resume her education. Because many mothers do not complete high school, and because the majority lack marketable skills and experience which would enable them to compete successfully for good jobs, most are unable to find employment that pays enough to provide for themselves and their children.[11] The fact that many of them are forced to depend upon welfare affects us all in that society will ultimately bear the burden of support.[12]

Adolescent pregnancy is a serious threat to the life and health of a young woman and her offspring—regardless of whether pregnancy occurs in or out of marriage. As maternal age drops below twenty, health and mortality risks for mother and child rise sharply. If maternal age dips below age fifteen, the death rate from pregnancy complications, birth and delivery escalates by 60 percent.[13] The most common complications of teenage pregnancy are toxemia, prolonged labor, anemia, poor nutrition, inadequate prenatal care and physical immaturity. At any stage of pregnancy or infancy, the very young mother is exposed to greater risks of losing her baby than her somewhat older counterparts. The incidence of prematurity and low birthweight is higher in teenage pregnancies, increasing the risk to the baby of such conditions as epilepsy, cerebral palsy and mental retardation. These underweight babies are also two to three times more likely to die in their first year than are babies whose mothers are over twenty years of age.[14]

Teenagers constitute a growing proportion of the United States population, and will continue to do so at least into the early 1990s. The phenomenon of a rapidly climbing teenage birthrate has important implications for population growth. If all teenage births could be eliminated, the result would be a population 15 percent smaller than the size projected with unchanged rates. The net population reproduction rate could be reduced to just over the value required for a stable population.[15] If stabilization could be achieved, it would ensure the availability of a better quality of life for all persons—including the growing ranks of teenagers.

Experts attribute the rash of teenage pregnancies to increased teenage sexual activity (which has more than outstripped easier access to contraceptives), ignorance of the reproductive process, ineffective or non-use of contraceptives, and lack of open discussion of human sexuality issues between adults and teenagers.[16] These factors, together with the precipitous drop in the age of physical maturity which has greatly lowered the age of possible parenthood, and the fact that teenagers make up a growing segment of the population, create the bases for an ecological problem in the United States of staggering proportions. Despite evidence indicating that one of the major reasons for unwanted teenage pregnancies is ignorance about human reproduction and the risks of pregnancy, and despite the fact that most teenagers would apparently choose to avoid pregnancy and childbirth if they could, young people continue to be denied information that would enable them to make responsible decisions related to their sexuality. Only three states and the District of Columbia *require* sex education in the schools, and only five states and the District of Columbia *encourage* including information on birth control in sex education classes.

There is a challenging need to establish accessible and appropriate facilities, sensitive to the needs and concerns of teenagers, where birth control information and services are available. Every state should adopt affirmative legislation which would permit minors to receive contraceptive and prophylactic information and services. Relevant sex education and information must be made available, in fact, *compulsory*, for all adolescents.

Policy Response

The Alan Guttmacher Institute has published data on thirty-seven more developed countries (MDCs) concerning the problems of teenage pregnancy, abortion and marriage.[17] Data from several European countries and Canada make an interesting contrast to data from the United States. In the former nations, programs for teenagers on sex education and information about contraceptive devices and technology are either widely available in the schools or readily available in social service agencies. Birthrates to women under the age of twenty are considerably lower for the European countries and Canada than for the United States. (See Figure 2.) Abortion rates are lower as well. In fact, the United States' teenage abortion rate *alone* is equal to the total teenage birthrates (married and unmarried) *plus* the teenage abortion rate for Canada, France, and England and Wales, and is considerably higher than the total teenage pregnancy rate for the Netherlands. The teenage birthrate in these countries is not lower due to less sexual activity or a greater reliance on abortion. European and Canadian teenagers simply become pregnant less frequently.

Why is this so? In the Netherlands, sexuality education is limited to the basics of sexual reproduction taught in science classes. However, the government provides mobile clinics which not only teach about sexuality, but also inform teenagers about the various methods of contraception as well as dispense contraceptive devices. In general, teenagers in European countries have greater access to both education on reproduction and contraceptive devices. The lower level of teenage pregnancies attests to the responsible use of the contraceptive knowledge that teenagers have made available to them.[18]

Sweden has traditionally been among the most liberal of European countries regarding nonmarital births and human sexuality. Nevertheless, the increased knowledge of prevention and contraception has kept the teenage pregnancy rate much lower than that of the United States. Information from the European countries and Canada indicates that differences in sexual activity among teenagers are not nearly so great as the differences in rates of teenage pregnancy. These differences can surely be accounted for primarily by the access to sexuality education and contraceptive information. The median age for first intercourse—

FIGURE 2

BIRTHS PER 1,000 WOMEN UNDER AGE 20, BY WOMEN'S AGE, CASE-STUDY COUNTRIES, 1981

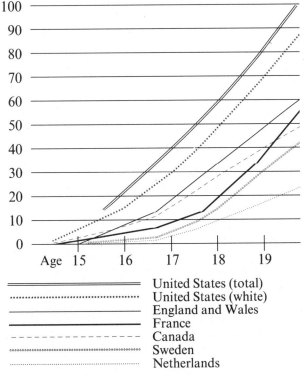

Source: Elise F. Jones, Jacqueline D. Forrest, Noreen Goldman, Stanley K. Henshaw, Richard Lincoln, Jeannie I. Rosoff, Charles S. Westoff and Deirdre Wulf, "Teenage Pregnancy in Developed Countries: Determinants and Policy Implications," *Family Planning Perspectives* 17: 2 (March/April 1985): 54, fig. 1.

slightly under the age of eighteen—is applicable for France, Great Britain and the Netherlands, as well as for the United States. The age of first intercourse for women is slightly lower in Sweden and slightly higher in Canada.[19]

It appears that if American teenagers are using contraceptives at all, they either use less effective contraceptives or do not use them correctly. This can be related to the reluctance of schools and agencies to provide this knowledge directly to the teenagers. In contrast, the Swedish government has carefully established links between the contraceptive clinic services and the schools; the Netherlands not only provides mobile clinic services, but also publishes and makes readily available materials on sex education and other sex-related topics. As a result, surveys among the teenage population in the Netherlands indicate that knowledge on how to avoid pregnancy is virtually universal. France has mandated that all adolescents be informed of sexual reproduction and birth control, and England and Wales have a national policy which includes sex and family life education in the curriculum. Canada, like the United States, delegates almost all education to the provinces (states) and localities and has no national policy. However, both Quebec and Ontario provide sex education as part of the school curriculum.

It is clear from examining the data in these six countries that the emphasis of policy formation is on the problem of preventing teenage pregnancy through responsible means—i.e., through the provision of reproductive information and contraceptive services to sexually active teenagers. All the while, respect for the privacy and confidentiality of the individual is maintained. The focus of the successful policies in Europe and Canada has been upon the pragmatic question of preventing unwanted teenage pregnancies, and not upon the moral question of early sexual activity.

The intent here is not to paint an ideal picture which is represented by enlightened Europeans. There has been controversy there on the issue of providing contraceptives to unmarried teenagers, and on the role of their parents. However, the specter of rising abortion rates among teenagers persuaded them that such a policy was justified. In Sweden, the government made the decision to make contraceptive information accessible to teenagers with the understanding that prevention of the need for abortion could best be achieved by providing effective, confidential services to sexually active teenagers.

A particularly attractive aspect of European policies concerning teenage sexuality is that health services are most often provided through government-sponsored clinics and health agencies. The general public, as well as teenagers, are more accustomed to utilizing such services for a variety of health needs. Many of the psychological, social and financial barriers to contraceptive services are surely eased because of the citizens' familiarity with, and easy access to, the health care system. Use of government-sponsored facilities in Europe and Canada does not have the negative connotations of welfare services that are associated with charity clinic services in the United States. At the same time it must be mentioned that, perhaps with the exception of Canada, it is logistically more simple for the small European countries to manage these services than it is for the United States. While Canada must deal with a large geographical area, its population is much smaller than that of the United States and thus more comparable to most European countries. In addition, fundamentalist religious groups are more visible, vocal and influential in policymaking in the United States than in any of the European countries noted here. This helps account for the fact that the European countries place greater attention on the need to prevent teenage pregnancy, rather than focusing on the immorality of sexual activity as is done in the United States.

The divisiveness of American politics cannot be ignored in the development of policy on teenage pregnancy. The use of private funding to reach and hold political office creates a strong body of interest groups, each of which can exert varying levels of influence on policymakers. The American political system, with its multiple checks and balances, makes more difficult the articulation and implementation of a coherent national policy, especially in an area as emotionally charged as human sexuality. This is less true of the parliamentary democracies under discussion, which have more centralized structures of authority for policymaking. The many and varied levels of decisionmaking and bureaucracy that must be dealt with in the United States can overwhelm efforts which are aimed at reaching and implementing effective policy quickly. The net result is that teenagers may be one of the most neglected populations for health care services in the United States.[20]

An additional factor correlated with teenage pregnancy that is less crucial in the six other countries is the unequal distribution of family income. The wide gap separating the top income earners and the lower socioeconomic levels which characterizes the United States is not as acute in any of the European countries discussed.[21] Low socioeconomic levels and little hope of changing one's economic status have been related to teenage anomie and the hopelessness associated with the failure to understand or see a need for the prevention of pregnancy. While one does not wish to indicate that there is no poverty in the other six countries, it surely does not exist with the same pernicious effects that are found in many areas of the United States, especially among racial minority groups.

In contrast to the United States, the countries being discussed recognize the problems of youth employment and underemployment by providing a variety of social services including training programs, stipends and other means of support which, again, are provided without the stigma of government charity which is often present when such programs do exist in the United States. Teenagers are not excluded from participation in social activities in Europe simply because they are not yet voting members of society. Instead, government policies are those of inclusion through the provision of services which are needed by this very distinct population, which will soon become part of the electorate.

Benefits to women in the other nations discussed tend to be readily available regardless of their marital or reproductive status. Allowances for children and food supplements are more generous than in the United States.[22] Yet unwed motherhood and out-of-wedlock pregnancy are less common than in the United States. This would contradict critics in the United States who contend that welfare assistance encourages out-of-wedlock motherhood.

In the United States, policy formation seems to be premised on the fear that increased knowledge on the part of teenagers about sexuality and the use of contraceptive techniques will lead to increased sexual activity and promiscuity. This has resulted in a poor knowledge of the process of conception and reproduction among teenagers, the highest rate of teen pregnancy among the MDCs, the highest rate of teen abortion among the MDCs, and an increased risk to the health of teenage females through poor prenatal care and stress on an endocrine system which is not yet fully developed. The overall problem is aggravated because of the mixed message of romantic, sexual lifestyles and the imposed immorality of sexual activity.

Because each individual state assumes the responsibility for sex education policy and each local school board is responsible for the manner in which policy is implemented, essential information concerning reproduction and contraception is not consistent across the country and distributed unevenly to the teenage population. Where school-based clinics have been established (in St. Paul, Chicago, and Jackson, Mississippi, for example), the effort has been completely on a grass-roots level. No larger network of support has been available. Financing of school-based clinics has come largely from funds outside the control of the local school boards, and administrators and staff have been hired separately. Successful programs have been established in a growing number of areas (from less than twelve in 1984 to over forty in 1985 and possibly sixty additional clinics in 1986, at the time of this writing). [23] It might be said that these clinics have been established despite, rather than because of, policy. It is an empirical fact that the general policy is *not* to provide health services at schools in most states. Thus, teenagers do not have the opportunity to develop good health maintenance skills; indeed, even free clinics and low-cost health services usually are not readily available to them.

When policy has been established which would ease access to contraceptive information and services, for example, influential pressure groups move to have the regulations tightened so that privacy and confidentiality are not possible. The so-called "squeal law," which would inform parents if teenagers sought birth control information at family planning clinics or from private physicians, is a case in point.

Americans are unlikely to be impressed if told that sexual promiscuity and immoral behavior showed no discernible increase among European teenagers after increased access to contraceptive devices, coupled with sex education, was made available. One study in Baltimore, however, has shown that with increased access to information and contraceptive devices, the age at which sexual activity began was actually delayed.[24] In addition, the study indicated that teenagers were also decreasing their rate of sexual activity. This implies that fears that sex education in the schools will lead teenagers into a more immoral lifestyle are unfounded.

Minorities and Teenage Pregnancy

According to a 1985 Louis Harris telephone survey with two cross sections of adults nationwide (2,510 interviews),[25] the American public is quite aware of the problem of teenage pregnancy and the question of sex education in the public schools. Eighty-four percent of those surveyed indicated that the high incidence of teen pregnancy was a national problem. How to deal with the problem, though, was another question. Sixty-four percent of the adults surveyed did not feel that parents had much or any control over their teenagers' sexual activity. While 76 percent of those with children between the ages of six and eighteen indicated that they had initiated discussions with their children about sex, only 33 percent of those said that information about birth control was included in the discussion. Sex education in the schools was overwhelmingly supported by the participants (85 percent), but dispensation of contraceptives to teenagers was approved by only 47 percent of the respondents, while 48 percent indicated that they would want to be made aware if their child sought birth control devices. What this indicated to the pollsters was that while parents want their teenagers to be informed about sex, they also want to be able to have some degree of control over their teenagers' access to birth control information and devices.

The high rate of teenage pregnancy among blacks is well documented. Even though blacks represent only 14 percent of the fifteen-to-nineteen-year-old population, their rate is high enough to affect those for total teen pregnancy. Unpublished figures from the Alan Guttmacher Institute place black teen pregnancy at 163 per 1000 as opposed to the white teen pregnancy rate of 83 per 1000.[26] While the rate of teen pregnancy among blacks is higher than that of whites in the United States, the white rate alone is still significantly higher than in the MDCs discussed earlier. Where school-based clinics have been established in largely black areas, the teen pregnancy rate has been reduced drastically. For example, during the first three years of the school-based clinic in St. Paul, the overall rate of teen pregnancy (largely among black and Hispanic girls) was reduced by 56 percent (from 79 to 35 births per 1000).[27]

As noted earlier, the fastest growing minority population in the United States is the Mexican-American population. This group also has the greatest number of teenagers and, significantly, a disproportionate number of Mexican Americans "live well below national standards in income, education, housing, and health."[28] Predictive indicators for early pregnancy such as poverty, teenage anomie, substandard education and an overall general feeling of hopelessness are quite descriptive of a significant proportion of the Mexican-American population.

Disaggregated statistics on Mexican-American teen pregnancies are sorely lacking because minority populations other than blacks have rarely been distinguished. In addition, data on Mexican Americans are usually reported along with that of other Hispanic groups such as Puerto Ricans and Cubans. Moreover, Mexican Americans historically have not always sought nor had access to the general American model of health care, which has caused them to be disproportionately unreported in general statistical data. Given the fact that Mexican Americans are a young population, research indicates that Mexican-American teenagers are most likely to conform to the national trend of early sexual activity.[29] Sexual activity, poverty, and poor health services-seeking skills and resources all combine to produce an alarming trend in teen pregnancy among Mexican Americans, which some have speculated is twice that of the national average, i.e., 180 per 1000.[30] There are few or no reliable statistics on abortion and miscarriage.

In 1981, Texas ranked first in the number of pregnancies (births, abortions and miscarriages) to females aged fourteen and under (2,370), and second in the number of pregnancies (births, abortions and miscarriages) to females fifteen-to-nineteen years old (89,910). The pregnancy rate of fifteen-to-nineteen-year-old females in Texas was 139 per 1000 in 1981. This is 45 percent higher than the national average of 96 per 1000. Given the high percentage of Mexican Americans resident in Texas (20 percent of the population), it is a fair assumption that Mexican-American teens are a major contributor to this high statistic.

Texas has no state policy dealing expressly with sex education in the schools. As is the case elsewhere, the issue is primarily left up to the local school districts. While some areas of Texas are solidly part of the southern "Bible Belt," and would therefore be assumed to be against sex education in the schools, there is a growing public awareness of the problem of teen pregnancy. Dallas and Houston each are represented among the small, but growing, number of areas where clinics have been established in the school systems. As in other areas, the Dallas clinic has concentrated upon providing general health care services to teenagers, with family planning and other sex education services forming only part of the program.

The incidence of pregnancy among students in predominantly Mexican-American school districts in San Antonio, for example, warrants the high level of concern which has spread beyond health care personnel to the parents, school board members and administrators. The Edgewood School District in San Antonio, the student population of which is 95 percent Mexican American, has taken the initial steps to establish a school-based clinic which will not only deliver general health care services to the students, but will also provide other awareness services such as sex education and family planning. An advisory committee has been set up comprising school district residents, parents, administrators, and at least one parish priest. [31] This enlightened approach fosters the sort of hope that is crucial to sustained activity designed to meet head-on the problem of pregnancy among teenagers.

Summary

Data collected by the Alan Guttmacher Institute staff on thirty-seven MDCs, and data on six specific MDCs compared to the United States, indicate that with increased emphasis on education and knowledge— i.e., sex education, contraception and family planning—the teenage pregnancy rate can be reduced significantly. Data gathered by the same institute indicate that teenage pregnancy rates in the United States are alarmingly high; for example, abortion rates alone for the United States are about equal to total birth, miscarriage and abortion rates in three MDCs, and are continuing to increase. When black and Mexican-American data are distinguished from the general national data in the United States, an even higher, and more alarming, trend in teenage pregnancy begins to emerge. The presence of school-based clinics in several areas have shown that *with community support*, services can be provided to teenagers in places where they are comfortable and likely to seek help. Moreover, in addition to general health services, the presence of these school-based clinics and the availability of sex education and birth control information have had a direct relationship to the reduction of the teenage pregnancy rate and a decreased reliance on abortion.

Suggestions and Proposals

The key goal should be the improvement of the overall health status of teenagers. Until recently, it was largely assumed that adolescents made up the healthiest segment of the population. This belief undoubtedly contributed to the lack of concern about providing adequate health care to teenagers. The result has been, as already noted, that teenagers make up one of the most significantly underserved populations in the United States; in particular, teenagers lack information about finding and using health care services. Moreover, ignorance concerning the use of health care facilities has undoubtedly aggravated the alarming trend toward increased teenage pregnancy.

Within the larger goal of improving the overall health status of teenagers is the more specific, but no less important, goal of greatly reducing the rate of teenage pregnancies and abortions. This can only be achieved through a concerted effort to provide sex education, contraception services and family planning information. This must be accomplished in spite of the fears of some Americans that increased knowledge will lead to more promiscuous lifestyles.

In the past decade, several areas in the United States have established school-based clinics. Each of these clinics was established on a local need basis, and few if any of their administrators were in contact with others who were beginning the same kind of work. In fact, it was not until September 1984 that a national meeting was held, bringing together the administrators of such clinics in a setting where they could compare notes and share experiences.[32] These clinics were established by local groups and coalitions who recognized the need to address the problem of teenage pregnancy in an atmosphere that would not be charged with the controversies over birth control information and the subject of abortion. The successes of the already established school-based clinics should form the basis of recommendations and proposals for similar services elsewhere.

Any provision of health care services in a school system must be related to the perceived needs of the residents of that area. Promoting grass-roots movements is not a monumental task, but attempting to institute any change without such support will most likely be met with resistance and result in failure. School-based clinics in Chicago, St. Paul, and Jackson, Mississippi, for example, were established to provide basic health services to students. These included physical examinations for athletes, immunizations, nutritional education, drug and substance abuse programs, and dental services. Family counseling, sex education and birth control information were included as parts of the overall health program. The media, to its credit, did not attempt to exploit the situation by paying undue attention to these programs, even though the motivation behind the establishment of the services was definitely linked to the high incidence of teenage pregnancy and abortion.

In each case, the funding and budget of the school-based clinic were kept separate from that of the school system. Funding was obtained from both public and private sources, thus it could not be curtailed by opposition from a vocal minority that might influence school board decisions. The general health services of the clinics were emphasized to promote parental support, and while significant reductions in the rates of teenage pregnancy and abortion were achieved, attention was given to other successes. For example, in the Dallas school-based clinic, one hundred previously undetected heart murmurs were discovered, and each year at least 3200 youths have made about eleven thousand visits for a very wide variety of health problems.

While one can be greatly encouraged by the successes of school-based clinics and the services they render both in general health care and sex education, one must not forget that simply improving access to health care for the poor and underprivileged will not necessarily change the outlook of these teenagers unless the general quality of the entire educational program is also improved. This will, in turn, enhance the job opportunities and economic status of a significant and growing percentage of our population.

NOTES

[1]For reports of this phenomenon, see Alex F. Roche, "Secular Trends in Stature, Weight, and Maturation," in Alex F. Roche, ed., *Secular Trends in Human Growth, Maturation and Development*, Vol. 44, nos. 3-4, Serial No. 179,

Monographs of the Society for Research in Child Development (Chicago: University of Chicago Press, 1979), pp. 19-21; Bengt-Olov Ljung, Agneta Bergsten-Brucefors and Gurrilla Lindgren, "The Secular Trend in Physical Growth in Sweden," *Annals of Human Biology* 1 (1974): 245-256; James M. Tanner, "Trend Towards Earlier Menarche in London, Oslo, Copenhagen, The Netherlands and Hungary," *Nature* 243: 5402 (May 11, 1973): 95-96; and Geoffrey A. Harrison, Joseph S. Weiner, James M. Tanner and N. A. Barnicot, eds., *Human Biology: An Introduction to Human Evolution, Variation and Growth* (New York: Oxford University Press, 1964).

[2]Elise F. Jones, Jacqueline D. Forrest, Noreen Goldman, Stanley K. Henshaw, Richard Lincoln, Jeannie I. Rosoff, Charles F. Westoff and Deirdre Wulf, "Teenage Pregnancy in Developed Countries: Determinants and Policy Implications," *Family Planning Perspectives* 17: 2 (March/April 1985): 53-63.

[3]Ibid.

[4]San Antonio Metropolitan Health District Statistical Report (San Antonio, TX: 1984), p. 2.

[5]Arthur A. Campbell, "The Role of Family Planning in the Reduction of Poverty," *Journal of Marriage and the Family* 30: 2 (May 1968): 236-246 at 238.

[6]C. P. Green and K. Potteiger, *Teenage Pregnancy: A Major Problem for Minors* (Washington, D.C.: Zero Population Growth, Inc., 1977).

[7]Jane Menken, "The Health and Social Consequences of Teenage Childbearing," *Family Planning Perspectives* 4: 3 (July 1972): 45-53.

[8]Alan Guttmacher Institute, *Teenage Pregnancy: The Problem That Hasn't Gone Away* (New York: Alan Guttmacher Institute, 1981), p. 9.

[9]Ibid., p. 7.

[10]Alan Guttmacher Institute, *Eleven Million Teenagers: What Can Be Done About the Epidemic of Adolescent Pregnancies in the United States* (New York: Alan Guttmacher Institute, 1976).

[11]Marion Howard, "Pregnant School Age Girls," *Journal of School Health* 41: 7 (September 1971): 361-363.

[12]Ibid.

[13]Menken, op. cit. note 7, pp. 48-51.

[14]Ibid., pp. 45-53.

[15]Ibid.

[16]Personal communication with Kay Scott Bard, Chair, National Executive Direction Council of Planned Parenthood (April 1986).

[17]Jones, et al., op. cit. note 2.

[18]Ibid., pp. 56-61.

[19]Ibid., p. 56.

[20]Douglas Kirby, Jodie Levin-Epstein and Elaine Hadley, *School-Based Health Clinics* (Washington, D.C.: Center for Population Options, 1985), pp. 3-4.

[21]Jones, et al., op. cit. note 2.

[22]Ibid.

[23]"Clinic News," *Center for Population Options Newsletter* 1: 4 (1985): 3.

[24]Personal communication with Karen Glenney, Director of Public Affairs, Planned Parenthood, San Antonio, Texas (April 1986).

[25]Survey, "Public Attitudes About Sex Education, Family Planning, and Abortion in the United States" (New York: Louis Harris and Associates, Inc., 1985).

[26]Personal communication with Karen Glenney, op. cit. note 24.

[27]Kirby, et al., op. cit. note 20, p. 14.

[28]Maria Luisa Urdaneta, "Chicana Use of Abortion: The Case of Alcala," in Margarita B. Melville, ed., *Twice A Minority: Mexican American Women* (St. Louis: C. V. Mosby Co., 1980), pp. 33-51.

[29]Personal communication with Hector Gonzales, M.D., consultant to the Edgewood Independent School District, San Antonio, Texas (April 1986).

[30]Ibid.

[31]Ibid.

[32]Kirby, et al., op. cit. note 20, p. ii.

TRADITIONAL HEALTH PRACTICES: SIGNIFICANCE FOR MODERN HEALTH CARE

Laura M. Adams and Merritt E. Knox

University of Wisconsin-Oshkosh

Introduction

Health policies and practices in the United States have been formulated within the context of Western scientific and cultural values. Most studies of health policies and practices in this country have thus been based on these values. Examining other values, the culture of a group, can aid in the understanding of that group's design for living, defined as a shared set of socially transmitted assumptions about the goals of life and the approximate means of achieving them.[1]

Many individuals in the United States believe that health care is a human right and should be acceptable, accessible and available to all citizens. Today, however, there exists a health care delivery system where the quality of care is determined by race, language and socioeconomic level. Health care is viewed as a commodity to be purchased, with the government responsible for financing much of the cost of care. This results in poor or substandard care for a large segment of the population. The inequality in health status within our population is a major social policy issue which Congress, responsible for the development of health care policies affecting the entire social structure of the nation, must address. This chapter discusses a select population whose health status is among the lowest in the nation, and presents their concerns in a cultural context.

The differing perceptions of health and illness that exist among the various ethnic groups determine their health practices and future health status. A person's reactions to health, illness, changes in lifestyle and the various caring and treatment practices are linked to his or her cultural beliefs, values and life experiences. While cultural factors play an important role in the delivery of total health care services to a population, they are often overlooked or viewed from an ethnocentric perspective.

What does a person know and believe about the value of health to him/herself and society? How is the individual to decide upon a course of action to follow that will restore a state or sense of well-being? What influences the person in making a decision about what to do when presented with two different and possibly opposing systems of health care practices? These questions will aid us to examine traditional health practices of two cultural groups in the United States, the Menominee and the Oneida Indians, as well as their current use of and impact on the health care delivery system.[2]

Western Concepts of Health

The concept of health and healing in our present society is a topic that is constantly changing; it does not enjoy the luxury of clear-cut definitions. Health in Western society is a culturally-based concept which varies in both scope and context according to the perspective of the person who is defining it. The health care delivery system deals with the perceptive definitions of the client, the health care provider and the society. The most widely used and recognized definition of health is that of the World Health Organization: Health is "a state of complete physical, mental, and social well-being, not merely the absence of disease or infirmity."[3] In contrast, health care providers use more abstract definitions, and socialize their constituencies into individualized, professional definitions. In the nursing profession, health is defined as "a purposeful, adaptive response, physically, mentally, emotionally, and socially, to internal and external stimuli in order to maintain stability and comfort."[4] It is little wonder, with these varying definitions and the inability of the health care provider and client to conceptualize the meaning of health in a concise and universally accepted definition, that cultural conflict exists in the delivery of health care. Health is defined by the cultural system in which the individual lives, and is generally dealt with in terms of illness and treatment. Policies formulated within the American health care delivery system are based upon these varied cultural patterns.

All people need order and explanation as they experience their environment and the processes of disease and health. Each culture provides definitions for such phenomena, although the form of these explanations varies from one group to another. In the modern world of biotechnology, health and healing practices are extremely complex, and seemingly disconnected at times, but they take on meaning according to the cultural orientation of the society.[5] Western society places an emphasis on curative functions, at any cost, often at the expense of preventive techniques. Curative treatment is based on scientifically "proven" methods and research data to the exclusion of treatments which may not have a basis in research.

The individual's need for order and explanation in his/her experience with disease and health within the environment is apparent in both traditional and folk healing. Each American Indian tribe has its own history and belief system regarding health and illness and the traditional treatment of illness. The traditional belief that health reflects living in total harmony with nature and being able to survive or adapt under most circumstances is persistent among the majority of the tribes of North America, including most Wisconsin tribes.[6]

Traditional Concept of Health

Traditionally, health in the American Indian community has reflected a quest for total harmony with nature and the ability to survive under exceedingly difficult circumstances. In this scheme, each person has an intimate relationship with nature. The individual needs to treat the earth as well as the body with respect, since the earth is also a living organism which desires to be well. When a person harms one, he or she also harms the other.[7]

The traditional concept of health has been defined by the American Indian Health Care Association and was presented as part of the testimony to the Senate Select Committee on Indian Affairs regarding the Indian Health Promotion and Disease Prevention Act of 1985:

> The circle of life embodies the philosophical perspectives of harmony with life in the American Indian cultures. Understanding the circle of life is essential in comprehending the philosophical view of Indian people and their culture. It represents the continuity of sharing, oral traditions, consciousness, generosity, and extended family and harmony with all living things. In the circle of life, animals symbolize separate and different values; the eagle represents courage, knowledge, strength and foresight; the turtle represents resourcefulness. Each animal, tree, sky, moon, etc. have [sic] their own quality of spirit life. American Indians traditionally believe that they are a part of all living things. According to Indian health belief concepts, a human is composed of body, mind, and spirit. All three are interrelated and function together. Health to Indians is the power to exist and function harmoniously. The spiritual orientation influences the traditional practice. The spirit focuses on the relationships between patients and their surroundings and type of ceremony. The reasons for ceremonies are beliefs that disease and illness are the results of lack of harmony between a sick person and his surroundings. . . . [t]he emphasis is on unity of experience; to be sick is to be fragmented;

to be healed is to be whole; and to be whole one must be in harmony with family, friends, nature and themselves.[8]

In general, traditional Indian health practices have been looked upon by Western society as "witchcraft, magic, or superstition" which is invoked in images of dreams, rattles, feathers, blankets and charms. This imagery leads the individual to forget that healing is based on a philosophy of a Great Spirit, nature, humanity and the sciences. It is often difficult to separate medicine and religion in American Indian culture, a fact that further enhances the concept of ritualistic healing practices. In many of the Indian societies, the medicine man was both the religious leader and the healer. This ritualistic approach to treatment was only a part of the Indian healer's repertoire. The use of herbs and herbal medicine[9] was practiced in conjunction with primitive surgical procedures such as cupping, trephination (skull surgery), fracture reduction and the suturing of wounds. All of these procedures were accompanied with ritualistic ceremonies which linked medicine to religion in a holistic approach to health.[10]

Wisconsin Indians who have been converted to Christianity usually manage to make their local churches distinctively Indian, community institutions. All of the major tribal groups in Wisconsin, with the exception of the Oneida and Stockbridge who were Christianized long ago in the East, have active factions of traditionalists who hold their ancient rites in quiet but deep defiance of the white man's religions. Congregations of the Drum, or Dream Dance, religion are found among the Potawatomi, Chippewa and Menominee, while the peyote religion, chartered as the Native American Church, is strongest among the Winnebago but also has diffused to the Algonkian-speaking tribes, with the exception of the Stockbridge. These major pan-Indian revitalization or nativistic movements originated during the nineteenth century as self-help efforts to unite and uplift Indians spiritually and morally in a time of crisis and despair.[11]

Differences between Modern and Traditional Health Practices

Traditional health care practices tend to function in distinctive social structural settings. These settings include community groups, kinship groups, private homes and healers' shrines. One feature which appears across a variety of cultures is that traditional health care practices tend to occur more publicly than do modern or Western health care practices, which are apt to be much more private in nature. Most traditional health care systems are more pluralistic than modern ones. These traditional systems reflect the different beliefs, interests and treatment styles of the cultural group. Many traditional health practices are tied in some manner to the religious beliefs of the group.[12]

Traditional health care for the American Indian has also been described as being holistic in nature. It blends the physical and spiritual with the environment. Religious practices and herbal remedies are often combined in order to promote the individual's maintaining or regaining harmony with his/her environment. The health practices of the North American Indian have been described as

> a complex tapestry woven from disparate threads. Some may be described as relatively primitive and empirical, while others are more complex, sophisticated, and of a magico-religious nature. Indian medical treatment was designed to fit the apparent nature of the ailment, and for the North American Indian the treatment depended upon the cause of the condition in terms of Indian belief.[13]

When contrasted with the traditional practices of the American Indian, modern or Western health care tends to be impersonal in nature and highly dependent on technology. Modern health care practice is often an isolationist type of experience which, some say, tends to the needs of machines instead of the needs of individuals. The physician treats the patient in an office or hospital, while other practitioners are called in to do various procedures, the two often seeming not to be in conjunction with each other. This type of care is usually a very private affair. Individuals in the system often lose their unique identities as only the problem is dealt with, not the person in his/her total environment.

The major differences identified between traditional and Western health care beliefs and values can be summarized into three broad areas. First, the traditional health care practices of American Indians are holistic in nature and deal with all aspects of the person and his/her environment. Second, traditional health care practices tend to occur in more public settings and include extended family groups and others. Finally, the Western health care system is more private and fragmented and tends to treat specific conditions as separate entities. This system is much more dependent on professionalism and technology in the provision of health care.

In order to explore further the reasons for these differences, we shall examine the traditional and current health care practices of two Wisconsin tribes, the Oneida and the Menominee, to determine their impact on the Western health care system. These tribes will be discussed in terms of their present societal status, and their traditional health care practices will be reviewed.

The Oneida

The Oneida tribe is the second largest tribal group of Wisconsin Indians, with approximately 3500 members. Of this group, 76 percent are full-blooded and 91 percent are at least one-half Indian. The Oneida is a member tribe of the historic League of the Iroquois. The other five tribes, Seneca, Cayuga, Mohawk, Onondaga and Tuscarora, are found in their homelands in New York and Canada, with outlying communities of Seneca and Cayuga in Oklahoma, where they were resettled during the treaty period. The Oneida language, still spoken by older people, is Iroquoian and is related to the Algonkian languages of other Wisconsin tribes.[14] The Oneida tribe has settled in eastern Wisconsin in Outagamie and Brown counties, and most of the tribal members reside in the reservation community of Oneida.

The Oneida tribe has one of the highest tribal incomes in Wisconsin. Prior to the 1960s, many Oneida worked as skilled laborers in the nearby city of Green Bay and only a small percentage depended upon reservation employment. Since the early 1970s, their tribal enterprises have developed to the point of being self-sustaining. Today their major economic enterprises include developing the Oneida Industrial Park, the Irene Moore Activity Center, and the Oneida Rodeway Inn and Conference Center. These tribal enterprises provide employment for many of the tribal members. In addition, with the help of the tribal enterprises, the Oneida community has developed a nursing home and an ambulatory health care center. They provide health education and promotion activities through their outreach programs, utilizing indigenous community workers.

Traditional Oneida Health Practices

To understand the concept of traditional medicine fully, one must consider the cultural context from which these practices developed. Historically, the American Indian lived under a social order knit together by a set of religious beliefs in which the individual played a unique role and existed in a harmonious relationship with the environment, other societal beings and the gods.[15] The Iroquois, for example, had two kinds of traditional religious practices, one associated with the agricultural cycle and the other with the curing and prevention of disease. Medicinal societies, one of which was the False-face society of the Iroquois, were an integral part of the culture.

One of the historical health practices that had been retained by the Oneida through the years and was incorporated into the treatment of

illness by some tribal members was a form of the False-face ceremony.
Robert Ritzenthaler described the practice:

> One of these kits consisted of a small False-face carved of wood
> and painted red. This was in a small tobacco bag, which in turn
> was wrapped in a piece of silk and then in a white handkerchief,
> and the whole placed in a woven bag. It was worn suspended
> about the neck of the patient. The owner of the kit believed
> strongly in its effectiveness, and cited cases of rheumatism being
> cured by it. The False-face curing ceremony has undergone grad-
> ual disintegration until today only the barest elements remain.
> The ceremony was originally performed in a bark long house by a
> secret society with special rituals, dances, and initiations. The
> members wore hideous wooden masks to represent False-faces, a
> band of supernatural beings without arms, legs, or bodies; only
> faces. A sick person was placed in the center of the room, and the
> masked members would rush in shaking turtle-shell rattles. They
> danced around the nude patient, and reaching into the fire,
> dropped hot coals and ashes on his head.[16]

The ceremony incorporated the use of false-faces and participants
rushing into the room, shouting and stomping their feet while hot coals
and ashes were dropped on the patient's head. This cure was performed
mainly for nervous disorders. Another fact of the ritual was the use of
corn mush. The corn mush was burned in the fire, with some placed on
the patient's body and some placed outside on the steps of the building.
Shredded tobacco was also thrown on the fire as an offering and each
person who participated in the ritual was given a plug of tobacco to
take home.

An interesting aspect of a traditional practice that has been retained
among the Oneidas and meets both social and health maintenance
needs are the "Soup" societies:

> The "Soup" or Singing Societies are organized and levy dues for
> the purpose of paying sick and death benefits to their members.
> Meetings are held about once a week at the homes of the mem-
> bers. Corn soup, from whence comes the name of the group, is
> served, and the evening is devoted to conversation and the sing-
> ing of hymns. There are just two of these societies left since the
> Welcome Society decided to disband and split up the treasury.
> One group, the Oneida Helpers, sings their hymns in English
> rather than Oneida, but in other respects it is the same.[17]

The intent of Iroquois "Soup societies" parallels the concept of
health insurance as it exists today. It is interesting to note that health
insurance for specific groups did not enter the health care delivery system in the United States until the late 1930s, and at that time insurance was provided by groups modeled after European mutual aid societies. Small contributions or dues were collected from group members to

assist them by paying cash benefits during episodes of illness or disability due to accidents occurring in the work place.[18]

It was not until the late 1950s and 1960s that "the Blues" were incorporated into the health insurance conglomerate we know today. The authors currently are obtaining information about traditional health practices of the Oneida through oral histories. During one of the research interviews, information was gathered about the "Dodo" society,[19] which had been formed at Oneida in the past few years by one of the participants in the study.[20] Membership in this society encompasses many elders of the tribe and some of the younger people, although anyone who desires may join. It meets monthly at a community center in Oneida and seems to serve the same function as the "Soup Societies," i.e., health insurance of a type, social interaction, and assistance to tribal elders who are in need of funds or assistance with tasks.

Some members of the tribe still use Indian cures and herbal remedies, and information on their use is passed from the elders to their children. The most common herbs used are butterfly weed and golden seal for fevers; elm bark for coughs; willow and elm bark for rheumatism and sprains; tansy for intestinal problems; wild cherry for coughs and fevers and Virginia snakeroot for hemorrhages. The barks are usually applied as poultices and the other herbs are brewed into teas. Most of these remedies have some proven chemical efficacy, but the difficulty of measuring efficiency and the inability to determine dosage make it difficult to determine their pharmaceutical value as used by the tribe. In the acculturation process, traditional health practices seem to have persisted because individual groups liked them or found them to have some utility.

The use of "Indian medicines" or remedies still exists, although most of the population subscribes to the Western health care system for the diagnosis and treatment of illness and for primary health care. The Indian remedies are used most frequently either as preventive or health promotion measures or as a last resort in chronic and terminal illness, most often in conjunction with the modern health care system.

In 1985 the Oneida conducted a tribal-wide community survey to assist them in their planning and economic development efforts. In conjunction with the tribe's interest in health care delivery, the survey asked the participants what Indian medicines they used and for what purposes. Of the 163 tallied responses to the date of this writing, thirty respondents (18.4 percent) stated that they used some Indian medicines and described briefly their usages.[21] A review of the responses indicates that most of the remedies are used for common illnesses and as preventive medicines, while a few reported the use of herbs for ceremonial purposes. The most common seem to be herbal teas and external poultices. The herbs used most frequently were bergamot, used for influenza, colds and stomach problems, and worm wood and yellow root for upset stomachs.[22]

MOST COMMON USES OF HERBAL REMEDIES
BY FUNCTIONAL COMPLAINT

Functional Complaint	Remedy
Stomach problems	Peppermint tea, catnip and bergamot
Upset stomach	Worm wood, yellow root mint and rosehips
Colds	Witch hazel, bergamot and sweet flag
Sore throat	Comfrey, bergamot and sweet flag
Diarrhea	Elderberry flowers
Congestion	Bergamot and sweet flag
Headache	Tansy and sage
Ear infection	Skunk oil
Mouth sores	Dried raspberry leaves

Several respondents stated that they used what they defined as Indian medicine in the form of teas for colds, stomachaches, diabetes, irritable bowels, cramps, diarrhea, and headaches and fever. Two responded that they used Indian medicine for ceremonial purposes and meetings at night, while one reported the use of cedar for prayer meditation and white pine for cleansing. The use of weeds was also mentioned in the healing of sores, clearing of minds, and for minor injuries such as stepping on nails.

Today the Oneida tribe receives the majority of its primary health care through the Oneida Health Center. The center provides up-to-date technology, health promotion and prevention programs, and outreach programs. Community health nursing is also offered on the reservation. Tribal members also use the Western health care facilities of the surrounding area for secondary and tertiary care. The Oneida Health Center is frequently used as the referral source and is designed to meet the tribe's specific primary health care needs. As practiced by its personnel, the center attempts to deliver health care with a family-centered approach congruent with traditional Oneida culture and values, a philosophy that elders deserve respect and care, a delivery system that is in harmony with the total environment, and a commitment by the care providers to learn and understand traditional Indian health values and to incorporate these into their professional practice.[23]

The Menominee

The Menominee tribe is the third largest tribal group of Wisconsin Indians, with approximately 3300 tribal members. Few of the Menominee are full-blooded (about 8 percent), although 67 percent are at least one-half Indian. The Menominee is one of the tribal groups of the central Algonkian tribes, drawing on many practices of another central Algonkian tribe, the Chippewa. The native language of the Menominee is based on the Chippewa language and is spoken by relatively few tribal members, although there appears to be an interest in returning to the native tongue. The tribal homeland of the Menominee originally covered some nine and one-half million acres of dense forest stretching from Lake Michigan to central Wisconsin, and from Milwaukee to the Upper Peninsula of Michigan. A treaty signed in 1854 by Chief Oshkosh and Chief Keshena ceded all but 275,000 acres to the government. In 1856 another 40,000 acres were ceded to the Stockbridge tribe. The remaining land makes up the present Menominee reservation in Wisconsin.[24] Their former homeland was called Weesechosek or a "good place to live."

The Menominee today are economically one of the poorest tribal groups in Wisconsin. Many of the tribe's current financial difficulties stem from the ill-fated experiment with terminating tribal status, which lasted from 1961 to 1974. Some 90 percent of the reservation is still forested and is considered the major economic asset of the tribe. The sole tribal enterprise on the reservation is a lumbering and sawmill operation, which employs only a small portion of the tribal members. Many of the younger members thus seek employment in urban areas such as Milwaukee or Chicago.

Traditional Menominee Health Practices

Traditional Menominee health practices made wide use of plants as medicines. The use of these remedies was usually in the hands of the medicine man. Most health practices held a deep religious meaning for the Menominee and were a central feature of their religion.[25] The Menominee, as a central Algonkian tribe, had much ceremonialism attached to medicinal treatments, which was not as apparent in either the northern Algonkian (e.g., Cree, Salteaux) or the eastern Algonkian tribes (e.g., Micmac, Penobscot). The latter groups derived most treatments from ordinary herbalists and magicians, while the central Algonkian tribes, the Ojibwa, Chippewa, Menominee and Winnebago, were affected by the more intrusive Iroquoian element in the northeastern

United States. This Iroquoian influence is reflected in the greater use of ceremonialism and ritualistic practices.[26] Traditional health practices of the Menominee were performed by three major groups—the Midéwiwin, the juggler and the herbalist.

The central tribes, including the Menominee, developed a secret society called the Midéwiwin. This group was spiritual in nature and had as one of its prime purposes the worship of the spirits. The spirits were identified as being those from whom medical powers, as well as remedies which could be used to prolong life, came. Supernatural forces played a dominant role in other aspects of health-related practices as well, as in the requirement that plant products be gathered by people other than the medicine man.

The Midéwiwin relied heavily on the use of various herbal remedies in their practice. Those individuals who followed the rules of conduct set by this society and took the prescribed herbal remedies were assured of a happy and long life. The extension of earthly existence was a result of adhering to these prescribed medicinal practices, avoiding evil practices, and leading a good social life. The Midéwiwin societies were a moral force within the Algonkian tribes which fostered tribal ideals of good living practices, as well as passed on individual knowledge of herbal lore.

The central Algonkian tribes exhibited the highest development of medicinal societies. The Chippewa showed the most developed organizational structure of all these tribes, but the Menominee were not far behind. In these tribes it was considered a great honor to belong to the Midéwiwin. Admission into the society was usually purchased by a youth's parents at a great price. Once the price had been paid, a parent could replace the youth if he or she died before completing the training. Admission was not restricted by sex or by the number of individuals in the society. The candidate was initiated and socialized into the society and given a specific role in an elaborate ritual. The ceremony infused the applicant with the vital "spirit power," which had been handed down from Mä'näbŭsh. Mä'näbŭsh was the cultural hero, also known as Hiawatha, through whom the deities gave to humans tribal rituals and the right to use power in the form of medicine such as roots and herbs. The applicant was taught various methods of healing as well as the proper songs to be used in the healing process. Four members of the society presided over this ceremony, four being a holy number within the spiritual life of these tribes. The person was then a Mitä (member) of the Mitä'wit (medicine lodge). Annual attendance at the society's meetings helped keep the member's power at its fullest. There were various degrees within the society so that one could advance with more teaching from an individual member (mentor). The Mitä practiced with someone until advanced training was obtained, allowing the Mitä to then practice on his or her own. In some cases the Mitä actually specialized in a particular area, much as modern medical practitioners do today. As one advanced in the lodge the person received more knowledge and power, allowing the member to be qualified for general practice. Much of this knowledge involved the use of various herbal remedies. The practice of the member was guided by his or her personal dreams.

Part of the advanced training included learning about the forces of evil in order to enable the medicine man to combat the evil forces which might affect an individual's health; it was not meant to promote the practice of witchcraft. There was always the fear that members would use this knowledge for their own benefit rather than for the good of the tribe.

Members in these societies owned their own remedies, which they kept in their private medicine bag. Only the owner of the bag knew the contents; it was a secret to everyone else. The medicine bag was made of the skin of a small animal with feathers placed in the nostrils to signify its purpose. The bags were considered to be powerful because of their medicinal contents and the ritualistic uses with which they were associated. When a new remedy was added to the bag, a medicine song was also added, increasing the power of the owner. Chief Oshkosh, considered a powerful medicine man, had sixty different remedies in his bag.[27] The services of the Mitä were not free, but often cost the individual a great deal. The Menominee placed great emphasis on the value of these services and the necessity of paying for them.

Another group of individuals, the jugglers, practiced a different form of traditional medicine. The juggler did not use physical remedies, but rather worked to protect the person from the malpractice of another. This protection was demonstrated by the efforts to overcome sorcerers who had placed some form of curse or illness on the person:

> "Spirit intrusion," like so many aboriginal concepts, was an idea widely held in Europe during the Middle Ages, and even in America in colonial days. The numerous references in the Bible to persons being "possessed by devils" and to "casting out devils" provided a respectable background for such survivals of primitive lore. Dr. Walter C. Alvarez saw survivals of spirit-intrusion beliefs among white people in such figures of speech as "I wonder what possessed me to do that," and "I wonder what can have gotten into that child." He saw a similar signification in our calling apoplexy a "stroke," and the custom of "rapping on wood" to ward off evil, which appears to be no different in principle that the Indian custom of beating on drums and shaking rattles.

The Cherokees recognized several dozen disease-causing spirits, animal and human. The medicine man's task was to determine which spirit was causing the trouble, as a different curative agent was prescribed for each of them. Their linguistic relatives, the Iroquois, likewise held that pestilence and disease were often the work of evil spirits. Witches and enchanters, as well as poisonous roots and plants, were possessed of such spirits. At religious festivals, the aid of Ha-wen-nepyu (great spirit) and his entourage was invoked to shield them from the designs of bad spirits. When "the Quack comes to visit the Patient," Baron de Lahontan wrote of the Algonquins, "he examines him very carefully; If the Evil Spirit be here," says he, "we shall quickly dislodge him." According to Louis Hennepin, whose acquaintance was principally with the Illinois and Miami, the "juggler" examined the patient's body and then announced "there's a Charm or Spell in such a part, in the Head, Leg, or Stomach, or where he thinks fit; he adds, that he must remove this same Charm, and that it can't be done but with a great deal of difficulty."[28]

A third group who practiced in the Algonkian tribes were the herbalists. Not all herbal lore was held solely by the Midéwiwin; much was held in common by the tribe. The herbalists specialized in the use of a wide range of herbs and plant products for various ailments as well as in maintaining and promoting an individual's health. These various herbal remedies worked only if one invoked the spirits who were associated with them and actually believed in these spirits. A gift to the spirits, traditionally tobacco, was left when a root or part of a plant was taken.

The use of herbal remedies by the Menominee has been well documented.[29] In his study, Huron Smith found a wide range of herbal medicines still in use by this tribe. Because of the sanctity of most of their medicinal knowledge, not all the information about the uses of various plants as medicine is available. The Menominee know that there are proper seasons for gathering various plants for medicinal use in order for them to possess their greatest power. Most Menominee remedies are combinations of plants, as one herb represents just one man while the combination of herbs represents more strength, allowing the medicine to become more powerful.

Mä'näbŭsh, the culture hero, gave to the Menominee and the central Algonkian tribes the powers of these medicines:

The way of the Indian in the past, and his customs was this, that he did things even as the spirit powers gave it to him to do. And it was that nephew of us all, Me'napus, who first was given these herbs and roots, in all their various forms and as they taste. Then he in turn gave them on, that all the Indians might use them whenever they were ill, and grow well from their use of them. And as the Indian knows it, is to use these herbs in curing people. Now this earth is the grandmother of us all; it is from her that these roots spring forth which this Indian is to use.

The religio-medical lore of the Menomini[30] has been set out in some detail by Dr. Huron Smith; it would seem that most of the medicines, as the white man calls them, and the particular songs and rituals appropriate for their gathering, preparation and use are of great antiquity. This lore was always the sacred possession of individuals who had received it by "purchase" or else through dreams, and in turn passed it on to others at a worthy price.[31]

While some traditional health practices of the Menominee seem to be used no longer, many other practices remain to some degree. Members of the tribe still use herbal remedies widely, and use tobacco as payment to the spirits for these remedies.

The Menominee have a goodly number of "pagans," defined as those who cling to the old rites and customs of the tribe, and who are well versed in the aboriginal uses of plants for food, textiles and medicines. Nominally, some 90 percent of the Menominee are Catholic; the non-Catholic tribal members are considered pagan. The pagan Menominee are seen as being more deeply religious in nature and as careful of sacred things. Traditional practices are more deeply rooted in this group than in the Christian members of the tribe, who are seen by the pagans as the "drifters" in the society.[32] Traditional tribal practices include such things as burial rites, where the body is removed from the west window of the home to a burial hut which has been constructed by family members. Drums beat throughout the night while the family tells of the good things the person accomplished in life. The spirits listen to this recounting of events and the person is considered to be on the way to heaven.[33]

Because medical knowledge is considered so sacred, it is difficult for outsiders to obtain full information on the uses of plants as medications.[34] In fact, often not even other tribal members are privy to this information. It is believed that it is in dreams that the medicine man has revealed to him the uses of plants as medicine, thus they serve as the diagnostic part of someone's treatment. This knowledge is available only to a particular medicine man, and not to the entire tribe. It is true, though, that many traditional practices have been passed orally from parent or grandparent to child.

Spirit Rock is one of the Menominee traditions with both medicinal and spiritual values to the culture that is still followed by many tribal members. It is said that Mä'näbüsh, grandson of Ko-Ko-Mas-Sang-So-Now (the Earth), invited one of the Menominee to visit the god. A band of eight Menominee visited the god, who granted their request to make them successful hunters. One member, however, angered the god by asking for eternal life. Mä'näbŭsh thrust the warrior into the ground and made him into stone which would be everlasting. Spirits are said to visit the rock at night, so people place gifts of tobacco on the rock for the spirits to intercede for them in their requests for help. According to the legend, when Spirit Rock finally crumbles away the Menominee will be extinct.[35]

The Menominee of today still employ some traditional herbal practices to augment "modern" scientific health care. While no traditional medicine man appears to be practicing today, older tribal members are able to recall medicine men who practiced when they were younger. It has been reported that most tribal members who reside on the reservation use herbal medicines, and there have been hints that prayer services and ritualistic ceremonies are practiced by a small select number of the tribe. However, no one contacted by the authors was willing to document that ceremonial rites persist today.

Most of the primary care for tribal members living on the reservation is provided through the Menominee Tribal Clinic, with referrals to the outlying regions for secondary and tertiary care. The tribal clinic provides complete services, including community health nursing services, health education, health promotion and illness prevention, dentistry, nutrition counseling and a pharmacy. Approximately 60 percent of the reservation members use the clinic for their basic medical care, with referral to nearby cities such as Shawano, Green Bay and Antigo for hospitalization and nursing home care. Public health nursing services are provided through the Menominee County Public Health Department in cooperation with the tribal clinic.[36] The impact of traditional health practices of the Menominee (and other central Algonkian tribes) on "modern" health care is evident, if not always readily accepted as such by the non-Indian population.

Impact of Traditional and Modern Health Practices on Social Policy

Health care delivery in the United States is large, complex, system-oriented and extremely complicated organizationally, with a bewildering array of providers and institutions. The influx of technological changes demands provider specialization in managing certain highly sophisticated care and treatment plans (e.g., renal dialysis and organ transplants).[37] The size and complexity of the system have caused fragmentation in the provision of health care which affects us all in our search for better health. The issues of access, availability and the quality of care are compounded by this fragmentation. The health care delivery system has been less able to accommodate the disadvantaged population; problems with the system have affected the poor and minority groups the hardest.[38] When considering the health care needs of the American Indian community, social policymakers must be aware that health promotion and disease prevention are critical factors in improving this group's health status. Today's increasing emphasis on health care costs and the explosion of biomedical technology, with concomitant increased life expectancy, means that preventive health care needs must be addressed and reforms implemented that will ensure equal opportunities for healthful living for all disadvantaged population groups.

In most instances, preventive services are controlled by the individual tribes, which direct medical services under the control of the Indian Health Service. At present, it seems more emphasis and resources are being directed to the provision of direct, rather than preventive, health services, even though the distinction between the types of care is rather artificial. Regardless of need, the majority of federal funding ends up in the acute care system with little concern for health promotion and disease prevention. While it is known that many of the health problems that plague American Indians are preventable, policymakers need to design and support strategies that are acceptable to the tribes themselves.

Future health care delivery methods must be changed to recognize the bilateral use of both traditional and modern health care patterns and practices. These new delivery methods need to incorporate realistic health care priorities without impinging on American Indian traditions, thus taking traditional practices into account in policy discussions about improving the health care system. As was stated during the congressional hearings on the Indian Health Promotion and Disease Prevention Act, "Perhaps the best situation would be for health promotion and disease prevention programs to be integrated with direct medical services in the basic appropriations process; i.e., that these activities be considered part and parcel of the services provided through the Indian Health Service."[39]

The United States must, then, develop and nurture policies that will aid the American Indian to reach optimum health while still retaining traditional practices and beliefs. The system must provide the economic support necessary to allow the development of health care delivery systems to provide quality care which is accessible and acceptable to the recipient. The system must utilize the traditional belief systems of the American Indian and, above all, it must be one that is controlled by the cultural group for which it is providing service. Self-determination in health care practices is vital in order to reach the goal of a healthy population.

American Indians currently experience the poorest health of any group in the nation, with accompanying higher mortality rates. The major health problems are tuberculosis, pneumonia, influenza, alcoholism, automobile accidents, diabetes mellitus, homicide and suicide. The 1978 Bemidji Area Morbidity/Mortality statistics list the leading causes of death as diseases of the circulatory system, accidents, injuries and neoplasms.[40] Moreover, the accidental death rate for American Indians aged fifteen to twenty-four is five times greater than the national rate, their suicide rate between the ages of twenty-five to thirty-four is 3.3 times greater, and their alcoholism rate for the latter age group is also 3.3 times above the national level.[41]

In the past thirty years there has been a decrease in Indian health problems related to communicable diseases, and an increase in those problems assocciated with behavior and lifestyles that are not presently addressed adequately by the Western medical system. These problems require new approaches which draw upon the cultural values and strengths of the American Indian people themselves. Concepts of holistic health and wellness have traditionally been a part of the world view of American Indians, and should be considered when health policy and programs are developed to improve their health.[42]

The newfound interest in Indian health care practices results from Indians' basic philosophical concept of living in harmony with nature and their ability to survive under difficult circumstances. These concepts are congruent with the emphasis on health promotion and illness prevention that has occurred, albeit belatedly, in the last decade in the Western health care system. Traditional Indian practices of health promotion and illness prevention are now valued as legitimate, and are no longer cloaked in the imagery of magic, witchcraft and superstition. Today it is uncertain how many American Indians adhere to traditional health practices, but it is known that in the majority of cases where there is a population locus of Indians (e.g., a reservation or particular sector of a city), native healers can be found.

Martha Primeaux states that it is her opinion that the American Indian has retained the traditional health practices because of the fragmented care of the institutionalized health care system.[43] It is difficult for the Indian to comprehend why modern doctors in this system will treat signs and symptoms without attention to cause. In many instances the Indian medicine man will treat an entire family while treating the ill individual. In Western medicine the total being of the individual in conjunction with the well-being of his/her family have usually been ignored in the course of treatment, although today the system is moving into a more family-oriented philosophy of caregiving in an effort to reduce the fragmentation and overlapping of services found in a highly specialized delivery system. Despite differences in traditional and Western health care practices, much can be gained by understanding the differences and working together to provide optimal levels of health care for all people.

The use of herbal medicines in the American health care system is historical in nature, and dates back to colonial days. During that era the Indians introduced the white man to the indigenous plants and remedies of the continent. These eventually were included in the United States pharmacopoeia and the National Formulary and were assimilated into our present-day drug therapy. Hope Isaacs, in her studies of Iroquois herbalism over the past one hundred years, noted there was a trend toward herbal usage in the area of preventive medicine. She found an increase during this period in the use of herbs as tonics, strengtheners and restoratives, and noted continuity in the use of specific herbs gathered for medicinal purposes.[44] The application of these herbs has changed over time to usage that is pharmaceutically correct. The question then arises whether present-day Indian herbal users are influenced by the need to preserve cultural patterns, and/or whether they perceive that care delivered by today's Western practitioners is inadequate. They may feel that herbal use is one way of showing their adherence to traditional practices, while still relying on the Western health care system for medical care.

Concerns Resulting from Conflicting Ideologies

A major problem in the clash between traditional and Western health practices is the misunderstanding of cultural patterns; this frequently results in the minority client being labeled as uncooperative and exhibiting inappropriate behavior. In addition to this misunderstanding of culture, the problem of communication can produce conflict that can lead to a breakdown in the level of care given. The biggest mistake health care providers can make when attempting to deliver care to a client from another cultural background is to fail to recognize or understand the significance and importance of traditional health care practices. Very often health care providers become smug about their assumed knowledge of cultural patterns and differences, and make gross generalizations about an ethnic group. When dealing with the American Indian, one must remember that each tribe has a unique language and unique tribal customs which vary within the major tribal groupings (e.g., Algonkian, Iroquois), although ideas about the care of disease or illness and cure are held in common by most tribes.

Most health care professionals have been socialized into a given culture and then resocialized into a health care provider's culture that is a part of their professional development.[45] As students in the medical field become better educated and more knowledgeable, they move further from former belief systems and their understanding and values regarding health, illness and treatment patterns become much different from that of the population at large. The potential for cross-cultural conflict lies in the rigid adherence of health care providers to the Western system of health care delivery, because with few exceptions providers do not sanction methods of prevention or treatment not based in the biotechnological world of science. In their view, only those who have been properly educated and certified are recognized as being able to provide modern health care. The providers believe they understand and can interpret all facets of health, illness and treatment. They are socialized into the "territoriality of the health care professions," at best accepting grudgingly alternative health care delivery practices or methods. This impels Wolfgang Jilek and Norman Todd to observe that when Western trained physicians are faced with the challenge of treating patients from a non-Western society, their responsibility is greater than when treating Western patients.[46] They must acquire sufficient knowledge of the culture to be able to distinguish between generic illness and illness-like nonpathological states. They must be able to determine the degree of their patients' acculturation and to judge whether a therapist or indigenous healer of that culture would be of more benefit than Western medicine. This socialization process is necessary to assure delivery of the best possible care for the client and to break down the barriers that already exist.

Another area that poses the potential for ideological conflict between the Westernized health care provider and the non-Western client is the interpretation of the causes of illness. The modern approach to illness is rigidly hooked into the theoretical base of epidemiology, while the American Indian is acculturated into the concepts of social class, spirit possession and spells. Thus the preventive aspect of health takes on another meaning to American Indians, and their cures often fall outside the realm of the Western-socialized care provider.

The two health systems, tribal and traditional and modern American and scientific, need not be antagonistic, but do require that the health care provider has sufficient sophistication to overcome the barriers. The care providers' socialization process must take into consideration alternate caregiving systems and cultural sensitivity, and recognize the value of traditional medicine to the client for both health care and the prevention of illness.

Though Indian health seems to be improving today, it is still too early to state that problems are really under control. Much of the advance in the 1960s and early 1970s was due to the fact that young physicians went to the Indian Health Service as an alternative to the armed forces in the medical draft. This tended to increase the number of physicians available, even though many of them lacked the skills necessary to accomplish what was needed.

Decreases in Indian mortality figures are also dependent upon decreasing malnutrition, improving sanitation and raising the level of employment. Health care in itself is not enough. Obviously, Indians currently are in a better state than they were just a few years ago, at least as far as the substance of general health is concerned, but they still have far to go to tap fully the advantages of American society. Cultural differences and conflict go far to explain why this is so.[47]

NOTES

[1]See Benjamin D. Paul, "Anthropological Perspectives on Medicine and Public Health," in James K. Skipper, Jr. and Robert C. Leonard, eds., *Social Interactions and Patient Care* (Philadelphia: Lippincott, 1965), pp. 195-206, for a more detailed discussion of the study of health values in a culture.

[2]Nancy Oestreich Lurie, "Wisconsin Indians: Lives and Lands," *Wisconsin Magazine of History* 53: 1 (Autumn 1969): 2-20, has a good discussion of tribes in Wisconsin, including the Menominee and Oneida tribes discussed in this chapter.

[3]The World Health Organization's definition of health, formulated in the 1940s after World War II, is widely used but still considered controversial by many health care providers. This definition can be found in "The Constitution of the World Health Organization," *WHO Chronicle* 1 (1944): 29.

[4]Ruth Murray and Judith Zentner, *Nursing Concepts for Health Promotion* (Englewood Cliffs, NJ: Prentice-Hall, 1975), p. 6.

[5]Agnes M. Aamodt, "Observations of a Health and Healing System in a Papago Community," in Madeleine Leininger, ed., *Transcultural Health Care Issues and Conditions*, Vol. 3 of *Health Care Dimensions* (Philadelphia: Davis, 1976), pp. 23-36.

[6]Rachel E. Spector, *Cultural Diversity in Health and Illness*, 2nd ed. (Norwalk, CT: Appleton-Century-Crofts, 1985), p. 182.

[7]Ibid. See Spector's discussion of various cultural groups in our society and their views on health practices.

[8]See Senate Select Committee on Indian Affairs, Hearings on the Indian Health Promotion and Disease Prevention Act of 1985, 99th Congress, 1st Session (Gallup, NM: June 1, 1985), call number Y4.In 2/11:S, hrg. 99-276, pp. 303-304. The committee heard detailed testimony about the views of today's

prominent Indian tribes concerning the prevalence of major diseases among
the Indian people, the resources currently available to develop health care delivery systems, relationships to traditional health practices and the Indians'
perceptions about the need for better health care promotion and disease prevention systems.

[9]R. Gordon Moore, "Indian Remedies," *Ohio State Medical Journal* 71: 11
(September 1975): 661-664.

[10]Virgil J. Vogel, *American Indian Medicine* (Norman, OK: University of
Oklahoma Press, 1970).

[11]Lurie, op. cit. note 2.

[12]Mary C. Sobralske, "Transcultural Study of Navajo Health Within a
Family" (Unpublished thesis, University of Wisconsin-Oshkosh, 1982). This is
a qualitative study of the Navajo Indians and their health perceptions. The
study defines the concept of health and health perceptions from a non-Western
rather than a Western cultural background.

[13]S. Henry Wassen, "On Concepts of Disease Among American Indian Tribal Groups," *Journal of Ethnopharmacology* 1: 3 (October 1979): 285-293.

[14]Lurie, op. cit. note 2.

[15]Moore, op. cit. note 9.

[16]Robert E. Ritzenthaler, *The Oneida Indians of Wisconsin* (Milwaukee:
Board of Trustees, Public Museum of the City of Milwaukee, 1950), pp. 36-38.
This descriptive study resulted from the author's two-month stay among the
Oneida Indians. Ritzenthaler deals with the historical data, the transition of
the tribe following its move from the East to the Midwest, and the acculturation process in terms of socioeconomic factors, religion, politics, medicine and
health care.

[17]Ibid., pp. 31-32.

[18]Marshall W. Raffel, *The U.S. Health System: Origins and Functions* (New
York: John Wiley, 1980).

[19]"Dodo" means "grandparents" in the Oneida language.

[20]Interview with an older female member of the Oneida tribe at the Oneida
Multipurpose Center on March 27, 1986.

[21]Data from this survey were made available to the authors during the
spring of 1986. As of this writing, the final report on the survey had not been
completed.

[22]What is called bergamot in the text was number 6 on the survey, a plant
or weed with blue flowers also called burganomt [sic] or horse mint.

[23]Much of this information was collected during the authors' meetings with
Oneida tribal elders and visits to tribal facilities.

[24]Patricia Raymer, "Wisconsin's Menominees: Indians on a Seesaw," *National Geographic* 146: 2 (August 1974): 228-251. See also Lurie, op. cit. note 2.

[25]Huron Smith, "Ethnobotany of the Menomini Indians," *Bulletin of the Public Museum of the City of Milwaukee* 4: 1 (December 1923): 1-174.

[26]William Thomas Corlett, *The Medicine-Man of the American Indian and His Cultural Background* (Baltimore, MD: Charles C. Thomas, [1935]).

[27]Raymer, op. cit. note 24.

[28]Vogel, op. cit. note 10, pp. 18-19.

[29]Smith, op. cit. note 25, has an extensive discussion of the use of various herbal remedies by the Menominee.

[30]Many of the older documents spell Menomini with an "i" at the end; more recent publications, as well as tribal members, today spell the word with a double "e" at the end, i.e., Menominee.

[31]Felix M. Keesing, *The Menomini Indians of Wisconsin: A Study of Three Centuries of Cultural Contact and Change* (Philadelphia: American Philosophical Society, 1939), p. 46.

[32]Smith, op. cit. note 25.

[33]Raymer, op. cit. note 24.

[34]Smith, op. cit. note 25.

[35]Information on the Spirit Rock legend came from the State Historical Society of Wisconsin, Madison, Wisconsin, and from interviews with individual Menominee.

[36]Interview with staff members of the Menominee Tribal Clinic, Keshena, Wisconsin, on April 15, 1986.

[37]Steven Jonas and contributors, *Health Care Delivery in the the United State*, 3rd ed. (New York: Springer Publishing Co., 1986). Jonas provides a comprehensive description of the status of the American health care delivery system which includes a discussion of the various components of the system, health care financing, the role of legislatures, and the role of administrative agencies in formulating policies and regulations that affect the nation's health. The book includes discussions by nationally known health experts.

[38]Vern Bullough and Bonnie Bullough, *Health Care for the Other Americans* (New York: Appleton-Century-Crofts, 1982).

[39]Hearings on the Indian Health Promotion and Disease Prevention Act of 1985, op. cit. note 8, p. 27.

[40]Ibid., pp. 344-347.

[41]Ibid.

[42]Ibid., p. 308.

[43]Martha H. Primeaux, "American Indian Health Care Practices," *Nursing Clinics of North America* 12: 1 (March 1977): 55-65.

[44]Hope L. Isaacs, "Iroquois Herbalism: The Past 100 Years," *International Journal of Social Psychiatry* 22: 4 (Winter 1976): 272-281.

[45]Spector, op. cit. note 6.

[46]Wolfgang G. Jilek and Norman Todd, "Witchdoctors Succeed Where Doctors Fail: Psychotherapy Among Coast Salish Indians," *Canadian Psychiatric Association Journal* 19: 4 (August 1974): 351-356.

[47]Bullough and Bullough, op. cit. note 38.

MINORITY ELDERLY: HEALTH CARE AND POLICY ISSUES

Toni Tripp-Reimer and Bernard Sorofman

University of Iowa

Since 1945, research has demonstrated convincingly that patterns of aging vary dramatically across cultures, but only in the past fifteen years has serious attention been focused on the American ethnic aged.[1] Early on, the notion that ethnicity should be discounted or ignored influenced official policy and health service delivery. Recently, however, there has been evidence that ethnicity is a salient social and political factor which merits the attention of health care providers and policymakers.[2] These patterns have resulted in the emergence of the field of ethnogerontology, the newest area of social gerontology. As defined by Jacquelyne Johnson Jackson, the scope of ethnogerontology encompasses the "causes, processes, and consequences of race, national origin, and culture on individual and population aging."[3]

Research in ethnogerontology has identified differential eligibility for access to, and utilization of, established health and social programs by the ethnic aged. Subsequent to these findings, a controversy emerged over whether public policy should be rewritten to reduce inequities in health care between the elderly of majority and minority groups.[4] This issue is the major focus of this chapter. First, the historical development of public policy related to aging and health care is described. Second, the patterns of differential eligibility, access and utilization which exist for the elderly in different ethnic groups are identified. Finally, two propositions are outlined regarding the role of public policy in rectifying these inequities.

History of Public Policy Initiatives Related to Aging and Health Care

We should like to begin by presenting briefly two major aspects of public law that relate to the health of the elderly. These are provisions that fall under the Social Security Act and those that fall under the Older Americans Act.

The social security system in the United States was modeled after
Bismarck's plan for Germany and programs later developed in France
and England, and was developed in response to problems exacerbated
by the depression. The Social Security Act was signed into law by President Franklin Roosevelt in 1935, and the first benefits were paid in
1940. Currently the program is referred to as OASDHI, an acronym for
its four components of old age, survivor's, disability and health
insurance.[5]

- Old age insurance is an income maintenance program that provides workers with a monthly cash benefit after retirement. In
  most cases a person must have been employed for ten years
  (forty quarters) to be eligible for benefits. Payments are based
  on the average earnings over a period of years prior to retirement. Wives who have worked for wages may receive their own
  benefits or half the amount their husbands would receive
  (whichever is greater).

- Survivor's insurance provides cash benefits to a worker's de-
  pendents if the worker dies.

- Health insurance is provided through two major programs. In
  1965 the Social Security Act was amended to provide Medicare
  (Title 18)[6] and Medicaid (Title 19).[7] Medicare provides medical reimbursement to the elderly regardless of their financial
  situation. It is a federally administered health insurance program for qualified persons over sixty-five years and for the dis-
  abled of all ages. Medicare has two parts: Part A[8] is hospital
  insurance with a deductible ($356 in 1986); and Part B[9] is sup-
  plemental medical insurance. Ambulatory care fees[10] are paid
  for with a monthly premium ($12.50 to $14.60 per month in
  1986).

Even if one is covered by both Part A and Part B, however, there are
many exceptions to coverage. For example, service providers under
Part B are not obligated to accept Medicare assignment, which means
that their fee is often more than Medicare will pay. In these instances
the patient must make the payment "out-of-pocket" and then file
forms and submit proof of payment before receiving reimbursement.
More important, Medicare fails to cover the greatest medical need of
the elderly—chronic care for long-term diseases and disabilities. (Editor's note: Since this writing, the enactment of the Medicare Catastrophic Coverage Act of 1988 has served to address this need in part.)
Medications for non-hospitalized patients are not covered, and stays in

long-term care facilities are covered only for a limited time. Medicare is oriented toward short-term illnesses and accidents, and contains time limits which are wholly unrealistic for the needs of the elderly.

Medicaid, on the other hand, is a public assistance program for needy, low-income individuals. It was designed to cover areas that Medicare did not, and to defray expenses for those who could not meet the cost of Medicare contributions or who had exhausted their Medicare benefits. Medicaid is left to the discretion of individual states, and so it varies in coverage nationwide. It is now available in all states,[11] and is financed approximately 60 percent with federal money and 40 percent divided equally between state and county funds. Also to be mentioned here is Supplemental Security Income which, too, is a public assistance program and not an earned right. It is not available if a person has resources in excess of a certain limit ($1500 in 1986).[12]

The Older Americans Act (OAA), passed by Congress in 1965, signalled an acknowledgement of the need for a national program of services to improve the lives of the elderly. As first enacted, the purpose of the OAA was to finance the development of new or improved programs to assist the elderly: OAA Title II[13] established the Administration on Aging (AoA) within the then Department of Health, Education and Welfare to manage these programs, and OAA Title III[14] provided formula grants to states for community agencies on aging as well as money to states and communities to establish local agencies on aging.

In October 1978, Congress enacted extensive revisions to the OAA. The primary purpose of the Title III amendments was to stimulate and help state and local agencies concentrate resources to develop a comprehensive system of services to older individuals. Under Title III-B of the 1978 amendments, the following social services may be provided: information and referral services; transportation services; outreach services; housing services (including renovation); legal services; and health services.[15] States and local agencies are allowed some discretion regarding the types of social services provided to an area.[16]

The passage of the 1978 amendments was preceded by considerable testimony concerning the effect of OAA programs on the elderly, including complaints about the program's inadequate service to minorities. Title III requires funded areas to assure that senior citizens have reasonably convenient access to an information and referral system. It provides that in areas in which a significant number of the elderly do not speak English as their principal language, the service provider must make information and referral available in the relevant language.[17]

Although Congress mandated the U.S. Commission on Civil Rights to investigate allegations of discrimination against minorities in OAA programs, it deleted several statutory provisions and sections of the law that referred explicitly to the inclusion of minorities in these programs. For example, the 1975 amendments to the model project provisions of the OAA required the Commissioner on Aging to give special consideration to projects that provided needed services to minority, American Indian and limited-English-speaking elderly. The 1978 amendments removed these provisions.[18] Although the Commission's investigation of federally assisted programs did not document the existence of discrimination against minorities per se, it seemed evident that congressional concern about the lack of minority participation was justified. The data collected in both phases of the Commission's investigation strongly suggested that the policies and practices generally followed by AoA officials adversely affected minority participation in OAA programs.

Demographic Characteristics of the Minority Elderly

The elderly constitute the fastest growing segment of the American population. Since 1900 there has been an eightfold increase in their numbers. Currently, more than 11 percent of the population is elderly, and by the year 2000 the proportion of senior citizens is projected to exceed 13 percent. Comparatively, members of minority groups make up a small proportion of the aged population. In 1980, individuals aged sixty-five and over represented 12 percent of the white population, but only about 7.9 percent of the black, 4.9 percent of the Hispanic, 5.3 percent of the American Indian and 6 percent of the Asian populations. Minority populations tend to be younger than whites, with a much smaller proportion of elderly,[19] even though there has been significant growth in the number of minority elderly.

Some specific ethnic groups are not consistent with the broad demographic pattern depicted for the larger minority clusters. For example, Cubans have a much larger proportion of persons aged sixty-five or older than do other Hispanics and other minority groups.[20] Specifically, although Cubans make up only about 6 percent of the total Spanish-origin population in the United States, their elderly constitute 12 to 16 percent of all aged Hispanics. This is a result of the selective nature of Cuban migration. In 1980, it was estimated that 9.7 percent of Cuban-origin persons in the United States were sixty-five or over, compared with 3.7 percent of Mexicans and 2.7 percent of Puerto Ricans.[21]

The above estimates call attention to the important problem of racial/ethnic identification in census data. Census figures may vary dramatically from one measurement to another, due largely to changes in the criteria whereby given categories of classification are defined. Between the 1970 and 1980 census, the Asian population in the United States increased by 67 percent. In part, this resulted from the 1965 Immigration Act (Public Law 89-236) which repealed the immigration quota. It also came about, however, when individuals from India, who had been classified as white for many years, were now reclassified as "Asians." Consequently, between 1965 and 1976 the number of Asian immigrants increased by 1000 percent.[22] The problem of whether to define ethnic membership on racial or linguistic background or by self-identification is especially apparent in the 1980 census. The reduction in the proportion of persons of Spanish origin classified as white between the 1970 census and the 1980 census resulted, in part, from a decision made by the U.S. Bureau of the Census to not count Mexicans, Venezuelans, Colombians and others as white if they did not designate themselves as such.[23] Duran Bell and his colleagues write:

> Members of ethnic groups have repeatedly challenged these census estimates on the grounds that various impediments to accurate reporting result in census figures that understate their true numerical prominence in the population. This tendency toward underestimation may be due to a greater undercount of lower socioeconomic groups in which minority persons are more likely to be found. Such persons are less likely to have stable residences, be literate in English, or be secure in the legitimacy of their citizenship and general legal status. All of these factors militate against accurate census enumeration.[24]

The geographic distribution of minority groups also should be mentioned. Ethnic groups may be dispersed or concentrated to various extents in regions of the United States. For example, Japanese, Chinese and Filipinos are concentrated on the West Coast, while Mexican Americans are concentrated in the Southwest. American Indians are often concentrated within regions, either on reservations or in urban areas, most notably in California, Arizona, New Mexico and Oklahoma, which together account for 46 percent of the total Indian population. Blacks are the most widely distributed of the major racial minority groups, but most still reside in the southern states and relatively few in the West.[25] The southeastern United States is distinguished from other regions of the country by having a high proportion of older blacks who still live in the region. In contrast to the white elderly, of whom 31 percent lived in the South in 1980, 59 percent of black elderly were still living in that section of the country.[26]

In addition, even within a state or region, specific ethnic groups are characterized by differential patterns. For example, among Hispanic groups, disproportionately higher numbers of Puerto Ricans live in urban areas, Cubans in suburban, and Mexican Americans in rural areas. As a consequence, the demographic configuration of the minority elderly is highly complex.

Sex ratios also distinguish the minority elderly from the white elderly. In general, there is a growing number of females in each of the populations. The preponderance of females compared to males for persons under age seventy is more pronounced among blacks than whites. A major difference between blacks and whites is the greater presence of black females among younger adults. But in the later years of life, a sex ratio crossover occurs between blacks and whites. The increasing age for this sex ratio crossover is parallel to the increasing age for the racial crossover in mortality between blacks and whites.[27]

The socioeconomic status of minority elderly is another distinguishing characteristic. Generally, higher proportions of minority group members live below the poverty level. Lower socioeconomic status is closely related to a higher prevalence of disease and a higher age-specific death rate.[28]

With the exception of the Japanese and perhaps the Chinese, minority spokespersons point to the greater social and economic distress suffered by their senior citizens as a justification for heightened attention to their health and social service needs. Disproportionately, blacks, Mexican Americans and American Indians experience the severe burdens of discrimination and impoverishment, the cumulative effects of which have been to inflict special hardships on their elderly. The soundness of this observation is supported by census data.[29]

Senior citizens generally experience a major decline in income, which causes stress and often markedly affects the quality of their lives. For example, approximately 36 percent of elderly blacks fall below the federal poverty line, as compared to 30 percent of all blacks and 14 percent of elderly whites.[30] Minority women experience the most severe income deprivation in old age. Robert Atchley, for example, estimates that 96 percent of older black women live in poverty.[31]

Several factors account for these patterns. First, the minority elderly generally held the very lowest paying jobs when they were employed. Individuals in these jobs are often not covered by social security. Having been compensated at very low levels, they are eligible only for the most meager pension benefits. Second, the Supplemental Security Income Program, established in 1974 in part to provide additional income to older persons whose incomes were below an established minimum level, has not reached many persons who are eligible for these benefits.

Thomas Talley and Jerome Kaplan first applied the concept of double jeopardy in social gerontology to the risk engendered by being simultaneously black and old.[32] The Urban League contended subsequently that blacks carry into old age a lifetime of economic and social indignities caused by prejudice and discrimination.[33] Others have focused on triple or multiple jeopardy. Richard Crandall applied the term to all individuals who possess two or more traits that make them the objects of prejudice and discrimination.[34]

Health

Of people sixty-five years of age and older residing outside of institutions, 85 percent reported at least one chronic disease and 50 percent reported some limitation in functional capacity related to chronic health problems. [35] Chronic illness among the aged is degenerative and typically involves multiple conditions with physical, psychological and social components. The five most prevalent chronic conditions among the aged in the United States according to a 1978 study by the National Council on Aging are arthritis, hearing impairment, visual impairment, hypertension and heart conditions.[36] Diseases of the heart (notably ischemic heart disease) account for the largest number of deaths annually among persons sixty-five and older, regardless of race or ethnicity. Mortality data show that only five diseases account for most deaths at all ages, and claim a disproportionally higher number of lives among the aged. (Ordered decrementally, they are: ischemic heart disease, cardiovascular disease (stroke and generalized arteriosclerosis), malignant neoplasms, infectious diseases and diabetes.[37]) These diseases bear heavily upon the life expectancies of whites and nonwhites. There are clear indications that minority groups have shorter life expectancies than the majority population. In 1986, the life expectancy for white males was 72.0 years and 78.9 for white females. In contrast, for black males and females it was 65.5 and 73.6 years, respectively.[38]

Racial Crossover in Mortality

Since 1967, age-specific crude death rates of blacks and whites have been shown to demonstrate a racial crossover in the United States and other Western industrialized nations.[39] While some attribute this to an artifact of enumerative census errors, Jackson considers it a "function of differential environmental exposures and resources available to various racial or ethnic groups."[40]

With regard to morbidity data, indications are that minorities tend to have more chronic, debilitating health conditions. However, there are differing reports about the comparative health statuses of black elderly and white elderly. Some researchers believe that the health status of aged blacks is inferior to that of aged whites.[41] This position is disputed by others.[42] John Nowlin, for example, examined data from the longitudinal study of older people by the Duke University Center for the Study of Aging and Human Development and concluded that the medically determined health statuses of older blacks and whites were generally very similar. [43] On the other hand, Ethel Shanas analyzed data by race, with some controls for socioeconomic status, and reported racial differences in health and disability.[44] These conflicting results point to the fact that better data are needed concerning the actual correspondence between ethnicity and health status.

There also appear to be variations in the patterns of social and functional parameters of illness among the minority elderly. Beth Soldo reported that older blacks tend to experience greater functional disabilities than whites, and that they experience them at earlier ages. Older blacks cite health-related reasons for early retirement more often than their white counterparts. Furthermore, while the proportion of noninstitutionalized elderly who are totally bedridden is not great either for whites or blacks, a greater percentage of older blacks are completely incapacitated and are residing in community-based households. Soldo further indicated a considerable excess of older minority males with disease and death due to influenza, pneumonia and respiratory conditions such as bronchitis, emphysema and asthma. In an analogous pattern, minority women have higher mortality rates for diabetes.[45]

Finally, regarding mental health, blacks and other minority aged tend to be diagnosed differently than whites for similar behavioral problems. Whites are more likely to be diagnosed as having depressive disorders; black and other nonwhites are more likely to be diagnosed as schizophrenic. (See the observations on this matter in the chapter by Lawrence Gary.) One of the possible explanations for this is that many minority group members are not highly verbal with white therapists, and do not use the communication styles preferred by white psychiatrists, psychologists and social workers.[46]

These are but a few of the key characteristics that distinguish elderly nonwhites from their white counterparts. For all too long, elderly minority group members have been treated as if they were homogeneous. A scrutiny of their culture, life experiences, demography and health status indicates considerable variation among them, which is not gleaned easily from aggregated demographic data.

Patterns of Service Utilization by the Minority Elderly

The enactment of the Older Americans Act in 1965 and subsequent amendments to it have brought about a wide variety of programs and services to accommodate the special needs of the elderly. Given the extensive services currently available, John Colen observes that the basic issue is no longer the lack of services. To a considerable degree, the elderly have available nutritious meals, housing assistance, medical care, income assistance and other services, although the extent to which they are available varies by locale. Still, regardless of the extensiveness of services available to the aged in general, access to them by minority elders is at best problematic.[47]

Duran Bell, Patricia Kasschau and Gail Zellman reviewed critically the literature relevant to service delivery for elderly members of the following groups: Chinese, Japanese, Filipinos, Samoans, American Indians, Mexican Americans and blacks. Their report concluded that there are serious impediments regarding eligibility, use and satisfaction with existing health and social services by the minority aged.[48] A similar comprehensive study of the minority elderly's use of public services was conducted by David Guttmann. This project, funded through the AoA, investigated whether nonwhite elderly had an equitable share of public benefits as compared to white elderly. Guttmann focused upon four major areas: the needs of nonwhite elderly; their knowledge and information about public benefits; their use of government programs; and their perception of public benefits, including the barriers that prevented their seeking or using available services. The study sample consisted of black, Hispanic, Asian and white elders. One of the most significant findings regarding the nonwhite elderly's use of health and social services was that 20 percent of the population had unmet needs, yet did not seek publicly sponsored assistance. The study revealed that: 1) Minority group membership is a significant factor in under- and nonutilization of public benefits (fewer nonwhite elderly both knew about and used public benefits than did white elderly); and 2) Eligibility requirements and difficulties with procedures were the leading reasons for problems in applying for and in receiving public benefits.[49]

Research demonstrates that the nonwhite elderly use public services less frequently than do whites, and that in many cases the rates of service utilization are not commensurate with their levels of need.[50] The use rates of a variety of services and facilities are informative regarding minority elderly utilization patterns. For example, since the early 1970s, gerontologists have examined questions of utilization, satisfaction and access of the minority elderly to nursing home care. Investigations consistently report lower representation of minority elderly in long-term care facilities.[51]

Another important consideration is not only that minorities use long-term care facilities less frequently, but there is also differential use by type of facility. Cary Kant and Barry Beckham conducted an investigation of the use of seventeen categories of institutions in which aged individuals may reside. Using census data for 1950, 1960 and 1970, and using the state as the unit of analysis, they found substantial differences in the distribution of elderly blacks and whites by type of institution. The institutions included prisons and workhouses, mental hospitals, residential treatment centers, hospitals, chronic hospitals, homes for the aged and facilities for the mentally handicapped. Generally, blacks were overrepresented in state mental hospitals, while the obverse was true in nonprofit homes as well as in proprietary homes for the aged.[52] Differential representation in these three types of institutions is especially important, for they have traditionally housed the largest proportion of the institutionalized elderly.

In addition to different patterns of utilization of health care services between whites and nonwhites, major problems of physical access to these services obtain, and have not been addressed adequately by public policies. For example, Bell and his colleagues observe that, in some areas, offices where food stamps are distributed are not always readily accessible to persons without private transportation. Additionally, medical care providers may tend to locate in affluent areas, far from neighborhoods where many minority elderly live.[53] They also contend that apparent physical access problems are aggravated by fears of impolite treatment by service providers whose offices are outside minority neighborhoods. This may be one reason why urban blacks tend to seek routine care in the emergency outpatient units of hospitals, and are less likely than whites of the same socioeconomic level to visit physicians in their offices.[54] Many ethnogerontologists have identified barriers to minority participation in programs for the aged that are created by negative attitudes of dominant-group staff members toward minority participants.[55] Jeanne Thune, for example, found that the negative attitudes of white participants toward black participants in an on-site program for the aged was yet another barrier to the participation of aged minorities.[56] And so, even when eligibility is not an issue, the nonwhite elderly use available services less often than do the white elderly. A variety of factors, including public policies, inappropriate service structures and cultural preferences have been identified as contributing to these variations in utilization patterns.

The Role of Public Policy

Given the problems and inequities which have been raised in this chapter, one must ask what the role of public policy should be in addressing the lot of the minority elderly. Two major responses are currently proposed in the literature. These will be stated as positions, the strengths and weaknesses of which will be called out.

Position I

This position argues that because of unique historical and socioeconomic patterns, public policy should mandate differential services and eligibility for the minority elderly. There are several specific proposals which have been made for various ethnic groups. While the elderly are defined conventionally as people over age sixty-five, the salience of that definition for some racial minorities has been questioned.

Because of socioeconomic and racial discrimination, most older blacks are highly likely to be "multiply disadvantaged" by age, poverty and race in contrast to their white counterparts. It has thus been suggested that the black aged be provided more financial and health assistance than they receive currently. Proposals have ranged from a guaranteed minimum income that is higher than the current social security benefit, to increased food stamp and health service benefits to offset the disadvantages they suffer.

Another proposed policy change is that local civil rights commissions in all thirty-nine thousand governments receiving federal revenue sharing should have at least one part-time bicultural staff member. These individuals would be responsible for identifying discrimination against the minority elderly in their jurisdiction, and involved in corrective activities that upgrade the quality of life among those elderly.[57] One of the most controversial proposals for improving the economic status of older blacks is that they should become eligible for full social security benefits at an earlier age than other groups. This proposal rests on the evidence that blacks have lower life expectancies and, hence, fail to receive their fair share of the benefits earned during their working lives.[58]

Regarding Pacific Islander and Asian Americans, Paul Kim has called for a clear definition of the Asian elderly to be written into public laws and program policies. He also proposes the establishment of a unified Asian representative group (such as a caucus for the Asian aged) that would relate issues important to the Asian elderly to public agencies as does the National Caucus of the Black Aged for blacks. This group would act not only as an advocacy organization, but also as the recipient of public funds which would then be distributed to all designated Asian ethnic groups based on a specified appropriation formula. The rationale for this program is that present laws regarding the minority elderly benefit some Asians, but others are being served minimally or not at all.[59]

A policy change that would particularly affect the Hispanic aged would be to not reduce Supplemental Security Income (SSI) payments for the eligible elderly sharing a home with others. Additionally, the 1981 White House Mini-Conference on Hispanic Aging recommended that Medicare should be broadened to cover preventive and health maintenance services (including dental care), as well as expanded home health care services. It also noted that Medicaid should be expanded to cover home health services in all states. [60] The rationale for this position is that Hispanic persons have been identified as having a marked preference for home health care and a long tradition of preventive and health maintenance care.[61] Finally, it has been proposed that medically indigent individuals should be granted Medicaid in all states. Magaly Queralt contends that this is important particularly for aged Cubans because of their strong preference for private medical care.[62]

Turning to American Indians, it should be called out that the limited employment opportunities available on the reservation adversely affect their eligibility for social security benefits. They also have limited participation in private retirement programs.[63] American Indians suffer the impact of conflicting federal policies and are often refused access to public services on the grounds that the BIA should have jurisdiction. Some return to the reservation, and many others move frequently to other cities. This mobility means that a local agency is not in a good position to ascertain the eligibility of claimants for its services. As Bell, et al. point out, simple exhortation is unlikely to motivate local agencies to provide services at the expense of local taxpayers.[64] They recommend that the best resolution of this difficulty is to require local social and income support agencies to provide services to American Indians on the same basis as that specified for other persons, and for the federal government, after notification from the BIA, to subsidize local agencies by some percentage of service cost. This procedure would give the BIA, not the local agency, responsibility for compiling statistics on the movement of individuals among cities and between cities and reservations.[65]

The proposals identified under Position I have been questioned on several grounds. First, difficulties arise pertaining to the boundaries of ethnicity. Most of the literature in ethnogerontology focuses on blacks, Hispanics, American Indians and Asians/Pacific Islanders. As a corollary, the white elderly are generally viewed as homogeneous and not culturally diverse. Thus, ethnogerontology tends to be restricted to the four groups just mentioned. However, several investigators have found European ethnicity to be a highly salient factor as well. There is insufficient recognition of the specific problems and issues of the ethnic elderly of European descent, and of white ethnic groups of all ages in general. For example, David Guttmann studied eight white ethnic groups in the Washington, D.C./Baltimore area: Estonians, Greeks, Hungarians, Italians, Jews, Latvians, Lithuanians and two groups of Poles. He found significant differences in health and support service use among the elderly in these different ethnic groups.[66] Similarly, Tripp-Reimer and Schrock found significant differences in preference for care given a variety of life circumstances for Amish, Czech, Greek and Norwegian elderly. These differences must be taken into account in planning service delivery to the elderly.[67]

Second, Bell and his colleagues point out that there are severe problems in relying on existing literature. For example, Hispanic elderly have been studied primarily by anthropologists and black elderly by sociologists. The result is noncomparability of data.[68] In addition, comparisons that are restricted to culturally discrete and homogeneous groups are almost totally absent. Most of the data available are cross-sectional from surveys that are not supplemented by in-depth interviews or by ethnographic investigations. Thus, much of the literature that compares the sociocultural patterns of the white aged and the non-white aged is confusing. Other problems similarly result from the inappropriate grouping of racial subjects by the use of racially heterogeneous labels, divergent methods of statistical analysis, the use of nonrepresentative or geographically localized samples that prohibit the generalization of sample findings to their larger populations, and inadequate knowledge about the validity and reliability of survey or other instruments that are used to measure subjective conditions.

Furthermore, problems with the literature differ by minority group. There is almost no literature regarding elderly American Indians. The literature on the Japanese elderly tends to avoid a serious discussion of problems among the Issei (first generation), and only describes their relatively secure status. For Mexican Americans, the literature is largely ethnographic descriptions of life in traditional barrios.[69]

Finally, the proposal that blacks should become eligible for full social security benefits at an earlier age than other groups troubles many. As proposed by Jackson, it fails to consider the social relevance of the empirical fact that the life expectancies of Mexican Americans and American Indians are also shorter than that of whites. Given this fact, one might ask legitimately whether such a special privilege should not also be extended to Mexican Americans and American Indians. Moreover, Bell and his coresearchers observe that Jackson has proffered no evidence for a genetic basis for the observed difference in life expectancy between blacks and whites. While they allowed that blacks have been limited historically to poorly paying occupations, and that low income is associated with poor nutrition, poor housing, and lack of financial and physical access to medical care, they also noted that only if some groups are restricted by law or discrimination to jobs that present a health hazard can there be a reasonable claim that they deserve special retirement considerations. Thus, they concluded that the only proposition deserving consideration is that low-income workers should be allowed earlier eligibility, regardless of race.[70] As proposed by Jackson and other minority gerontologists, the policy changes based on race could well result in inequity for low-income white groups.

Position II

The second major public policy position advocates increasing access and flexibility in the delivery of existing services to the minority aged, without undergoing major policy changes. This position argues that ethnicity merits important consideration in the planning and delivery of health care. Because of cultural, historical and locational factors, "racial or ethnically neutral" programs preclude use by minorities and are therefore inequitable. When programs designed for white, middle-class elderly are administered without modification to minority elderly, the results are often frustrating and ineffective.

This view proposes ethnically sensitive health planning and delivery. Clients are deemphasized as the objects of change in improving service delivery; the focus is on modifying organizations and programs to achieve maximum participation. A variety of approaches have been proposed to maximize minority elderly participation in health and social service programs. These may be grouped into the following categories:

> **Attention to ethnic factors in program content:** Program revisions which fall into this category include the provision of ethnic foods in nutrition programs. A second important factor is the acceptance of traditional (i.e., folk) explanations for illness, with treatment being prescribed in a culturally consistent manner.

> **Attention to ethnic factors in staffing:** This includes not only hiring bilingual/bicultural staff when possible, but also

training other staff in the importance of cultural diversity and sensitivity in the planning and delivery of programs. Some innovative staff proposals include having the minority aged trained as paraprofessionals in order to serve as liaisons between other staff and clients.

Attention to locational factors: When possible, sites of health care delivery should be located in or close to the targeted ethnic community. When this is not feasible, transportation should be organized (perhaps through volunteers) to aid the elderly in need.

Outreach programs should be aggressive in recruiting minority participation: Using the existing indigenous community organizations that are already in contact with the elderly in the community is one way to provide more acceptable services. These informal systems may be key factors in identifying persons at risk and determining help-seeking behaviors, and can be tremendous resources in the actual provision of services.

Mass media campaigns through ethnic newspapers, radio and/or television programs have been shown to be an effective approach in mobilizing the ethnic elderly to seek out information on aging services.[71] Additionally, publicizing services at community centers (e.g., churches) is another method of reaching the elderly. Any public service media campaigns of this type should be addressed not only to the elderly, but also to other family members who might serve as brokers between their elderly and the health and social service delivery system.

Ethnic representation in program planning design and operation of the organization: For blacks, Asians, Mexican Americans and American Indians, the level of consumer input into major decisions has proven to be a distinguishing factor in programs which have been successful in reaching the minority elderly.[72]

The problems with the recommendations made in Position II are twofold. First are the difficulties in organizing, monitoring and evaluating such flexible programs. It is difficult to evaluate health services programs that serve the minority elderly because there are few measures of the extent to which such programs and services are effectively organized, structured and administered. The second problem is the potential, or perhaps likely, increase in cost if there is increased use of services. However, it is our position that program cost should not be an excuse for maintaining inequities. If the proverb that "health is wealth" is true, no material cost should be too great to assure the best possible health/health care for the largest possible number of the citizenry.

In bringing our observations to a close, we should like to call out that a flexible policy, tailored to the needs of targeted minority elderly, could increase participation and satisfaction. This will have to suffice until the advent of a true national health and social insurance program. Because the basic issue revolves around economics, it is unlikely that health and social service delivery will be truly equitable without major reformulations of the sociopolitical structure of the United States.

NOTES

[1]Leo Simmons, *The Role of the Aged in Primitive Society* (New Haven, CT: Yale University Press, 1945).

[2]During the late 1950s and on into the 1960s, a small number of gerontological publications written primarily by sociologists focused on ethnic differences and the social status of aged minorities. The most prominent of these publications include Thomas Talley and Jerome Kaplan, "The Negro Aged," *Newsletter of the Gerontological Society*, (December 1956), p. 6; National Urban League, Inc., *Double Jeopardy: The Older Negro in America Today* (New York: National Urban League, Inc., 1964); Margaret M. Clark and Barbara G. Anderson, *Culture and Aging: An Anthropological Study of Older Americans* (Springfield, IL: Charles C. Thomas, 1967); E. Grant Youmans, ed., *Older Rural Americans: A Sociological Perspective* (Lexington, KY: University of Kentucky Press, 1967); and Frances M. Carp, *Factors in Utilization of Services by the Mexican-American Elderly* (Palo Alto, CA: American Institute for Research, 1986). During this period, anthropological studies focused on cross-cultural differences in the aging experience. See, for example, Austin J. Shelton, "Ibo Aging and Eldership: Notes for Gerontologists and Others," *The Gerontologist* 5: 1 (March 1965): 20-23; and Paul Spencer, *The Samburu: A Study of Gerontocracy in a Nomadic Tribe* (London: Routledge & Kegan Paul, 1965).

[3]Jacquelyne Johnson Jackson, "Race, National Origin, Ethnicity, and Aging," in Robert H. Binstock and Ethel Shanas, *Handbook of Aging and the Social Sciences*, 2nd ed. (New York: Van Nostrand Reinhold Co., 1985), pp. 264-303 at 265.

[4]See Jackson, ibid. at p. 285; Jacquelyne Johnson Jackson, "Aged Blacks: A Potpourri in the Direction of the Reduction of Inequities," *Phylon* 32: 3 (Fall 1971): 260-280; 1971 White House Conference on Aging and Aging Blacks, *Special Concerns Report of the White House Conference on Aging, 1971* (Washington, D.C.: U.S. Government Printing Office, 1972); Rosemary McCaslin

and Welton R. Calvert, "Social Indicators in Black and White: Some Ethnic Considerations in Delivery of Service to the Elderly," *Journal of Gerontology* 30: 1 (January 1975): 60-66; William Bechill, "Politics of Aging and Ethnicity," in Donald E. Gelfand and Alfred J. Kutzik, eds., *Ethnicity and Aging: Theory, Research, and Policy* (New York: Springer Publishing Co., 1979), pp. 137-148; David E. Biegel and Wendy R. Sherman, "Neighborhood Capacity Building and the Ethnic Aged," in Gelfand and Kutzik, op. cit. this note, pp. 320-340; Federal Council on Aging, Mental Health, and the Elderly, *Recommendations for Action*, DHEW Publication No. (OHDS) 80-20960 (Washington, D.C.: U.S. Government Printing Office, 1979); Douglas Holmes, Monica Holmes, Leonard Steinbach, Tory Hausner and Bruce Rocheleau, *The Use of Community-Based Services in Long-Term Care by Older Minority Persons* (Denton, TX: North Texas State University Press, 1979); Elizabeth W. Markson, "Ethnicity as a Factor in the Institutionalization of the Ethnic Elderly," in Gelfand and Kutzick, op. cit. this note, pp. 341-356; Jose B. Cuellar and John R. Weeks, *Minority Elderly Americans: A Prototype for Area Agencies on Aging—Executive Summary*, Administration on Aging Grant No. 90-A-1667 (01) (San Diego, CA: Allied Home Health Association, 1979); Frank Cota-Robles Newton, "Issues in Research and Service Delivery Among Mexican American Elderly: A Concise Statement with Recommendations," *The Gerontologist* 20: 2 (April 1980): 208-212; and U.S. Commission on Civil Rights, *Minority Elderly Services: New Programs, Old Problems*, Part I (Washington D.C.: U.S. Commission on Civil Rights, 1982).

[5]Title II of the Social Security Act, codified at 42 U.S.C. Secs. 401-431.

[6]Title 18 is codified at 42 U.S.C. Sec. 1395-1395pp.

[7]Title 19 is codified at 42 U.S.C. Sec. 1396-1396i.

[8]Medicare Part A is codified at 42 U.S.C. Sec. 1395c-1395i.

[9]Medicare Part B is codified at 42 U.S.C. Sec. 1395j-1395w.

[10]At the time this chapter was written in 1986, Medicare included the following: acute and skilled nursing care; home health care; diagnosis and x-ray; physical therapy and speech treatment; ambulance if transportation otherwise would endanger health; chiropractic care for subluxation of spine demonstrated by x-ray exam; kidney dialysis or transplant; drugs given in a hospital or nursing home (skilled); care in a Christian Science sanatorium; physician's care for medical and surgical treatment, tests and procedures; outpatient and emergency room care for illness or accident; prosthetic devices for limb, arm and back, and neck braces; durable medical equipment (wheelchairs, home dialysis); medical supplies; casts and splints; home health aides (one hundred visits in one year); skilled part-time nursing care in home; and hospital benefit eligibility, maximum of $6500.00 is reimbursable.

Areas not covered included care in most foreign hospitals; drugs that can be self-administered; custodial care; nontraditional care (acupuncture, naturopathy, chiropractic—with one exception); health adjuncts (homemaker services, dental care, glasses, podiatry, hearing aids, immunizations, orthopedic shoes); and care not judged reasonable and necessary (frequent visits or prolonged hospital stays). A further major limitation restricted psychiatric care to 190 days in a lifetime and a maximum of $250.00 annually for outpatient mental health services.

(Editor's note: The recently enacted Medicare Catastrophic Coverage Act of 1988 includes provisions which affect the above.)

[11]Arizona, in 1982, was the last state to obtain Medicaid.

[12]Supplemental Security Income is granted by Title 16 of the Social Security Act, codified at 42 U.S.C. Secs. 1381-1383c.

[13]Codified at 42 U.S.C. Secs. 3011-3020d.

[14]Codified at 42 U.S.C. Secs. 3021-3030jj. In 1967 following HEW's reorganization, the Administration on Aging was placed under the Social and Rehabilitation Service. The 1973 amendments to the OAA placed the AoA in the office of the HEW Secretary.

[15]A major statutory change occurred in 1973 when the Older Americans Act was amended to revise the Title III state grant programs. To participate in the new Title III programs, each state was required to divide itself into planning and service areas (PSAs) and to designate an area agency on aging (AAA) to administer all local programs within the PSA. In 1978, Titles III, V and VII were consolidated under a new Title III, combining social service, nutrition and multipurpose senior service programs. Formerly, Title III had provided social services, Title V had provided senior centers, and Title VII had provided nutrition services.

[16]For example, under Title C, nutrition services include the establishment and operation of nutrition projects that provide at least one hot or other appropriate meal five or more days a week, in two areas: congregate settings and home delivery. These meals are to be provided in a group setting when appropriate.

[17]Codified at 42 U.S.C. Sec. 3027(a)(20).

[18]The AoA, following Congress' lead, revised the OAA regulations to eliminate requirements for establishing preferences or priorities for minorities. The regulations issued under the 1978 amendments had no explicit requirement for minority participation in contracts or grants. In addition, most references to service delivery priority for minorities were replaced by references to priority for those in greatest social and economic need. See U.S. Commission on Civil Rights, *Minority Elderly Services: New Programs, Old Problems*, Parts I and II, op. cit. note 4.

[19]R. L. McNeely and John N. Colen, eds., *Aging in Minority Groups* (Beverly Hills, CA: Sage Publications, 1983), pp. 25-26.

[20]Magaly Queralt, "The Elderly of Cuban Origin: Characteristics and Problems," in McNeely and Colen, ibid., pp. 50-65 at 50.

[21]Ibid., p. 53.

[22]See Paul K. H. Kim, "Demography of the Asian-Pacific Elderly: Selected Problems and Implications," in McNeely and Colen, op. cit. note 19, pp. 29-41 at 31.

[23]U.S. Bureau of the Census, *Supplementary Reports, 1980 Census of the Population* (Washington, D.C.: U.S. Government Printing Office, 1980).

[24]Duran Bell, Patricia Kasschau and Gail Zellman, *Delivering Services to Elderly Members of Minority Groups: A Critical Review of the Literature*, sponsored by the HEW Office of Human Development (Santa Monica: Rand Corporation, 1976), p. 2.

[25]Forty-one percent of Mexican Americans reside in California; approximately 36 percent are in Texas. Ibid., p. 3.

[26]U.S. Bureau of the Census, *Demographic Aspects of Aging and the Older Population in the United States*, Series P-23, No. 59 (Washington, D.C.: U.S. Government Printing Office, May 1976); U.S. Bureau of the Census, *1980 Census of the Population by Age, Sex, Race and Spanish Origin of the Population by Regions, Division and State* (Washington, D.C.: U.S. Government Printing Office, 1980), Table 1.

[27]For a discussion of the concept of sex ratio crossover, see Jackson, op. cit. note 3, pp. 273 and 284-285.

[28]Ethel Shanas and George L. Maddox, "Health, Health Resources, and the Utilization of Care," in Binstock and Shanas, op. cit. note 3, pp. 697-726 at 708.

[29]Bell, et al., op. cit. note 24, p. v.

[30]Steven Zarit, *Aging and Mental Disorders: Psychological Approaches to Assessment and Treatment* (New York: Free Press, 1980), p. 80.

[31]Robert Atchley, *The Social Forces in Later Life: An Introduction to Social Gerontology*, 2nd ed. (Belmont, CA: Wadsworth Publishing Co., 1977), p. 125.

[32]See Talley and Kaplan, op. cit. note 2.

[33]See National Urban League, op. cit. note 2.

[34]See Richard C. Crandall, *Gerontology: A Behavioral Science Approach* (Reading, MA: Addison-Wesley Publishing, 1980).

[35]Shanas and Maddox, op. cit. note 28, p. 708.

[36]The same patterns of chronic disability and disease were observed in a survey of the Hispanic aged. See Jean K. Crawford, *A National Study to Assess the Service Needs of the Hispanic Elderly: Final Report* (Los Angeles: Asociación Nacional pro Personas Majores, 1980). Arthritis was reportedly the most prevalent condition among the Hispanic aged (48 percent of Mexican Americans; 55 percent of Cubans Americans; and 59 percent of Puerto Ricans), while diabetes ranked third for Mexican Americans. Cataracts and glaucoma also ranked high, as did heart disease. See Barbara Jones Morrison, "Physical Health and the Minority Aged," in McNeely and Colen, op. cit. note 19, pp. 161-173 at 162.

[37]See Shanas and Maddox, op. cit. note 28, p. 708.

[38]U.S. Bureau of the Census, *Statistical Abstract of the United States: 1988*, 108th ed. (Washington, D.C.: U.S. Government Printing Office, 1987), Table 106, p. 170.

[39]Steve Wing, Kenneth Manton, Eric Stallard, Curtis Hames and H. A. Tryoler, "The Black/White Mortality Cross-Over: Investigation in a Community-Based Study," *Journal of Gerontology* 40: 1 (January 1985): 78-84; and Kenneth Manton, "Changing Concepts of Morbidity and Mortality in the Elderly Population," *Milbank Memorial Fund Quarterly* 60: 2 (Spring 1982): 183-244 at 213.

[40]Jackson, op. cit. note 3, p. 285.

[41]See Ethel Shanas, *The Health of Older People* (Cambridge, MA: Harvard University Press, 1962); see also Jackson, op. cit. note 3, p. 290; Ron C. Manuel and John Reid, "A Comparative Demographic Profile of the Minority and Nonminority Aged," in Ron C. Manuel, ed., *Minority Aging: Sociological and Social Psychological Issues* (Westwood, CT: Greenwood Press, 1982), pp. 31-52 at 45-48; and Helen Foster Giles, "Differential Life Expectancy Among White and Nonwhite Americans: Some Explanations during Youth and Middle Age," in Manuel, op. cit. this note, pp. 53-62.

[42]John Nowlin, "Geriatric Health Status: Influence of Race and Socioeconomic Status," *Journal of Minority Aging* 4: 4 (September 1979): 93-98; and Jackson, op. cit. note 3, p. 291.

[43]Nowlin, ibid., p. 97; and Jackson, ibid., p. 267.

[44]Reported in Jackson, ibid.

[45]Beth J. Soldo, "American Elderly in the 1980s," *Population Bulletin* 35: 4 (November 1980): 3-47.

[46]Josephine A. Allen, "Mental Health, Service Delivery in Institutions, and the Minority Aged," in McNeely and Colen, op. cit. note 19, pp. 174-184 at 180.

[47]John N. Colen, "Facilitating Service Delivery to the Minority Aged," in McNeely and Colen, ibid., pp. 250-259 at 250.

[48]See Bell, et al., op. cit. note 24, pp. v-xiii.

[49]David Guttman, *Perspectives on Equitable Share in Public Benefits by Minority Elderly: Executive Summary* (Washington, D.C.: National Catholic School of Social Service, Catholic University of America, 1980); also see discussion in Jackson, op. cit. note 3, pp. 285-288.

[50]Jacquelyne Johnson Jackson, "The Blacklands of Gerontology," *Aging and Human Development* 2: 3 (August 1971): 156-171 at 161; and Colen, op. cit. note 47, p. 251.

[51]Gretchen Schafft, "Nursing Home Care and Minority Elderly," *Journal of Long Term Care Administration* 8: 4 (Winter 1980): 131; Richard Eribes and Martha Bradley-Rawls, "The Underutilization of Nursing Home Facilities by Mexican-American Elderly in the Southwest," *The Gerontologist* 18: 4 (August 1978): 363-371; and E. Percil Standford, ed., *Minority Aging: Policy Issues for*

the 1980s: Proceedings of the Seventh National Institute on Minority Aging (San Diego, CA: Campanile Press, 1981).

[52]Cary S. Kant and Barry L. Beckham, "Black-White Differentials in the Institutionalization of the Elderly: A Temporal Analysis," Social Forces 54: 4 (June 1976): 901-910 at 905.

[53]Bell, et al., op. cit. note 24, p. x.

[54]Ibid.

[55]Ibid.; Robert L. Schneider, "Barriers to Effective Outreach in Title VII Nutrition Programs," The Gerontologist 19: 2 (April 1979): 163-168 at 165-166; and Cuellar and Weeks, op. cit. note 4. See also Oliver W. Slaughter and Mignon G. Batey, "Service Delivery and the Black Aged: Identifying Barriers to Utilization of Mental Health Services," in Manuel, op. cit. note 41, pp. 171-177.

[56]Jeanne Thune, "Racial Attitudes of Older Adults," The Gerontologist 7: 3 (September 1967): 179-182.

[57]See McNeely and Colen, op. cit. note 19.

[58]Jackson, op. cit. note 3, pp. 285-287.

[59]Kim, op. cit. note 22, p. 36. An Asian-oriented research agency was established, but it went out of existence after three years. Subsequently, another resource agency was established, but it is identified as serving only selected Asian elderly populations residing in certain areas. There are three major organizations serving the Asian elderly: the Pacific Asian Coalition in California, the Asian American Mental Health Research Center in Illinois, and the National Pacific/Asian Resource Center on Aging in the state of Washington. There are also more than 2800 Filipino organizations in the United States.

[60]Queralt, op. cit. note 20, p. 60.

[61]Ibid.

[62]Ibid.

[63]E. Daniel Edwards, "Native-American Elders: Current Issues and Social Policy Implications," in McNeely and Colen, op. cit. note 19, pp. 74-82 at 77.

[64]Bell, et al., op. cit. note 24, p. xi.

[65]Ibid.

[66]See David Guttman, Informal and Formal Support Systems and Their Effect on the Lives of the Elderly in Selected Ethnic Groups, AoA Final Report 90-A-1007 (Washington, D.C.: National Clearinghouse on Aging, 1979).

[67]Toni Tripp-Reimer and Miriam Schrock, "Residential Patterns and Preferences Among Ethnic Aged," in Joan Uhl, ed., Proceedings of the Seventh Annual Transcultural Nursing Society Meetings (Salt Lake City: Transcultural Nursing Society, 1982), pp. 144-157.

[68]Bell, et al., op. cit. note 24, p. 2.

[69]Ibid., pp. xi-xii.

[70]Ibid., p. 94.

[71]Queralt, op. cit. note 20, p. 59.

[72]John Colen and David Soto, *Service Delivery to Aged Minorities: Techniques of Successful Programs* (Sacramento, CA: School of Social Work, California State University, 1979), cited in Jackson, op. cit. note 3, p. 265.

HOMICIDE IN BLACK COMMUNITIES: A PUBLIC HEALTH PERSPECTIVE

Julius Debro

Atlanta University

Introduction

Time relentlessly saps the vitality of the body as nature makes use of death in the unending cycle of birth, death and rebirth. Death by nature fits the natural order of the being and becoming of life. Wrongful death by human hand, though, abridges this order, as well as the social order, and violates the first law of nature which admonishes every individual to preserve his/her life. This violation and abridgement have been all too troublesome in the lives of black people in the United States.

The purpose of this chapter is to trace homicide in black communities in the United States from 1880 to the late 1980s. Eighteen-eighty was selected because it is the first year that the Bureau of the Census collected data on crime. Sketchy data on crime prior to 1880 are available, but are very limited in content. Most violence committed against blacks prior to 1880 was by slave masters and other white citizens. Whites perpetrated massive violence against blacks throughout the slavery and Reconstruction periods, and lynchings, which were a commonplace at the end of the nineteenth century and the outset of the twentieth, have occurred as late as the 1970s. In most cases prior to the 1940s, blacks were victims and not offenders in the use of violence.

The socioeconomic position of most blacks has not changed appreciably over the years. As slaves, some blacks worked in the white man's house and others worked in his fields. In today's world, some blacks are still "in the house" and many others are in the ghettoes of our cities. Many blacks still suffer from acute racial and class isolation, removed from both white and black middle-class Americans. Some few are now middle class, but all too many fill the ranks of the underclass. The latter are usually the victims and perpetrators of black homicide.

While the problem of black homicide has persisted since blacks first came to this country as slaves, little research has been devoted to the causes or consequences of the phenomenon. How serious is the problem of black homicide? What are its root causes? What are the solutions? Why has the framework of study about black homicide shifted from that of a social problem to a medical problem? What are the policy implications of this shift? This chapter addresses these questions.

It is maintained here that this shift in definition is not the result of changing public attitudes toward health or increases in black homicide statistics, but rather of a new political trend. A number of issues formerly addressed by the social sciences are now considered to be in the medical and psychological domain. Labeling certain conditions and issues as social problems is part of a political process arising from social change. The economic, social and political milieux in which social problems are defined, particularly the political and polemical powers of the defining groups, determine what sets of conditions become problems and what solutions are acceptable. In the case of black homicide, a group of powerful organizations in the medical and psychological communities has succeeded in transforming the definition of this phenomenon from a social to a medical problem.

This definitional transformation has been facilitated by certain popular and academic trends, including the growing strength of the medical model as an explanation of human behavior. Advances in the medical field over infectious diseases have created the need for epidemiologists to look for new frontiers. The general popularity of the medical model, along with its prestigious and politically powerful interest groups, and the proclivity of Americans to reduce complicated behavioral models to individual "blame models" of behavior, have fostered the change from a social to a medical definition of homicide. Structural models (e.g., economic, social and demographic) have been discarded or weakened. All of this has contributed to a reconceptualization of black homicide.

The overview of the causes of violence in the black community which follows touches upon genetic myths as well as discusses socioeconomic models and control theories. The chapter concludes with a discussion of the move to a public health perspective of black homicide—a model that includes the behavioral science approach to human conduct.

Historical Overview

In order to assess accurately the nature and extent of black homicide, one must first look at the wider problem of violence in this country. The history of the United States is steeped in violence. Explorers and colonists faced an unwelcome and hostile physical environment. Frontier life was harsh, savage and brutal. Millions of American Indians lost their land and lives in the "peopling" of the continent. Many American heroes were Indian fighters. The Revolutionary War pitted rebellious colonists against Englishmen and colonist against colonist. Violent uprisings, culminating in the bloody Civil War, characterize American history. The West and Southwest were taken from Mexico via warfare. Outlaws versus sheriffs, cattlemen against sheepmen, and "brave" vigilantes versus the lawless were a commonplace. Violence between the "cowboys and Indians" became a metaphor.

To this day, men of violence—bear fighters, Indian fighters, outlaws (e.g., the James brothers), gamblers, plantation owners, confederate officers and rebel southerners—constitute a noteworthy part of the historical collection of American heroes. We adore the John Wayne-type of macho man. The good guys in our stories and movies must eventually kill the bad guys. The violent "cops and robbers" on television reflect a violent culture. The macho man, the model for our male children, is a physical and visceral type who resorts to violence and sexual exploitation to maintain his identity and respectability. Violence rather than compromise is his way of solving problems, and the redress of personal wrong is not done through the legal process. A real man stands up and fights whenever he must. The macho man drinks (holds his liquor well), gambles, fights, and seduces all of the females he can (married or single). He generally does not become emotionally involved with the women he seduces. Still, many women are intrigued by this image.

Violence takes many forms in the United States depending on the social situation of the individual and his or her degree of integration into the society. Blacks have never been fully integrated into the social mainstream. During slavery they were bought, sold and exploited as chattels. Not seen as real humans, slaves had few if any rights and were practically subject to the whim of any white person on or off the plantation. Free blacks were treated a little better, but were still considered subhuman. Physical violence and threats against blacks were a common occurrence. Over the course of slavery (and to some degree until the civil rights movement), white men subjected black women to sexual exploitation. Of course, the black male was lynched for looking at a white woman the "wrong way." This sexual caste system led to a long history of one-sided exploitation and violence.

Until the end of the Civil War, blacks were not allowed to participate in the political, economic and social mainstream of American society. They were taught and forced to be dependent upon whites for their livelihood, self-gratification and self-esteem. The system of slavery promoted dependency and negative self-concepts, particularly among black males. Moreover, slavery constrained severely the expression of dissatisfaction by blacks, which, in turn, tended to foster violence within the group, i.e., black-on-black. Today, the lower-class black male's inability to fulfill his obligations as a good family provider contributes significantly to his low self-esteem. This tends to engender frustration and violence, much of which is directed toward his fellow blacks of both sexes.

Studies show that children who are abused by parents grow up to become abusers themselves. Blacks who have been continually abused by whites may well be inclined to perpetuate physical violence (most of it internalized against themselves). Certainly, ghetto blacks who suffer from discrimination, poverty, low self-concepts and frustration are prone to violence. The abuse today has changed in form but not in substance. It is fostered not only by racism, but also by socioeconomic factors which strike at the heart of the individual. Poor schools, neglected communities, deteriorating family relationships, limited employment opportunities and continuous covert discrimination have decreased the self-esteem of many black individuals—especially the black male who moves from childhood to adulthood often feeling trapped in a situation of deprivation. Unable to assume the traditional role of provider and family leader, the male may resort to violence to ease the frustration of his impotence in a society that is not responsive to his needs and denies his entrance into the mainstream. Certainly the black male in many instances has resorted to a ghetto lifestyle that encourages deviance and violence, e.g., drinking, gambling, hustling, serial mating and bravado. Such a lifestyle has complicated his relationship with the black female, who many times unrealistically expects him to approximate the successful white male role model. The resulting conflict between black men and black women frequently leads to domestic violence.

The Population

In the early 1900s approximately 90 percent of blacks (about ten million) lived in the South. By the late 1960s the black population had doubled and only about 48 percent lived in the South. The majority of blacks now live in metropolitan areas.[1] Between 1970 and 1980 the black population in the United States increased by 17.3 percent (from 22.5 million to 26.5 million). In 1980, blacks represented approximately 12 percent of the total American population.[2] Blacks are now congregated in the largest cities. New York has the largest black population (1,788,377), followed by Chicago (1,197,174), Detroit (758,468), Philadelphia (638,788) and Los Angeles (504,301).[3]

Black Homicide Rate

Data on black homicide rates prior to 1910 are not available. Black homicide rates per 100,000 in 1910 and in some subsequent years are as follows:

$$
\begin{array}{ll}
1910 & \ldots 28.5 \\
1920 & \ldots 28.5 \\
1930 & \ldots 37.9 \\
1940 & \ldots 60.5 \\
1960 & \ldots 21.9 \\
1974 & \ldots 39.7
\end{array}
$$

By 1976 the black homicide rate was approximately 80 per 100,000 for blacks *between the ages of fifteen to twenty-four*, actually a decrease from a high of more than 100 per 100,000 in 1970-72.[4] In 1978 the homicide rate for blacks in the same age group was 72.5 deaths per 100,000, compared with a rate of 13.2 per 100,000 for *all* persons aged fifteen to twenty-four.[5] By 1984 the homicide rate had decreased to 70 deaths per 100,000 for blacks aged fifteen to twenty-four, compared to a rate of 12 per 100,000 for all other persons in the same age group.

The black homicide rate is officially about six times higher than that for whites; this official rate, however, is subject to disagreement because the FBI rates, on which the official homicide rate is based, are different from statistics compiled by the National Center for Health Statistics.[6] FBI data can be helpful in studying black homicide beginning in 1976, but are not useful for long-term studies involving the race of the offender and victim before that date because local police departments' supplementary homicide reports before 1976 were essentially reports about the victims. The National Center for Health Statistics provides information on deaths based on death certificates completed by local medical examiners, coroners and physicians throughout the United States.[7] The data differ because the FBI includes murder and nonnegligent manslaughter, but excludes deaths due to negligence, justifiable homicides and excusable homicides. The NCHS data include any violent killing committed by one human being against another.

It is an empirical fact that the overall general crime rate among blacks is higher than that among whites, and this leads many to ask whether a relationship exists between race and crime. There is a direct

correlation between race and crime—but it varies with social conditions. Societal structures in black communities are not as strong as
they are in white communities. (See Figures 1 and 2.) Blacks have
fewer economic opportunities, and historically have been segregated
into areas with declining economic bases. (See Figures 3 and 4.) As a
result, blacks have less money and capital; in addition, black children
are segregated in schools with lower tax bases and, concomitantly, receive an inadequate education. Their neighborhoods are often characterized by violence and social disorganization. The statistical relationship between race and crime is fundamentally a product of class
differences rather than racial differences. A much larger proportion of
the black population than the white population is lower class. Moreover, a much higher percentage of blacks than whites live at the poverty level, and poor blacks are worse off than poor whites. Finally, the
level of relative deprivation is much higher among blacks than among
whites.

FIGURE 1

BLACK FAMILIES BY TYPE: 1970 AND 1982

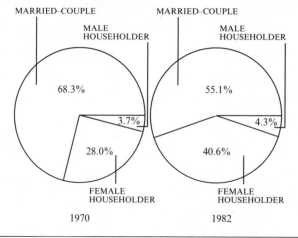

Source: William C. Manthey and Dwight L. Johnson, *America's Black Population: 1970
to 1982, A Statistical View* (Washington, D.C.: U.S. Bureau of the Census,
1983), Chart 7, p. 19.

FIGURE 2

BIRTHS OUT OF WEDLOCK BY RACE: 1970 AND 1980

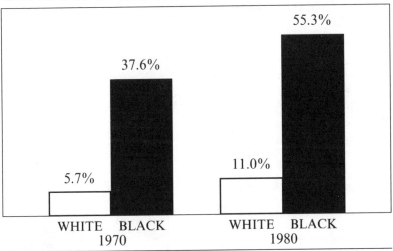

Source: William C. Manthey and Dwight L. Johnson, *America's Black Population: 1970 to 1982, A Statistical View* (Washington, D.C.: U.S. Bureau of the Census, 1983), Chart 9, p. 22.

FIGURE 3

NUMBER OF PERSONS BELOW POVERTY LEVEL BY RACE: 1970 TO 1981

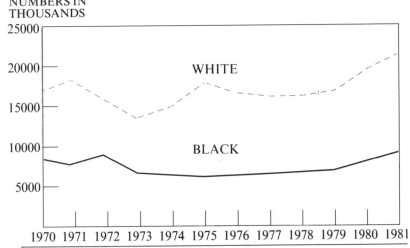

Source: William C. Manthey and Dwight L. Johnson, *America's Black Population: 1970 to 1982, A Statistical View* (Washington, D.C.: U.S. Bureau of the Census, 1983), Chart 4, p. 8.

FIGURE 4

MEDIAN FAMILY INCOME BY TYPE OF FAMILY
AND RACE OF HOUSEHOLDER: 1971 AND 1981
(1981 DOLLARS)

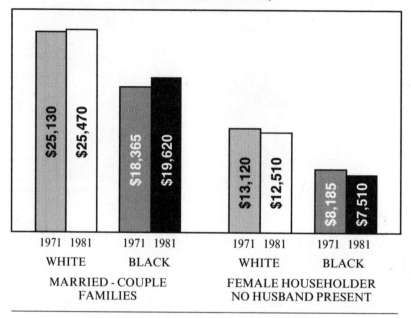

Source: William C. Manthey and Dwight L. Johnson, *America's Black Population: 1970 to 1982, A Statistical View* (Washington, D.C.: U.S. Bureau of the Census, 1983), Chart 2, p. 6.

Homicides: A Global Perspective

How does the homicide rate in the United States compare with other countries? Its national homicide rate is more than six times higher than England's, and about twice that of the general European average. Murder is practically nonexistent in the following countries:*

Norway	0.80
Morocco	0.84
Ivory Coast	1.12
England	1.63
Malaysia.......	2.60

But in some other countries it occurs even more frequently than in the United States:[8]

Kuwait	13.59
Guyana	20.70
Turkey	27.29
Nigeria	80.70
Lesotho	136.75

*Rate per 100,000 population

FBI statistics for the United States indicate that in 1983, 19,308 persons died as a result of either murder or nonnegligent manslaughter. Fifty percent of the people arrested for these offenses were black, and 42.5 percent of the victims were black.[9] In 1986, 20,613 people were killed according to FBI statistics.[10] Of that number, 48 percent of the people arrested were black, as were 47 percent of the victims.[11] Within the last few years, there seems to have been a gradual decrease in the number of homicides committed by blacks. There is insufficient evidence to indicate whether what has been observed constitutes a trend that will continue. An important related fact, though, is that the migration of blacks from the South to the North in large numbers has decreased. Between 1975 and 1980, approximately 415,000 blacks moved to the South and only about 220,000 left, reversing the longstanding pattern of black movement away from the South. In 1980 the proportion of the total black population residing in the South was 53 percent, the same as in 1970.[12] Perhaps the small decrease in the amount of homicides committed by blacks is not only related to this change in migratory patterns, but also due to more blacks learning to cope with life in large metropolitan areas.

The concern of American society is not with "legitimate" acts of violence as defined by cultural norms and legal institutions, but with illegitimate violence directed at individuals. The most insidious act of violence is, of course, homicide. Blacks commit nearly half of all homicides that are recorded in the United States. What are the characteristics of black crime?

- Black crime is primarily a phenomenon of large cities.

- Black crime is overwhelmingly committed by black males.

- Black crime is committed primarily by youths between the ages of fifteen and twenty-four.

- Black crime is clearly a phenomenon of the ghetto.[13]

Most young black male homicide victims were/are killed by persons known to them, usually acquaintances or family members. From 1976 to 1982, 46.2 percent were killed by acquaintances, 19.9 percent by strangers and 8 percent by family members. The victim-offender relationship was unknown for 26 percent of murders involving young black male victims.[14]

Granted that homicide rates are higher for blacks than whites, is violent behavior an inheritable trait of black males? Most psychologists and social scientists do not regard aggression as fundamentally spontaneous or instinctive, and none claim any genetic, racial proclivities to aggression. Most social scientists see aggression as an emotional response to socially-induced frustrations — a learned ply to specific situations. If this is indeed the case, then there is little wonder that blacks, given their prevailing social state, especially their disproportionate representation in the underclass, seem statistically prone to violent behavior.

The increase in black crime, and especially in black violence, is a relatively new phenomenon. Harold Rose indicates that even though the South has the highest crime rates in the country, the number of criminal convictions of blacks is not much greater on the average than their proportion in the population.[15] He did note that blacks serve longer terms for crimes against whites than for those against blacks, and that blacks are pardoned and paroled much less frequently than are whites in similar circumstances.[16]

Review of the Literature

Race and Crime

Early studies were not offense specific, but primarily concerned black crime in black communities. These studies were usually conducted by black scholars. The first major study concerning black crime, conducted by W.E.B. DuBois, is contained in *The Philadelphia Negro*.[17] DuBois examined the conditions of four thousand blacks in Philadelphia and found that most of their offenses involved minor criminal behavior. He referred to black crime as "social degradation," and observed that it was difficult to measure because of different reporting standards utilized in different regions of the country. Richard Korn and Lloyd McCorkle reached the same conclusion decades later, pointing out that the data available from 1900 to 1930 not only were collected under different standards than those used today, but were also "poorly standardized and consequently useless."[18]

In 1904 DuBois noted that 125,093 prisoners had been sentenced in the United States. Of them, 15.8 percent were blacks, who then made up 11.5 percent of the population.[19] He did not consider the measurement of the black rate to be fair because of the influence of racial prejudice in the arrest and conviction process, and indicated that over half the black prisoners sentenced in the United States received life sentences. DuBois' explanation of these long sentences was that most were for rape, and called out that black conviction rates for raping white women exceeded the actual rate of rape. This long-term sentencing beyond that required for fair punishment served to guarantee states a pool of cheap black labor. DuBois saw most actual black crimes as stemming from petty stealing and quarreling, revenge against whites, altercations arising between employers and laborers, and fights and murders arising from the strained contact of the races.[20]

In an article entitled "Negro and Strong Drink," Booker T. Washington refered to a "Biennial Report of the Attorney General of the State of Alabama" for the years 1908-1909 which reported 236 homicides. One hundred forty-two of the defendants were black and ninety-four were white. In ninety-seven of the cases, the defendant or the deceased was drunk or drinking at the time of the homicide. Washington thus attributed the high homicide rate to alcohol.[21] (Today, alcohol abuse is considered a major health problem among blacks, and its relationship to homicide cannot be disputed. Frederick Harper observes that alcohol abuse is the number one health and social problem in black America.[22])

In 1927 William Root wrote that black inmates from urban Pennsylvania occupied the poorest homes in the poorest districts, where vice and crime flourished, and that they lacked educational and vocational skills and used leisure time improperly. He noted that they were the victims of a caste system, and concluded that blacks, because of social and economic conditions, were forced to feel inferior and were humiliated in a variety of ways.[23]

Ira deA. Reid observed that the major causes of crime among blacks were unemployment and underemployment. In his 1932 study of black prisoners in New York, he found that the factors causing the commission of crimes had "roots deep in the social status of a minority population."[24] In "Negro Homicides in the United States," Kenneth Barnhart maintained that the factor of race was not as important as the factors of location and illiteracy.[25] Other scholars of that period also looked at the racial factor in capital cases.[26] Earl Moses, for example, published a study on community factors in black delinquency which also considered the zonal theories of Shaw and McKay. He attributed crime in the black community to the settlement of blacks in the areas of

deterioration where crime flourishes.[27] Later, studies began to focus
upon the racial disparities in arrests and sentencing. Several in the
early 1960s have indicated that blacks were more likely to be arrested,
incarcerated and sentenced to longer terms than whites,[28] a fact that
DuBois pointed out years earlier.

In 1958 Marvin Wolfgang published a comprehensive study of
homicides in Philadelphia.[29] He analyzed records of homicides from
the Philadelphia police over a five-year period from 1948 to 1952 and
found that 73 percent of the victims were black, as were 75 percent of
the offenders. The highest rate for victims was in the age group of
twenty-five to thirty-four. The highest rate for offenders was for
twenty to twenty-four year olds. [30] Other studies have found similar
results.[31] Wolfgang attributed the high homicide and crime rates to a
subculture of poverty and violence, one that still exists among young,
undereducated, segregated, underemployed and unskilled ghetto
blacks.

Black Violence as a Social Problem

Black violence did not become a major issue in the United States until
the rebellions of the 1960s when blacks began to destroy the black sections of large cities.[32] The President's Commission on Law Enforcement and the Administration of Justice focused primarily upon serious
offenses, but gave little consideration to black homicide because it was
considered primarily an intraracial offense. The commission concluded
that blacks were disproportionately both homicide offenders and victims in large cities, and that most of this violence was concentrated
among family members and friends or acquaintances:

> In general, the disparity of rates for offenses of violence is much
> greater than comparable differences between the races for offenses
> against property. For instance, the Negro arrest rate for murder
> is 24.1 compared to 2.5 for whites, or almost 10 times as high.[33]

As more data became available, studies began to indicate that maximum criminality was a product of the young, and that crime rates varied by offense, sex, place and time. Edwin Sutherland's and Donald
Cressey's theory of "differential association" played a vital part in directing the attention of criminologists to the subcultural support of
criminal behavior.[34] Thorsten Sellin's theory of "culture conflict" has
also been used as an explanation for subcultural crime. He argued that
norms of conduct are present for every defined group to which the individual belongs, and that culture conflict results when those norms

clash.[35] Additional studies have indicated that there is a subculture of violence and that blacks are the locus of this subculture.[36]

Theoretical Diversity

William Chambliss compared functional and conflict theories pertaining to the causes of crime. He observed that sociological constructs, including labeling theory, that comprise the functionalist approach, perceive criminal law as a reflection of value consensus within a given society. Chambliss argued that empirical data collected for functionalist studies forced these data to fit into value consensus theories. Criminal law, he claimed, does not reflect custom; rather, it reflects the desire of the ruling class to maintain its own interests at the expense of those being ruled. He viewed most criminal behavior as a reflection and consequence of the struggle between the rulers and the ruled, as the former strived to preserve the existing social order and the latter endeavored to change it.[37]

In the late 1970s and early 1980s, the crime control school of thought became quite prevalent. "Law and order," i.e., law and order regarding street crime, became the shibboleth. White collar crime was relegated to a lesser concern. The federal government began to place more emphasis upon the police and their acquisition of additional equipment, primarily weapons and related hardware, to fight crime. Rehabilitation programs were de-emphasized and less money was made available to study crime as a social problem, while commissions to study street violence and drugs were supported. Former Attorney General William French Smith appointed a task force to combat violent crime, and its membership lacked any sociologists. The federal government moved away from "liberal" sociologists and criminologists to more conservative persons such as James Q. Wilson, a political scientist, to study the crime problem. [38] Wilson stresses the individual, psychological and biological causes of crime, downgrading its sociological aspects.[39]

The Shift

Within the last few years the shift in the study of black homicide from cultural and socioeconomic causes to medical, biological and psychological ones has been dramatic. Since the work of Caesar Lombroso, the medical profession has emphasized a biological model to study crime and criminals and downplayed the sociological aspects of crime. This shift also involves a move into the popular field of violence epidemiology. In 1979 the Department of Health, Education and Welfare published a document, *Healthy People: The Surgeon General's Report on Health Promotion and Disease Prevention*, which pointed out the changes within the public health field and introduced a new focus on violence. The report indicated that there had been great success in dealing with infectious diseases and that the "principal killers and disablers of the past" had declined and, in some cases, "have fallen off the charts."[40]

With the most notable exception being cancer, the majority of the major health problems arising before 1983 have been eradicated or attenuated. In a search for new directions, health professionals have begun to concentrate upon the prevention rather than the management of infectious diseases:

> Health problems in the United States have changed radically over this century. This is in large measure due to dramatic advances in the prevention, treatment, and management of infectious disease. . . . [T]hese successes have caused many of the most feared health problems to decline and even disappear as causes of disability and death.[41]

The new orientation maintains that public health should concern itself with prevention and health promotion on a broad basis, i.e., improving the quality of life. Violence, including homicide, affects the quality of life and is thus a health problem. Therefore, so the argument goes, there is a need to move into violence prevention because, as is true of other health problems: (1) it is more effective to prevent than to cure or rehabilitate; (2) prevention must be directed toward reducing premature or unnecessary death or disability; (3) the quality of life must be improved; and (4) health education and behavioral changes are keys to the prevention of disease and crime and violence.

The Department of Health and Human Services began to focus upon the homicide issue in 1982. In 1983, Janine Jason, Melinda Flock and Carl Tyler, Jr., of the Centers for Disease Control (CDC) published their finding that homicide was one of the five leading causes of death for all persons between the ages of one and forty-four.[42] They found that over half of the homicides did not involve the perpetration of another crime. These homicides were defined as primary homicides. They then suggested that those deaths that did not involve the perpetration of another crime could be defined as a public health problem. [43]

Jason and her coauthors acknowledge that criminal homicide has been studied extensively by social scientists, criminologists and psychologists, but that now is the time for public health and preventive medicine specialists and epidemiologists to enter the picture.[44] To Jason, Flock and Tyler, the study of homicide as a health problem makes sense because the application of epidemiological techniques (i.e., those used in morbidity and mortality studies) could be utilized to construct causation and prevention models. In looking at the characteristics of primary homicides in the United States, they found that they were overwhelmingly intraracial involving male offenders and victims during their peak work years.[45]

The Centers for Disease Control, since their inception in 1942, have evolved from the study of malaria to involvement in chronic diseases, birth defects, family planning, diabetes and infectious diseases.[46] In 1980 the CDC was reorganized into five divisions, one of which was the Center for Health Promotion and Education. This division was given the responsibility of investigating the problem of purposeful injury or violence, which impelled the CDC to move into the area of violence epidemiology. The rationale was that homicide could be analyzed abstractly as a disease because it has an offender, a victim, and circumstances surrounding the incident. One could assess the risks to a particular class of offenders or victims, and one could look at the environment from which they came.

The strategy of the Centers for Disease Control is to attempt to implement preventive measures in the area of intrafamilial violence. Studies such as the one by Lawrence Sherman and Richard Berk have shown that police officers should begin to arrest more batterers as a control measure.[47] Crisis centers and shelters for battered wives are now a commonplace in many cities. Complete counseling services, housing facilities, protective shelters, referrals to community agencies and follow-up services are provided by these centers at city, county, state and federal cost. Parenting education concerning child discipline and development is widely provided. The Centers for Disease Control recommend public school health education on family interactions, stress reduction through neighborhood support systems, and family counseling and therapy related to family violence.[48]

The Centers for Disease Control are also examining violence between acquaintances or strangers which is not associated with crime; how to diffuse aggressive or stressful situations; how to effectively avoid physical conflict; and how to determine what situations are associated with a heightened risk of violence (e.g., arguments with acquaintances over money or property, altercations with strangers, etc.).[49] CDC prevention measures include attempts to alter male/male and male/female interaction patterns.[50]

A major objective of the Department of Health and Human Services, under whose jurisdiction the CDC falls, is the improvement in the health of Americans through the reduction of homicide among

black males ages fifteen to twenty-four from the current rate of 70 per
100,000 to below 60 per 100,000 by 1990. For all people in the same age
range, the rate is 12 per 100,000. Among black males in this age group,
homicide is the leading cause of death.[51]

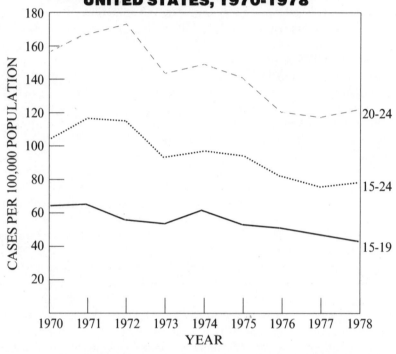

FIGURE 5

HOMICIDE RATES FOR BLACK MALES
15-24 YEARS OF AGE, BY AGE GROUP –
UNITED STATES, 1970-1978

Source: "Violent Deaths Among Persons 15-24 Years of Age – United States, 1970-
        1978," *Morbidity and Mortality Weekly Report* 32: 35 (September 9, 1983):
        453-457, Figure 3, p. 456.

The Politics of Black Homicide

The problem of black homicide was discussed in 1980 at a symposium
sponsored by Dr. James Ralph, then chief of the Center for Minority
Group Mental Health at the National Institute of Mental Health
(NIMH), but it did not receive the publicity that CDC received when
it made its announcement later. At this symposium, specific suggestions for the study of black homicides were made. Participants recom-

mended studies of the following and their relationship to high homicide rates: drug and alcohol abuse; stress and homicide; racism; use of deadly force by the police; public housing intervention projects; and interpersonal behavior and relationships in the black community. These recommendations were forwarded to the Secretary of the Department of Health and Human Services. In December 1980, Robert Tractenberg, the deputy administrator, responded that $1,000,000 should be set aside for the study of black male homicide in 1982-83. He recommended some broad research areas for those who intended to submit research proposals:

- A comprehensive, state-of-the-art review of the literature.

- A study of the different psychosocial and environmental circumstances that contribute to high rates of homicide.

- What coping styles are used among black males who do not get killed.

- A study of the psychosocial and economic costs of homicide.

- Research on the relationship of alcohol and drugs to homicide.

- Longitudinal studies on the life adjustments of black males.

- Roles of major social institutions in fostering attitudes and values conducive to high homicide rates in black communities.

- Stability and change over time in homicide rates.

- Ways to develop gainful, beneficial, nontraditional work opportunities for young black males.[52]

Tractenberg also recommended specific community projects and called for evaluation procedures to test the effectiveness of these intervention strategies: conflict resolution training; police-community domestic violence reduction teams; community organization and development; and strengthened community support systems.

The Department of Health and Human Services also recommended additional studies on hospital emergency room usage. Such research has shown that many assault victims who came in for care have previously been assaulted. Thus, for the first time, black-on-black homicide was being defined by the public health community as a medical/health problem. This current definition of homicide is different from that utilized in the past, when black homicide was defined as a "criminal problem."

Color Blindness

The psychiatric treatment of blacks has suffered from "color blindness." That is, white psychiatrists have had difficulty in relating to the
experiences of their black patients. Color blindness is the assumption
that blacks are psychologically no different from white patients, and
thus should be treated exactly the same as white patients who manifest
the same symptoms. By using mental health standards based on white
middle-class patients, and by adopting a similar value system in their
treatment procedures, white psychologists and psychiatrists have erro-
neously diagnosed any deviations from middle-class white standards as
pathological. This is particularly the case in the related areas of court-
ship, sexuality and mating, as well as in the redressing of personal
wrongs. Feeling as though they are without police protection, isolated
ghetto blacks frequently resort to violence to redress wrongs. The sexual mores and religious values and practices within black culture have
always varied from those of the dominant society. Most blacks live in
an isolated, precarious and threatening world, which has rendered
them less "objective," open, phlegmatic and optimistic than whites.
Their world views are generally different and they react among themselves in a more personal and emotional fashion than do whites.

Melvin Sabshin, Herman Diesenhaus and Raymond Wilkerson
demonstrated that the field of psychiatry abounds with stereotypes
used to describe blacks, such as blacks are "innately lazy, unintelligent
and criminal." Black psychiatric patients, according to these stereotypes, are "hostile and not motivated for treatment, having [a] primitive character structure, not psychologically minded, and impulse-rid-
den."[53] In *Black Rage*, William Grier and Price Cobbs observed that
blacks developed a cultural paranoia against white people as part of
their upbringing, *which could be more appropriately viewed as a norm
rather than as aberrant behavior*.[54] This cultural paranoia is often con-
fused by white mental health specialists with an actual paranoia. Some
well-meaning whites who try to associate with blacks on an equal basis
become painfully aware of this cultural paranoia. Also, some middle-
class blacks confront the same phenomenon when associating with
lower-class blacks. Indeed, middle-class blacks are frequently isolated
not only from whites, but also from their lower-class counterparts.
This isolation may or may not be purposeful.

Summary

The change of the public health treatment and control model to a prevention model in relation to violence is a relatively new development for public health professionals in our society. The Centers for Disease Control are now treating black homicide as if it were an epidemic. By employing the epidemiological model, researchers at CDC track the patterns of crime and violence in the same manner that they employ to study disease patterns in natural populations such as communities or nations.

The epidemiological approach holds that the occurrence and spread of disease result from multiple interacting medical *and* social factors, rather than from a single, root cause. This approach emphasizes the surveillance and measurement of violence within an ecological and social context, which parallels the "ecological-social disorganization" frame of reference and methodology utilized by the Chicago School of criminology dating from the 1930s. The epidemiological approach today has benefitted greatly from advances in data gathering and processing, and thus avoids some of the biases of earlier studies. Researchers are more able today than in the past to measure accurately, survey and analyze violence, and to do so within the context of neighborhoods. This has facilitated a shift from an emphasis on individual cause and prevention to a combination model including both societal and individual causes and preventive measures.

Health officials publicly attribute this shift to a change in attitude regarding the health risks Americans face, and to a recognition of the disproportionately high number of homicides in black communities. But as called out earlier, the disproportionate number of black homicides has not just suddenly been discovered and recognized. Rather, these differential rates can be traced back over several decades, which reinforces the point that objective conditions alone do not account for (1) the recognition of certain phenomena as social problems; (2) an agreed-upon definition of the problem; and (3) an agreed-upon causal and preventive treatment model. Acknowledging certain conditions to be social problems involves a complex process in which various economic, social and political interests interact to structure a given phenomenon. The current recognition of black homicide as both a public health and a social problem illustrates and reflects this process. Whether the use of this new perspective will actually lead to a reduction in homicide and violence remains to be seen. Certainly, if the public health approach encompasses sociological variables in its frame of reference, research methodology and control techniques, the chances for success will be greater.

NOTES

[1]William Manthey and Dwight L. Johnson, *America's Black Population: 1970 to 1982, A Statistical View* (Washington, D.C.: U.S. Bureau of the Census, 1983), p. 1.

[2]See U.S. Bureau of the Census, *U.S. Summary—General Social and Economic Characteristics* (Washington, D.C.: U.S. Government Printing Office, December 1983), Table 77, "Nativity By Race, 1900-1980," pp. 1-15.

[3]Ibid., Table 248, "Persons by Race for Areas and Places: 1980, Places of 50,000 or More and Central Cities of MSAs," pp. 1-393-1-400.

[4]"Violent Death Among Persons 15-24 Years of Age—United States, 1970-1978," *Morbidity and Mortality Weekly Report* 32: 35 (September 9, 1983): 453-457 at 454.

[5]Ibid., pp. 454-455.

[6]See, for instance, the information provided in Federal Bureau of Investigation, *Uniform Crime Reports for the United States: 1986* (Washington, D.C.: Federal Bureau of Investigation, U.S. Department of Justice, 1987).

[7]See, for instance, National Center for Health Statistics, *Advance Report: Final Mortality Statistics: 1980* (Washington, D.C.: U.S. Government Printing Office, 1981).

[8]International Criminal Police Organization (INTERPOL), *1975-1976 Statistiques Criminelles Internationales* (Saint Cloud, France: INTERPOL General Secretariat, n.d.), "Volume of Crime" tables at pp. 19 (Ivory Coast), 34 (Guyana), 44 (Kuwait), 46 (Lesotho), 54 (Malaysia), 55 (Morocco), 60 (Nigeria), 62 (Norway), 71 (United Kingdom) and 84 (Turkey).

[9]Federal Bureau of Investigation, *Uniform Crime Reports for the United States: 1983* (Washington, D.C.: Federal Bureau of Investigation, U.S. Department of Justice, 1984), pp. 7, 8 and 187.

[10]Federal Bureau of Investigation, *Uniform Crime Reports for the United States: 1986*, op. cit. note 6, p. 8.

[11]Ibid., pp. 9 and 182-184.

[12]Manthey and Johnson, op. cit. note 1, p. 1.

[13]National Advisory Commission on Civil Disorders, *Report of the National Advisory Commission on Civil Disorders* (Washington, D.C.: U.S. Government Printing Office, 1968), pp. 134-136.

[14]These figures are reported by the Center for Studies of Anti-Social and Violent Behavior, National Institute of Mental Health: Violence Epidemiology Branch of the Center for Health Promotion and Education at the Centers for Disease Control (Atlanta, GA).

[15]Harold M. Rose, "The Changing Spatial Dimension of Black Homicide in Selected Cities," paper presented at the Academy of Science, Justice Sciences Meeting (Oklahoma City, OK: March 1980).

[16]Ibid.

[17]W.E.B. DuBois, *The Philadelphia Negro: A Social Study* (New York: Schocken Books, 1967, orig. pub. Philadelphia, PA: University of Pennsylvania, 1899).

[18]Richard Korn and Lloyd W. McCorkle, eds., *Criminology and Penology* (New York: Holt, 1959), p. 50.

[19]See W.E.B. DuBois, ed., *Notes on Negro Crime, Particularly in Georgia*, The Atlanta University Publications, No. 9 (Atlanta: The Atlanta University Press, 1904).

[20]Ibid., pp. 16 and 56-58.

[21]Booker T. Washington, "Prohibition and the Negro," *The Colored American Magazine* 14: 5 (May 1908): 266-269.

[22]Frederick D. Harper, "Overview: Alcohol and Blacks," in Frederick D. Harper, ed., *Alcohol Abuse and Black America* (Alexandria, VA: Douglass Publishers, 1976), pp. 1-12 at 1.

[23]William T. Root, *A Psychological and Educational Survey of 1916 Prisoners in the Western Penitentiary of Pennsylvania* (Pittsburgh, PA: Board of Trustees of the Western Penitentiary, 1927).

[24]Ira deA. Reid, "The Negro Goes to Sing Sing," *Opportunity: A Journal of Negro Life* X: 7 (July 1932): 215-217 at 217.

[25]Kenneth A. Barnhart, "Negro Homicides in the United States," *Opportunity: A Journal of Negro Life* X: 7 (July 1932): 212-214.

[26]See, for instance, Guy B. Johnson, "The Negro and Crime," *Annals of the American Academy of Political and Social Sciences* 217 (September 1941): 93-104; and Harold Garfinkel, "Research Note on Inter- and Intra-Racial Homicides," *Social Forces* 27 (May 1949): 369-381.

[27]Earl Moses, "Community Factors in Negro Delinquency," *Journal of Negro Education* V: 2 (April 1936): 220-227.

[28]See Edward Green, *Judicial Attitudes in Sentencing* (New York: St. Martin's Press, 1961), pp. 55-62 and 76-96; and Henry Allen Bullock, "Significance of the Racial Factor in the Length of Prison Sentences," *Journal of Criminal Law, Criminology and Police Science* 52: 4 (November-December 1961): 411-417.

[29]Marvin E. Wolfgang, *Patterns in Criminal Homicide* (Philadelphia: PA: University of Pennsylvania Press, 1958).

[30]Ibid., pp. 5, 31 and 65.

[31]See, for example, Julius Debro, "Homicides/Suicides in the City of Atlanta, 1979-1981," a report prepared for the Centers for Disease Control, Environmental Health Services (Atlanta, GA: 1981).

[32]See discussion in President's Commission on Law Enforcement and the Administration of Justice, *The Challenge of Crime in a Free Society: A Report* (New York: Dutton, 1968), p. 101.

[33]Ibid., p. 149.

[34]See the discussion of this theory in Edwin H. Sutherland and Donald R. Cressey, *Criminology* (Philadelphia: J.P. Lippincott, 1970), pp. 75-91.

[35]See Thorsten Sellin and Marvin Wolfgang, eds., *Delinquency: Selected Studies* (New York: Wiley and Sons, 1969).

[36]For example, Marvin Wolfgang and Franco Ferracuti, *The Subculture of Violence: Towards an Integrated Theory in Criminology*, English edition (Beverly Hills, CA: Sage Publishing, 1982), pp. 263-264 and 298.

[37]William J. Chambliss, "The State, the Law, and the Definition of Behavior as Criminal or Delinquent," in Daniel Glaser, ed., *Handbook of Criminology* (Chicago: Rand McNally, College Publishing Co., 1974), pp. 7-43.

[38]A good example of this trend can be found in James Q. Wilson, *Thinking About Crime* (New York: Vintage Books, 1975).

[39]See Wilson's theory, laid out in James Q. Wilson and Richard J. Herrnstein, *Crime and Human Nature* (New York: Simon and Schuster, 1985), pp. 41-66.

[40]U.S. Department of Health, Education and Welfare, *Healthy People: The Surgeon General's Report on Health Promotion and Disease Prevention*, Publication no. (PHS) 79-55071 (Washington, D.C.: U.S. Government Printing Office, 1979), pp. vii and 3-6.

[41]Janine Jason, *CDC and the Epidemiology of Violence* (Atlanta, GA: CDC, Center for Health Promotion and Education, 1983), p. 1.

[42]Janine Jason, Melinda Flock and Carl W. Tyler, Jr., "Epidemiologic Characteristics of Primary Homicides in the United States," *American Journal of Epidemiology* 117: 4 (April 1983): 419-428 at 419.

[43]Ibid., p. 420.

[44]Ibid., p. 426.

[45]Ibid.

[46]Jason, op. cit. note 41, p. 3.

[47]Lawrence W. Sherman and Richard A. Berk, "The Specific Deterrent Effects of Arrest for Domestic Assault," *American Sociological Review* 49: 2 (April 1984): 261-272.

[48]Jason, et al., op. cit. note 42, p. 427.

[49]Ibid.

[50]Ibid., p. 428.

[51]*Morbidity and Mortality Weekly Report*, op. cit. note 4.

[52]Information on the specific outcomes that emanated from the above research suggestions may be obtained from the office of Robert L. Tractenberg, Deputy Administrator, Department of Health and Human Services, Washington, D.C.

[53]Melvin Sabshin, Herman Diesenhaus and Raymond Wilkerson, "Dimensions of Institutional Racism in Psychiatry," *American Journal of Psychiatry* 127: 6 (December 1970): 787-793 at 788. For other research, see Mark L. Rosenberg, Evan Stark and Margaret A. Zahn, "Interpersonal Violence: Homicide and Spouse Abuse," in John M. Last, ed., *Maxcy-Rosenau Public Health and Preventive Medicine* (Norwalk, CT: Appleton-Century-Crofts, 1986), pp. 1399-1426; and Fred Loya and James A. Mercy, *The Epidemiology of Homicide in the City of Los Angeles, 1970-79: A Collaborative Study* (Atlanta, GA: U.S. Department of Health and Human Services, Public Health Service, Centers for Disease Control, Center for Health Promotion and Education, Violence Epidemiology Branch, 1985).

[54]William Grier and Price Cobbs, *Black Rage* (New York: Basic Books, 1968), p. 135. (Author's italics.)

CONCLUSION

Winston A. Van Horne

University of Wisconsin-Milwaukee

As one reads the *Proverbs*, one is impelled by the striking beauty and power of its intricately woven aphorisms to reflect upon the human condition and its possibilities. Of these, one is especially compelling in relation to the substance and purpose of this book, namely, ". . . the tongue of the wise *is* health."[1] The two key terms here are *wise* (wisdom) and *health*, Wisdom is not just the capacity to construct sound hypotheses and theories about the empirical world, nor the ability to organize innumerable bits of information into categories, nor the possession of vast knowledge about sentient beings and inanimate bodies. Rather, it is the faculty of the mind and the disposition of the spirit that incline the will to act aright by making the best possible use of knowledge, experience, intelligence and understanding. Where wisdom abounds good judgment overflows, and health luxuriates as right and proper conduct flourishes.

Health is not just the absence of disease, deformity, defect, pain and/or suffering. It is, instead, the presence and persistence of a state of physical, mental, and spiritual well-being that frees the individual to strive unceasingly to make objectively real the subjective possibilities of his/her being. In this sense, health is indeed wealth, for wealth is not merely the abundance of material possessions but the richness of the possibilities of the subjective being of the individual made objectively real, regardless of the form this takes. An so the *Proverbs* hits the mark in observing that "the tongue of the wise *is* health," for wisdom nurtures health, which is wealth, without which no man fulfills the striving purpose of his being and imprints himself to the fullest possible measure on the world around him. Wisdom, health and wealth, then, are the triad that opens to human beings the boundless possibilities for good—evil is the antithesis of wisdom—in the worlds that dwell within and without them. This is not a flight of fancy of speculative metaphysics; it is grounded in the timeless reproduction of cultures, as can be observed clearly in the preceding chapters by Eugene Farley as well as by Laura Adams and Merritt Knox.

These authors, as well as other contributors to this volume, call out with great clarity and force the fact that it is imperative, nay, absolutely obligatory, that health care policymakers and providers learn of, and act wisely upon, the cultural moorings of belief pertaining to good and evil, right and wrong, and proper and improper conduct that animate the behavior of the ones for whose health they care. In calling attention to the significance of the Great Spirit in relation to the health and well-being of American Indians, Adams and Knox are not archaeologists digging amidst cultural ruins to discover artifacts that engage the antiquarian interests of contemporary Americans. They are making it known to policymakers and providers of health care that American Indians do perceive a relation between evil and disease as well as between good and health, thus it is critical that the form and substance of these relations be known and understood in the context of the experiences and behaviors they structure. This is especially true if decisions and activities regarding the health of American Indians are to serve their intended purpose. Put differently, the wisdom of given decisions and activities concerning the health/health care of American Indians cannot but be called into question insofar as they ignore, fail to consider, or underestimate the significance of the intrinsic good of the Great Spirit who nurtures and sustains health. Both Adams and Knox make plain that the tongue of the wise is not to be found in modern medicine, grounded in the empirical sciences and technology, insofar as it dismisses any real-life physical relation between good spirit and good health and evil spirit and ill health, as far as the American Indian is concerned. They most assuredly do not argue that American Indians are not attuned fully to the value of the role of the empirical sciences and technology in modern medicine. What they, as well as Farley, have done, with remarkable success, is to draw out vividly before one's eyes the value, yet limits, of knowledge (empirically grounded medical knowledge), and make a plea for wisdom if those limits are to be transcended. It is, they believe correctly, only by wisdom's transcendence of knowledge in decisionmaking and policy implementation that the full and true value of modern medicine will be procured by American Indians—or anyone else for that matter. Modern medicine must speak not only with the tongue of the knowledgeable, but also with the tongue of the wise, if its preventive, curative, and nurturing functions and purposes are to become what they can be.

If Adams' and Knox's construction of American Indian sentiment concerning good health is sound, a clear relation obtains between good health and good conduct. The belief that such a relationship exists is obviously not limited to American Indians. Was this relationship not called out more than two millennia ago by Socrates when he observed that "we should set the highest value, not on living, but on living well?"[2] And what does living well entail? Socrates believes that it entails the unremitting and unswerving pursuit of excellence; for "every ... good thing which men have, whether in public or in private, comes from excellence."[3] The pursuit of human excellence is the touchstone not only of living well, but also of dying well. It is Socrates' firm conviction that "it is a much harder thing to escape from wickedness than from death, for wickedness is swifter than death. ... [Thus no] man of any worth at all ought to reckon the chances of life and death when he acts, or ... think of anything but whether he is acting justly or unjustly, and as a good or a bad man would act."[4] Such conduct assures that the individual lives well and dies well as he/she pursues excellence by wisdom's guide of knowledge.

The continuum of living well and dying well presumes the continuum of the body and the spirit. This is recognized by Socrates, and in a point of timeless profundity he observes that "no evil can happen to a good man, either in life or after death."[5] And why? Because "[h]is affairs are not neglected by the gods."[6] Surely, Socrates is not oblivious to the fact that many evils do befall a good man in life. What he is saying here is that a good man does not fall to these evils, which assures that all is well with him in life and after death. This is awfully, awfully tough, and Socrates knows it all too well. Innumerable are the evils that trouble the body and the spirit of man, and becloud his vision, if not blind the eye of his soul, to the imperative of the pursuit of excellence.

The good health of the body and the spirit that good conduct fosters is not easy to attain, for just as wickedness is swifter than death, so too is evil swifter than good. Did not William Shakespeare have Mark Antony say in his funeral oration for the assassinated Julius Caesar that "[t]he evil that men do lives after them; [t]he good is oft interred with their bones?"[7] Still, good health and good conduct sustain living well and dying well, and make possible the unending pursuit of excellence in life as well as the rewards that attend it both in life and after death. This is the most profound conclusion that emerges from this volume, which, in a very real sense, bridges time, space and cultures. Here Socrates and the American Indian become one, a oneness in which countless others participate. Health is not just of the body, but of the spirit also, and there is no dying well where there is no living well, which presumes an abiding respect for human dignity.

As one reads the pages of this volume, one cannot escape the resonance of human dignity that echoes in each of the chapters. B. F. Skinner, for example, believes that dignity is merely an emotive term, the content of which is captured far more accurately within the framework of the scientific constructs of operant conditioning and schedules of reinforcement.[8] Many behaviorists share Skinner's conviction, but untold numbers of persons believe that dignity is not simply an epiphenomenon of the behavior of axons and dendrites, nerves and muscles, all in relation to given schedules of reinforcement. They believe that man possesses an intrinsic value and worth in his person, in virtue of being human, which should be recognized and esteemed. It is the individual's instrinsic value and worth that impel each to strive for excellence, and in doing so live well and die well. There is, here, a conceptual as well as an empirical relation between human dignity, human excellence, and human health. None whose dignity is not nurtured strives for excellence; none who does not strive for excellence either lives well or dies well; and none who neither lives well nor dies well experiences true health. Wisdom's guiding light thus makes plain that the tongue should speak of policies and activities pertaining to health and health care which nurture to the utmost the dignity of the individual. This is exactly what the contributors to this volume have done.

In calling out the inordinately high risk of black males between the ages of fifteen and twenty-four to death by homicide, and the vexingly high rate of homicides, especially the deaths of blacks at the hands of other blacks, that now bedevil the black population in the United States, Julius Debro does not merely seek to shock his readers and make them conscious of a major problem in the society. True, he no doubt desires to do this, but his aim is to do more. In comparing the mortality and morbidity rates of American Indian infants and black infants, Joyce Kramer does not simply wish to make known the empirical fact that American Indian infants fare better than black infants. Her aim is to do more. In focusing attention on the lot of the elderly among racial/ethnic minorities, Toni Tripp-Reimer and Bernard Sorofman do not merely desire to bring to notice the all-too-often wretchedness of their health and health care. They aim to do more. In bringing into sharp focus the problems of health and health care pertaining to the high rate of pregnancy among Mexican-American and other teenagers, Maria Luisa Urdaneta and Tom Thompson do not just wish to make the public conscious of obtuse moral considerations that ofttimes deflect attention and activity from important biological elements of the problem. They aim to do more. In drawing out the relation between poverty, stress and mental health in black America, Lawrence Gary does not simply wish to reinforce with abundant data the fact that poverty and stress extract an inordinately high toll in terms of the mental health of black Americans. He aims to do more. What more, then, do these authors aim to do? This question can be answered only after another is asked and answered.

What is the substratum that binds together the "more" at which the aforementioned authors aim? It is human dignity made manifest in the life of each individual. In the life of every individual there is value and worth, the nurturing of which grounds the ultimate purpose of political society. Individuals did not come together in political society for the sake of the security of their persons and property, in order that each may pursue his/her egoistic self-interest, as Thomas Hobbes and John Locke thought, nor to dissolve their individuality into the good of the collectivity, as both Jean Jacques Rousseau and Karl Marx believed. They came together in political society for the purpose of establishing and maintaining a nurturing environment, whereby the value and worth of each might be maximized through the process of everyone's participation in the unending quest for human excellence. Participation in this process entails the recognition of, and commitment in activity to, human dignity as an ultimate value. It is the nurturing of human dignity to the end of human excellence that constitutes the ultimate purpose of political society. All other purposes of political society are ancillary to this purpose. With this clarification, one may now return to the question that was set aside momentarily.

The authors mentioned earlier all seek to expand the horizon of human dignity, and by extension human excellence, in American society by calling out, both explicitly and implicitly, the need for policies and activities designed to foster better health and health care for those with whom they are concerned. They are acutely mindful of the fact that without good health it is nigh impossible for one either to live well or die well, and that human dignity is trammelled and brutalized where one neither lives nor dies well. They do not believe that living well entails the possession of material abundance; they do believe that it entails a threshold of need satisfaction without which the value and worth of the individual *qua* individual are diminished. Such a diminution of value and worth degrades one's person and invariably lowers one's self-esteem.

It may well be that the potentialities for self-esteem are formed in the womb. If this is so, insofar as these potentialities are not nurtured, particularly in youth but also over the course of one's life through old age, serious doubts concerning one's self-worth cannot but haunt one. Kramer as well as Urdaneta and Thompson are most mindful of this, and it impels them to be strong advocates of public policies designed to provide good and readily available pre- and postnatal care. Attaining a threshold of need satisfaction in relation to the health and the health care of Americans, especially for the groups of their immediate concern, thus constitutes the *more* at which Debro, Gary, Kramer, Tripp-Reimer and Sorofman as well as Urdaneta and Thompson aim. They do not delineate in detail all the elements of this threshold; nonetheless, they do provide sufficient elements for one to grasp its minima.

These minima lie somewhere between Victor Rodwin's weak equity criterion and stronger equity criterion—the former being most sensitive to the limits of a society's resources, the latter necessitating a reordering of societal priorities in relation to those limits. The threshold of need satisfaction in relation to Rodwin's equity criteria enjoins policymakers to broaden the access of all Americans to high quality health care. Doing so should serve to improve the health of racial/ethnic minorities in the United States, and thus enhance their prospects for living well, which benefits the society as a whole insofar as each who truly lives well pursues excellence unfailingly.

Love of excellence and respect for human dignity presume a measure of wholesome tolerance and intolerance. Excellence loathes mediocrity, which implies intolerance. But this intolerance is neither haughty nor perverse. In loathing mediocrity, excellence does not degrade the dignity of the individual. It does rebuke and chastise one for failing to strive unceasingly to become the very best that one can be within the limits of one's potentialities and capacities. Excellence's respect for human dignity thus makes it intolerant not of differences in human potentialities and capacities, nor of dissimilarities in the activities through which these are made manifest, but of the lowering of the individual's striving purpose. The intolerance of excellence for the lowering of the striving purpose of the individual conflates with its tolerance of different kinds of striving purpose, as long as the latter draws individuals toward the limits of their abilities. Those who contributed to this volume know this all too well, and one can feel across the pages of this book the wholesome tolerance and intolerance that animate its authors.

Reading the chapters by Farley as well as by Adams and Knox, one discerns clearly their strong belief that knowledge, truth, insight, foresight, wisdom and excellence are the monopoly of no one religion, race, ethnic grouping, set of individuals or culture. This is critical to their constructions pertaining to human health and the possibilities of the health care system in the United States. The point of singular importance which emerges from their observations is that deontological recognition must be accorded to the legitimacy of different conceptions of health and approaches to health care that treat the dignity of the individual as an inviolable, ultimate value. This is not easy, for there is no universal agreement on what constitutes the dignity of the individual. The absence of agreement does not, however, entail that each individual does not possess an inherent dignity in his/her person. Did not Saint Augustine, in his brilliant and ageless discourse on time, ask, "...

what is time? Who can easily and briefly explain it? . . . But what in speaking do we refer to more familiarly and knowingly than time? . . . And certainly we understand when we speak of it; we understand also when we hear it spoken of by another. What, then, is time? If no one ask of me, I know; if I wish to explain to him who asks, I know not."[9] Just as everyone knows but may not be able to explain what time is, so too everyone knows but may not be able to explain what human dignity is. This knowledge is assumed in this book as policymakers and providers of health care are enjoined to take the sorts of action that assure the sanctity of human dignity, even as dissimilar conceptions of health and approaches to health care are accorded the kind of recognition that gives them standing, that is, good repute, in the society.

It is a profound sense of tolerance, and an unequivocal respect for the sanctity of human dignity, that impel Urdaneta and Thompson to take the rather controversial stance that in the context of the health of the individuals concerned, as well as the well-being of the society at large, conflicting and unsettled moral constructs should not be allowed to override agreed-upon biological facts in the formulation and implementation of public policy designed to at least ameliorate, if not solve, the problem of teenage pregnancy. This courageous position is likely to trouble many. However, its bedrock grounding in the sanctity of human dignity positions it as one alternative that should be considered seriously by those who are charged with the responsibility and authorized to act in behalf of the interest and good of the citizenry. It is the presumption of tolerance that makes the articulation of a position such as this possible, and it is the presumption of tolerance that holds out the hope that its potential benefits will be recognized widely and acted upon.

Still, the very tolerance that Urdaneta and Thompson evince is but the flip side of an intolerance that is grounded in their love of excellence and respect for human dignity. Believing that the exponential increase of pregnancy among teenage women constitutes a major societal problem, sensitive to the role that biology plays in the problem at hand, attuned to the intractability of the moral disagreements that attend the problem, and convinced that an early pregnancy out-of-wedlock affects adversely the dignity of the child who bears a child—with all its accompanying individual and societal costs—Urdaneta and Thompson are unwilling to permit the problem to continue to fester while possible ameliorative activities, if not solutions, get bogged down in persistent ethical and moral controversy. They are most intolerant of this and rightfully so. Was it not said that while Nero fiddled Rome burned? The wages of sin may well be death, as Saint Paul believed, but Urdaneta and Thompson are not willing to construct teenage pregnancy as sin. They perceive and are troubled by the threat it poses to human dignity, and it is this of which they are intolerant. Put differently, concerns pertaining to human dignity, and not the eschatology of sin, fuel the intolerance of Urdaneta and Thompson for decisions and activities that fail to come to grips with the centrality of biology concerning the problem of teenage pregnancy. If the sort of policies that Urdaneta and Thompson desire are to obtain, there has to be some kind of partnership in a shared purpose between those whose interests are complementary as well as contradictory.

Reflecting on the revolution in France, Edmund Burke observed that society entails a partnership between the living, the dead and the yet unborn.[10] Burke was correct. Society is indeed a partnership, one in which every man/woman has the responsibility and duty to act to assure the integrity and honor of his/her own personal dignity, as well as nurture the dignity of others, to the end that none is without the opportunity to participate in the quest for individual and collective excellence. This construction of the idea of society animates this book.

Partnership entails responsibility and duty both at the level of the individual and the collective. The contributors to this volume are keenly attuned to this, and it guides their vision of what ought to be done to enhance the health and the health care of Americans, especially racial and ethnic minorities. If homicide is the leading cause of death for black males between the ages of fifteen and twenty-four; if murder confronts a murderer with four stark realities, namely, being killed in turn, rotting away in prison, running forever in the underground or going into foreign exile—the least likely prospect for one with limited resources; if prisons make individuals worse, violating the moral precept that no man should be subjected to conditions that make him worse in his being by standards of human excellence; and if poverty, de facto segregation, poor education, problems of socialization in childhood, and a constricted horizon of life's possibilities all conjoin as contributory factors to the public health problem of blacks killing blacks, does not the partnership of social life necessitate by responsibility and duty policies and activities that undo progressively this problem? Debro most assuredly thinks so. Although he does not present an explicit set of policy prescriptions, his data and arguments have but one unmistakable purpose—the mobilization of opinion in favor of concerted action both locally and nationally to increase the life chances of blacks and, correspondingly, decrease the waste that homicide wreaks in black communities.

It is not without good reason that it has been said time and time again that a society's greatest resource is its human capital. From this resource comes everything that is good, valuable, precious, dear, enduring, praiseworthy and excellent. Prosperity issues from it, and it is the wellspring of progress. Happy, then, is the society that husbands its human capital by nurturing each individual to be a full partner in its benefits and burdens. Such husbanding is antithetical to any waste of this resource, which waxes and wanes transgenerationally. The partnership of society bridges generations, and each has a responsibility and duty, emanating from the intrinsic dignity of man and the timeless becoming of his pursuit of excellence, to pass onto the next burdens no greater and benefits more abundant than those which it inherited. This has not, of course, been the legacy of all the generations of American society, yet this principle has animated the aspirations of each.

It is known all too well, though not always acted upon with prudence and wisdom, that generational waste carries weighty transgenerational costs in its wake. Knowledge of this has impelled the contributors to this volume to tackle problems of health and health care that bring to the fore the generational and transgenerational responsibilities and duties of Americans pertaining to the waste of human capital. This is not always done explicitly, but it nonetheless suffuses their work. For example, when Kramer zeroes in on the lives lost and the suffering occasioned by the high rates of mortality and morbidity among black infants, she seeks to do two things simultaneously: bring into very sharp focus this waste of human capital and its attendant costs, and admonish Americans about their responsibility and duty to handle this resource wisely. Likewise, when Tripp-Reimer and Sorofman call out the acute problems of health and health care that harass the elderly, especially those of racial/ethnic minorities who, for the most part, live off very limited means, they desire to make known that healthy elderly persons possess a wealth of knowledge and experience that constitutes a resource of no little value. This resource should not be wasted. Good partners do not waste one another's resources. And so it is in the interest of all that the society cares for the health of its elderly no less than it cares for the health of its young.

There is an adage that the young may die but the old must die. Nature renews itself timelessly through its unending cycles of birth, death and rebirth. When death comes in consequence of nature's orderly renewal of itself, one cannot but sense the power, mystery and majesty of a teleology that transcends man's striving purpose. When death issues from human foible, ignorance, bigotry, neglect, niggardliness, avarice, rapaciousness and/or misjudgment, one feels a certain betrayal of man's striving purpose. The wasting of human life—whether young, mature or old—by untimely death or retrograde living scandalizes human dignity and palls the quest for excellence. The recognition of this impels the authors of this book to articulate a case, though more implicitly than explicitly, for public policies regarding the health and the health care of Americans which are attuned as closely as possible with nature's rhythm for the renewal of the species. One observes in Farley's preface, for example, an unmistakable striving for a measure of harmony between the natural order and the human order of things, for the sake of conjoining the teleologies of nature and man to the end of sound health and a system of health care that recognize and act upon the proper symmetry between life and death. Were such to obtain, not only would all Americans experience more robust health, but racial/ ethnic minorities would also come to enjoy from youth through old age a quality of health/health care markedly better than that which has been known to them heretofore.

In bringing this conclusion to a close, and reflecting upon all that has been said, one is forced to contemplate this question: Wherein lies the lasting value of this book? This is a question of singular importance in an age quickened by immediacy. Terms that are a commonplace such as the "quick fix," "looking out for number one," "I want mine now," "winning is everything," "what have you done for me lately?," and "the future is now" all capture with remarkable accuracy the spirit of the age. If the future is now, and now is the present, the future is the present; "[b]ut should the present be always present, and should it not pass into time past, truly it would not be time, but eternity."[11] The present is now, which is an endless succession of ever-so-fleeting presents. The present of time does not endure, for no sooner than it is the present it is past, succeeded instantaneously in the now by another present, endlessly. The terms that are most germane here are *fleeting* and *endure*.

If the future is the present, and the present is fleeting and does not endure, one's horizon of time cannot but be bounded by the immediate. To the extent that this metaphysic animates conduct, that which is of lasting value inevitably remains veiled insofar as its immediate value is not readily apparent. Happily, the immediate value of this book is all too clear and distinct. But long after its authors are deceased, its data dated, it hypotheses corroborated or confuted and its prescriptions accepted or rejected, its evaluation of the human condition of racial/ethnic minorities in the United States in terms of the relation between health and well-being will persist. In directing attention to the relation between health, human dignity, human capital, societal partnership, wisdom and the love of excellence, it calls upon a people to be attentive to the immediate, but ever mindful of the lasting.

NOTES

[1]*Proverbs*, 12:18.

[2]Plato, *Crito*, VIII, 48, trans. F. J. Church in Robert D. Cumming, ed., *Euthyphro, Apology, Crito* (Indianapolis and New York: The Bobbs-Merrill Company, Inc., 1956).

[3]*Apology*, XVII, 30.

[4]Ibid., XXIX, 39, and XVI, 28.

[5]Ibid., XXXIII, 42.

[6]Ibid.

[7]William Shakespeare, *Julius Caesar*, III, 2:75, in Stanley Wells and Gary Taylor, gen. eds., *William Shakespeare, The Complete Works* (Oxford: Clarendon Press, 1986).

[8]See B. F. Skinner, *Beyond Freedom and Dignity* (New York: Alfred A. Knopf, 1971).

[9]Saint Augustine, *Confessions*, XI, 14, trans. J. G. Pilkington in Whitney J. Oates, ed., *Basic Writings of Saint Augustine*, Vol. I (New York: Random House, 1948).

[10]Edmund Burke, *Reflections on the Revolution in France* (New York: E. P. Dutton; and London: J. M. Dent and Sons, 1967), p. 93.

[11]*Confessions*, XI, 14.